Social Change and Creative Activism in the 21st Century

Social Change and Creative Activism in the 21st Century

The Mirror Effect

Silas F. Harrebye
Roskilde University, Denmark

SOCIAL CHANGE AND CREATIVE ACTIVISM IN THE 21ST CENTURY: THE MIRROR EFFECT
Copyright © Silas F. Harrebye 2016
Softcover reprint of the hardcover 1st edition 2016 978-1-137-49867-0

All rights reserved. No reproduction, copy or transmission of this publication may be made without written permission. No portion of this publication may be reproduced, copied or transmitted save with written permission. In accordance with the provisions of the Copyright, Designs and Patents Act 1988, or under the terms of any licence permitting limited copying issued by the Copyright Licensing Agency, Saffron House, 6–10 Kirby Street, London EC1N 8TS.

Any person who does any unauthorized act in relation to this publication may be liable to criminal prosecution and civil claims for damages.

First published 2016 by
PALGRAVE MACMILLAN

The author has asserted his right to be identified as the author of this work in accordance with the Copyright, Designs and Patents Act 1988.

Palgrave Macmillan in the UK is an imprint of Macmillan Publishers Limited, registered in England, company number 785998, of Houndmills, Basingstoke, Hampshire RG21 6XS.

Palgrave Macmillan in the US is a division of Nature America, Inc., One New York Plaza, Suite 4500, New York, NY 10004-1562.

Palgrave Macmillan is the global academic imprint of the above companies and has companies and representatives throughout the world.

ISBN 978–1–349–69824–0
E-PDF ISBN: 978–1–137–49869–4
DOI: 10.1057/9781137498694

Distribution in the UK, Europe and the rest of the world is by Palgrave Macmillan®, a division of Macmillan Publishers Limited, registered in England, company number 785998, of Houndmills, Basingstoke, Hampshire RG21 6XS.

Library of Congress Cataloging-in-Publication Data
Names: Harrebye, Silas F., author.
Title: Social change and creative activism in the 21st century : the mirror effect / Silas F. Harrebye.
Description: Houndmills, Basingstoke, Hampshire ; New York, NY : Palgrave Macmillan, 2016. | Includes index.
Identifiers: LCCN 2015037099 |
Subjects: LCSH: Social action. | Political participation. | Social movements. | Social change.
Classification: LCC HN18.3 .H366 2016 | DDC 303.4—dc23
LC record available at http://lccn.loc.gov/2015037099

A catalog record for this book is available from the Library of Congress.

A catalogue record for the book is available from the British Library.

Typeset by MPS Limited, Chennai, India.

To all the real heroes out there

Contents

List of Figures and Tables	viii
Preface	ix
Acknowledgments	xii

Part I Identifying the Phenomenon – More Than an Ethical Spectacle

1 Occupying the Space In-Between	3
2 Creative Activism Today	25

Part II Mapping the Field – Using the Terrain to Your Advantage

3 First Movers and Circular Cycles of Contention	47
4 Paradoxes of Participation	72

Part III Exploring the Practice – New Theoretical Framework

5 The Ambivalence of Cynicism, Irony, and Utopia	93
6 Mirroring Counter Strategies	120

Part IV Questioning the Impact – New Trends and Future Dilemmas

7 Professionalization and Cooptation	161
8 The Gordian Knot – Measuring Effect and Revisiting Theories of Change	189
Notes	222
Bibliography	227
Index	243

List of Figures and Tables

Figures

4.1 Cross-country comparison of the relationship between dissatisfaction and participation — 76
4.2 Relationship between dissatisfaction and participation on the individual level within different welfare state regimes — 78
5.1 Creative filter bubbles and ideological echo chambers — 112
6.1 The functionality of critical alternative mirrors — 144
6.2 The functionality of alternative proposing mirrors — 145

Tables

4.1 Country clusters — 77
4.2 Typology of activism — 83
6.1 The development in critical theorizing over social struggles for justice — 149
7.1 Activism Inc. — 178
8.1 Key variables of time and intention — 195
8.2 Key variables of space and politics — 199

Preface

My earliest memory as an activist is one of me lying in a pram that I am way too big for. I hear clanking beer bottles underneath me. Looking up at the blue sky above, a red flag is blowing in the wind. According to Bob Dylan the answer, then, was right in front of me. It was the 1st of May in early 1980s Copenhagen. On International Worker's Day my parents always met their socialist comrades, with whom they also shared a farmhouse in Sweden, to commemorate the historical struggle with which they sympathized and identified. I later realized that I did not. Not in the same way, at least. I did not grow up in a working-class family, as opposed to them, but in a middle-class family of intellectuals. Already as a child, therefore, I started to question the answers hovering above me and strategies applied all around me. The question of whether my generation's political struggle is different than that of my parents still resonates.

My first participation in a *creative* activist happening took place in the very early days of my life – and it happened in the mayor's office. My parents couldn't find daycare for their child because the local politicians didn't provide any. Their reaction was to have a sit-in – with a twist. They brought their child, placed him on the mayor's desk and left. So there I am looking up at the mayor. The direct action disrupted business-as-usual and in a way that made it impossible for those responsible to just shrug their shoulders and leave – as I was probably hungry. The strength of the action was a combination of undamaging pressure tactics (it might have left me emotionally scarred, though) with a prefigurative statement clearly illustrating my parents' problem, their need, and who (in their mind) was responsible.

Time passed and I didn't grow up to be much of an activist. I was active in the periphery of Børne- and Ungdomshuset, and I do participate in the occasional demonstration. I have also been part of starting up two new political parties and continually use my writing to express my opinions. I guess we try to make a difference the best way we can. For some it is organizing rallies, for others community gardening maybe. Today I am a board member of the new Danish movement and political party Alternativet (The Alternative).

When I finished my masters degree in political philosophy I went on to work as a consultant in Ramboll Management with donor-financed development projects in Eastern Europe and Africa. During those years I joined a small independent research group, Critical Sociology, and we would meet every other Wednesday night to discuss critical theory and map the current local terrain of creative activism. These meetings began to function as therapeutic sessions for me, since my doubts about my involvement with the neo-liberal management regime of consultancy were only strengthened by talking to this group of skeptics. My participation in this group not only encouraged me to pursue a PhD, but also suggested the issues it would address.

During my time in New York I got in contact with a bunch of veteran and cutting-edge activists. One of them was Andrew Boyd who was in the process of editing a book together with relevant organizations and inspirational single campaigners from around the world. I was fortunate enough to be invited to participate and to make a minor contribution. Beautiful Trouble is a toolbox for the next generation of change-makers as it lays out core tactics, principles, and theoretical concepts that drive creative activism while also providing case studies to illustrate just how these may be applied in practice (Boyd, 2012 and beautifultrouble.org). When the book and living web archive was launched in 2012 I was thrilled that the world had finally got a systematic, approachable, and practically inspirational coverage of creative forms of activism. Beautiful Trouble is a fun and useful entry into the world of creative activism for budding social entrepreneurs and offers plenty of suggestions for further exploration in books, films, people, websites, and organizations. I was also a little worried, though, that this ambitious project would make my work seem needless. I am glad to say that I don't think that's the case. Much work still needs to be done in this ever-evolving field of activist artistry and participatory democracy.

My motivation for doing this project has been threefold: firstly, a fundamental belief in the importance of the social bottom-up struggle against injustice; secondly, a curiosity about theory's relevance for our understanding of these struggles; and, thirdly, a sense of being part of a new generation's own way of expressing discontent and experimenting with alternatives to the dominating way of life – the global social movements and the local 'project politics' of creative activists are both expressions of that development.

With this book I question, not the legitimacy of my parents' struggle, but the relevance and sufficiency of its form and intention today. Different forms of open capitalism and closed totalitarianism have to create new forms of repression and exploitation; thus new forms of protest emerge – they have to. That is my short story of *Self, Us, and Now*.

This dialectic process has always challenged and developed democracy, and thus necessitates empirically based and theoretically inspired analyses that enable us to reflect upon how these power struggles affect our society. Creative activism as a particular type of engagement and facilitation of other's participation today seems to do so, balancing as it does between critique, cooperation, and cooptation on the margins of the repertoire of contention.

Acknowledgments

First of all I would like to thank my colleagues at the Institute for Society and Globalization at Roskilde University for their professional support in research groups and seminars – not least Thomas P. Boje, who has not only been a patient, critical, and open-minded advisor, but also become a dear friend.

In the spring of 2011 I attended the New School for Social Research in New York where I studied under Nancy Fraser. Thank you for agreeing to become my co-advisor in the last phase of my PhD fellowship. It has been an honor to have one of my heroines challenging my ideas – as I challenge hers here.

Stephen Duncombe (NYU and Director, Center for Artistic Activism) has headed the way into this particular field and continues to be a trusted collaborator. Your insistence and ability to combine academic research and political activism is exemplary.

My time in New York also snowballed into a series of interviews with renowned creative activists and leading scholars in the field from around the world. I want to thank all of them for taking the time to talk to me – not least Jacques Servin (aka Andy Bichlbaum, co-founder of The Yes Men), Srda Popovic (leading figure in Otpor! and co-founder of CANVAS), Andrew Boyd (behind the Billionaires for Bush campaign, founder of The Other 98%, and AgitPop), John Jordan (co-founder of Reclaim the Streets and Clandestine Insurgent Rebels Clown Army), David Solnit (main organizer at the Battle of Seattle and co-founder of Art and Revolution), Sixten Kai Nielsen and Martin Rosengaard (founders and directors of Wooloo), along with Evé Chiapello, Marshall Ganz, Nancy Fraser, Deva Woodly, all the people in Action Aid and Alternativet, and many other organizers and change-makers whose voices can be heard and whose bravery is present throughout the book.

I also wish to thank Palgrave Macmillan for their professional collaboration in making this book. The editors have shown me why scientific meticulousness must be combined with narrative and persistency in order to have value.

I also need to thank the editorial teams at *Comparative European Politics* (Palgrave Macmillan) and *Culture and Organization* (Taylor & Francis) for allowing me to reuse parts of articles that I have published here – the former for "European patterns of participation – How dissatisfaction motivates extra-parliamentary activities given the right institutional conditions," co-authored with my colleague Anders Ejrnæs, and the latter for "The ambivalence of creative activism as a reorganization of critique." Finally, I am grateful to my family who support me with patience and curiosity, not least my children, Joël and Lilja, who have taught me so much more than I will ever be able to teach them. I owe this work to the love of my life, Stine. Thank you for your love, your smile, and your dreams. You have been a healthy counterbalance to the instrumental rationality of academia throughout this process. You inspire so much more than words.

This book is the fruit of years of work. I hope it tastes ripe.

Part I
Identifying the Phenomenon – More Than an Ethical Spectacle

1
Occupying the Space In-Between

The following campaigns all have one thing in common. Whether it be KONY 2012, Greenpeace's surprise appearance at the Danish Queen's gala party, *Top Goon: Diaries of a Little Dictator in Syria*, The Yes Men's fake *New York Times*, or Antanas Mockus' symbolic violence vaccines and mime-controlled traffic-squads in Bogota, Colombia, they function as creative critique meant to challenge regimes, habitual ways of thinking, and, in a way, the very notion of politics. Sometimes they even lead to innovative solutions to wicked problems.

According to *Time* Magazine, the person of the year in 2011 was The Protester. And, sure enough, protesters are currently turning the world upside down with their demands for bottom-up democracy. But who are they? And what do they want? From Tahrir Square to Zuccotti Park, from Madrid to Kiev, from everyday makers to political artists and social entrepreneurs, people from all around the world have been busy occupying public space and challenging illegitimate governments, vulture capitalism, and business as usual. In addition to that, people have participated in a large number of minor happenings, campaigns, and revolts that may never see the light of flashing cameras. In a way, these demonstrations are a part of the traditional repertoire of contention. But they also push the boundaries of the established repertoire of resistance and dialogue. In *The Battle in Seattle* in 1999 the slogan was *another world is possible*. It shut down the World Trade Organization (WTO) conference and gave birth to the alter-globalization movement. But the demonstrators never really succeeded in showing what that other world might look like. Activism in the 21st century seems determined not only to *demonstrate against* the status quo but also *demonstrate how* the world could be different.

It is a myth, however, that these masses are merely spontaneous manifestations coincidentally erupting in conjunction. A small group of proficient organizers most often inspire, coordinate, and facilitate these events. At the heart of this vanguard is the creative activist.

In this chapter I will give a tentative definition of creative activism, which involves narrowing down how I understand and use the terms activism, critique, and creativity – as well as explaining how these change agents operate in the cracks that we are all scared to fall into, and how they in doing so occupy the space in-between.

Activism as political theater

Creative activism often engages artistic skills but the term refers to a phenomenon much broader than artistic activism. It doesn't involve violence, but creative activism is a more specific type of practice than peaceful activism. In an interview with legendary activist John Jordan (co-founder of Reclaim the Streets and Clandestine Insurgent Rebels Clown Army, today working with the laboratory of Insurrectionary Imagination), I asked whether he saw himself as an artist or an activist and if he was perhaps both – and if so, how these 'professions' are related. Jordan replied:

> A lot of the work that we do (...) is bringing artist and activist together and actually trying to use the poetic, creative, outside-the-box imaginative working methods of artists and bringing those together with the kind of much more courageous, much more critical and much more confrontational imaginations of activists.

Creative activism includes many different kinds of pranks and protests, as well as participation in various happenings, street art, tactical media, social utopian experiments, viral campaigns, flash mobs, subvertisement, the-emperor-has-no-clothes disruptions, invisible theater, and minor additions or twists to the already known traditional repertoire of demonstrations, sit-ins, strikes, barricades, lobbyism, information campaigns, boycotts, mass petitions, the urban insurrection, etc. I will not cover all of the above but focus on the ones that best illustrate the shared characteristics of creative activism.

In the United States of America one out of five women are sexually assaulted during their time at college (Kessler, 2014). In 2013 Emma Sulkowicz was allegedly raped by a fellow student in her dorm room (he was never convicted). For a whole year (from September 2014 until she graduated in May 2015) she walked around Columbia University campus with a twenty kilos heavy mattress on her shoulders, that is the mattress she is said to have been raped on. She literally carried the weight of her (and so many others') experience on her shoulders. This provocative performative endurance-action as it turned out, was able to raise hell.

There is an art to every practice. Activism is no exception. That is the fundamental rationale of many new activist training centers (articulated by artisticactivism.org). This book investigates new forms of critical democratic participation in a globalized world. It does so through investigation of a particular form of political participation in the civil sphere. Thus I delimit myself from party politics and more institutionally anchored voluntary labor, which is usually the focus of most of the existing political analysis and civil society research. Instead my focus will be on activism – more precisely the unorthodox and creative kind, which I claim is both a typical and telling trend of our time. In this book I explore what I call creative activism – both as a societal symptom and as a strategic reaction with democratic potential. I do so in order to capture the ambivalence of such critical practices.[1]

I argue that the creative activist is in many ways one of our time's most influential critics. Her practices constitute both a subtle and spectacular critique and, when successful, can function as a priming pump for the political imagination.

In modern society, Guy Debord argues (*Society of the Spectacle*, 1967), that the world is dominated by carefully manufactured displays designed to spellbind "the masses" in order to transform them into mind-numbed consumers. But in contrast to Adorno and Horkheimer's critique of the culture industry, Debord believes that the powers of the spectacle could be turned against itself. One such counter tactic is the so-called 'détournement' developed by the Situationist International. A type of political jiu-jitsu often used by creative activists.

"Everything is theatrical," says David Solnit, founder of Art and Revolution and key activist during the shutdown of Seattle in 1999, which is said to be the birth of what was later known as the anti-globalization movement some thirty years after Debord's diagnosis. The question is whether the traditional demonstration, besides displaying the size and unity of the mass, is always great political theater. The traditional repertoire of contention is challenged by creative activists such as Debord and Solnit, who point out that the power relation between the media and the politicians has shifted. To phrase the mediatization of politics polemically, one might say that where the journalists used to chase the politicians, the politicians now chase the journalists. The way in which the media sets the political agenda today means that activists now have to adjust to the way their actions are portrayed, if they want to avoid ending up as victims of the 'politics of circulation of content'.

In the media, activism is often associated, by politicians and authorities alike, with conflict and dissent. In the *Oxford English Dictionary* activism is defined as "the use of vigorous campaigning to bring about political or social change." Activists do however have a variety of different orientations and use a wide range of strategies and tactics in their practices. In a later chapter, a typology of activism is therefore developed in order to further our understanding of and deliberation on activists and their differences with regard to their goals, their logic, and their activities. Here I distinguish between the radical, the confrontational, the creative, the professional, and the occasional activist – and the everyday maker.

There seems to be a widespread agreement that a 'proper' activist needs to "live the issue, demonstrate relentless dedication, and contribute a sustained effort to duly merit the label" (Bobel, 2007, p. 147). Chris Bobel (along with other contemporary scholars in the field, e.g. Sørensen, 2012) raises questions regarding the assumption that collective action necessarily depends on the alignment between personal and collective identity. He suggests that it can be problematic if our standards for what 'counts' as an activist are too high, as it will then be 'out of reach' for many social movement actors and more low-risk and loosely tied activists.

Creativity is visible throughout the repertoire of contention – from TV shows to street demonstrations and from guerilla campaigns to more artistic social sculptures. Now, one could have chosen to focus on only one of these forms of tactics, on one type of critique, thereby delimiting and clearly defining the research field. But from Cairo to cyberspace, from Wall Street to Main Street social activism has got a creative sense to it that is obscuring the boundaries between artist and activist, protester, pop art, pranks, PR, and policy production. I have chosen to include several critical tactics since I explore the phenomenon of creative activism on a phenomenological level. The challenge is then to define a clear demarcation of the research field; the advantage is that I am able to speak about more general tendencies in diagnostic terms.

Creative critics

Activists are by definition critical. Nevertheless, it is important to be aware that not all activists are left-wing socialists who challenge the power elites – take activist fascists, for example. That being said, the ideological or party-political division has not been the focus of my investigation, as I am more interested in the emancipatory potential of critique. Critical thinking about practical forms of critique and critical theorists pervades my entire text. For empirical and theoretical reasons, it is therefore important to clarify what I mean by 'critique' and how I use this concept – and where I position myself in the critical landscape. Critique is a key concept in this book in the following three ways. Firstly, my analysis points towards a critical *zeitdiagnose* of capitalism and its protesters; secondly, the object of my investigation, the creative activist, is a critical agent; and thirdly, I use known critical theorists and their concepts throughout my analysis.

Etymologically the word 'critique' derives from the Greek *krinein* and *krisis*, which connote judgment and crisis. Today critique is almost always related to a certain individual, social, or societal crisis where the criticism in whichever form it might take constitutes a verdict, diagnosis, or modification – according to my analysis of regimes of repression or conformation and its related pathologies.

Now, a distinction can be made between two different critical strategies. One involves a critical phraseology and often appeals to an intuitive feeling of what is wrong with a certain matter. This kind of critique manifests itself at all levels of our society, from gossip in the workplace to political public debates where it needs to adjust to the popular discourses at the time (what I later call the grumbling phase of social movements). The other form of critique entails an explicit normative fundament that takes into account the historical and structural conditions that shape our society. This kind of critique is referenced in the ideological manifestos of political parties and debated in cliquish academic journals (in this regard, I consider my work to be a sociology of critique rather than critical sociology). In his book on the subject *Til Forsvar for Kritikken (In Defense of Critique)*, Rasmus Willig (2007, p. 11) concludes that: "While the one preserves the daily, normative order by virtue of its continual critical corrections, the other maintains a reflexive distance as a form of second order observation of the first" (own translation). One might also distinguish between the private and the public sphere. It is my assumption that there is a third way, namely a critical practice that challenges the two aforementioned strategies as well as the institutional conditions that gave rise to them. The creative activists in this book serve as principal examples of practitioners of this third kind of critique as they attempt to bridge the other two:

The association of Critical Shareholders (http://kritiskeaktier.dk/) buy just enough stocks in selected companies, e.g. Carlsberg, Novo Nordisk, Danisco, etc. to allow them to vote and pose critical questions and suggestions at these big corporations' annual general assemblies.

As Frank Aaen (member of the Danish Parliament for The Red-Green Alliance / Enhedslisten) steps up to address the assembly at A. P. Møller Mærsk the friendly atmosphere turns frosty: "Oh no, God have mercy on us" someone in the crowd yells (Rasmussen, May 1, 2009, Personal communication). As the black sheep of the family, a critical shareholder for over a decade, he raises the topic of working conditions in China and asks uncomfortable questions about Mærsk's responsibility in the aftermath of 2008 financial crisis.

As I am conducting a sociological study of practical forms of critique, I doubt that it is at all possible to discuss abstract justice claims without grounding them in actual experiences, although not many convincing typological examinations have been made of the concept of critique within a sociological context. But for our specific purposes, it makes sense to distinguish between a practical and a theoretical critique. I delink myself from Kant's purely epistemological critical project and the scientific tradition where critique is first and foremost a textual academic theoretical exercise. The phenomenon that I study is a socio-political practice. Karl Marx broke with the Kantian tradition when he emphasized the necessity of 'practical critical action' (*Thesen über Feuerbach*, Marx, 1968, Ch. VIII, A). Foucault, though with a different understanding and approach to politics altogether, did the same when he accentuated the 'critical attitude.' Where Kant is interested in the limits of reason (Kant, 2007 – Orig. 1781), Foucault is preoccupied with the ability of practical critique to transgress these limits (Foucault, 2007). Kant's critical philosophy sees the theoretical implications of critique as a speculative procedure. Karl Marx deals with a theoretical critique, one that involves immanent critique, as the description of the capitalist production logic itself constitutes a critique – and one that does not prevent him from advocating critical practical activities meant to change the world.

Theorists such as Marx and Foucault share their attempt to distance themselves from the epistemological endeavors of Kant, but post-structuralism and cultural studies have in their rejection of idealism in several different ways also launched an epistemological challenge to critical theory, as illustrated by the Frankfurt School – from its first generation to today's critical theorists. In this tradition (revolving around the Institut für Sozialforschung) a, however not very homogeneous, set of theorists have shared a common normative ground and a belief that considerations about the anthropological and psychological dynamics that motivate the masses as well as structuring ideologies must be investigated in order to formulate a useful critique of modernity, capitalist society, and the perceived pathologies that are derived therefrom. I will critically revisit a fundamental premise of certain strands of critical theory, namely the claim that you need an idea of what constitutes the good life to be able to pose a valid critique. I do so based on my analysis of creative activism's insistence in doing so.

However, the study of social movements, strands of activism, and more formal civil society associations that challenge power, daily practices, and our way of life, highlights how "the sociological study of critical action does not have to choose between the observation of practices carried out as small symbolic acts, circumscribed and situated, or alternatively, as the philosophical valuation of general appeals to inevitable and transcendent values" (Rebughini, 2010, p. 477). But there is tension between the normative unity of the theory and the pluralism of the critical practices immersed in common sense that can be seen in different social contexts and which carries with it a vision of critique that can only have a localized and temporary valence. Both the practical and the theoretical critique will always be normative. But whereas the former is more contingent in nature and not necessarily conscious or explicit about its normative impetus, the latter commonly aspires to universalistic criteria. Whereas pragmatic forms of critique are sociologically pluralistic, in that they can take on any form not necessarily compatible at a level of principle, the transcendental kind poses its questions within the field of political philosophy.

Even though a locally born and situated practical critique is often consolidated and legitimized by universal types of critique transcendent to the context, the creation and the validation process are analytically distinct (Benhabib, 1992). Where one is an abstract exercise that can be tested by how it holds up against good counter-arguments, the other adapts a more direct manner – a result of how the practical political circumstances condition the possibility to express lived experiences that can be tested by comparing their relevance for one's own life. Furthermore, many activists, especially the young and ideologically eclectic activists of today, do not always feel the need for a universal validity or stable solutions. They are often content with posing destabilizing questions. So, in a way I do agree with Rebughini (2010, p. 477) that "thanks to new forms of communication, mobilization and protest, it becomes possible to create, on the one hand, a link between local and contingent fragmentation of specific issues and, on the other, the ambition to give this very critique a more general capacity that also acquires a normative value." However, even though critical activist practices allow us to link the normative 'why' to the pragmatic 'how' that manifests its expression in specific demonstrations of contempt or inspiration, it is important not to mix the evaluation criteria of right and just with effective and representative.

It is not uncommon that theorists change position with regard to this question during the course of their career – and it can go both ways. For example, it has been argued (e.g. Holst, 2005) that Nancy Fraser, a central figure in the book, did exactly that. In the early years of her career, she believed that social critique should not (necessarily) be philosophically substantiated, whereas later on, she clearly states in her debates with Habermas (Fraser & Habermas, 2003), that her point of departure is in a morally based theory of justice (e.g. her universalistic principle of 'parity of participation').

In my analysis I will contextually include and nuance the practical concept of critique through a description of what it is that characterizes the critical practices of creative activists. The overall distinctions made here about what counts as which kind of critique in my research allow me to move to a sublevel of categories of critique where I can concentrate on exactly what it is that characterizes particular types of creative practical critique. This includes considerations of two particular types of critique: The strategic implications of *immanent critique* and the suggestive potential of *utopian critique* (based on a romanticized view of the past or a hopeful belief in the future), including thoughts on whether normative critique necessitates a clear idea of what you want or just a clear sense of what is wrong with the world. In other words, I will be looking at the suggestive nature of creative critical practices and their (lack of) ability to transcend the existing categories.

From a pragmatic and political perspective, critique should be more than a gesture of negation or a predictable ritual of rejection. On the other hand: "The idea of critique (...) only makes sense if there is a discrepancy between a desirable and an actual state of things" (Boltanski & Chiapello in Nowotny, 2011, p. 12). Conceptually, words such as protest, resistance, dissent, defiance, contentious politics, and social struggle are relevant and used throughout the book, given the environments that I am exploring and engaging with. They do however remain as a politically conditioned sub-terminology under the overall heading of *practical creative critique* (whether it takes an immanent or a utopian form), because they are too laden with certain traditional academic disciplines to be able to stand alone. Resistance is often used as a negative term in the dialectic struggle for power. But resistance, understood as creative critique, can also be viewed as an action that transforms oneself and the world at the same time as it opens up the present to becoming (Dufour, 2010; Brighenti, 2011; Beasley & Hager, 2014). So, having narrowed down how critique functions as an underlying, overarching concept, the transformative potential of 'becoming' begs the question: What is creativity?

The Rebel Sell

Just like critique, in a historical sense, has managed to free itself from the monopoly of abstraction and negation, creativity has gone through a de-theologization and also to some extent broken with the mythical tradition of geniuses related to religious beliefs. The artist himself has taken on several roles – from craftsman to court artist and from revolutionary artist to bohemian. Creativity stems from the Latin word *creare*, which means to create. For centuries God was the sole creator and he who created everything out of nothing (*creatio ex nihilo*). In those days man was thought of, at best, as an imitation of divine ideas (Plato) or as a follower of the natural order (Aristotle). In the Renaissance philosophers began to write about the free will of human beings as something that allows us, as the privileged species that we are, to rise above nature, though still only within the limits that God has set for us. From the 16th to the 19th century the perception of man changes from a created being to a being with the ability to create. The rare artist as a genius is glorified. But during the 20th century the development of human psychology in particular meant that we have gone from a view of creativity as something a few men were born with, to something all of us can be – a universal potential – that allows us to break free from our naturally, socially, and culturally pre-determined faith – and take charge of our own destiny and create our own identity and society. Philosophically speaking, creativity went from being a solely religious matter to an aesthetic and then existential one. In sociology creative abilities were related to particular processes and different environments. Pedagogically it was concerned with one's upbringing and education.

As we have entered the 21st century, the creative individual is once again celebrated. Not deified but worshipped. The creative class is growing and in most lines of work creativity is a sought-after quality in a marketplace where one constantly has to stay flexible as capitalist production is increasingly dependent on innovation to reach its growth margins and create new needs and markets in a global economy that struggles to keep up with its own standards. One may go as far as to say that creativity today is not a privilege but rather a necessary requirement – and with compulsory creativity we are eliminating the freedom that was once the end goal of creativity (Larsen, 2011, pp. 24–29). The correlation between cognitive capitalism, where unlimited resources such as knowledge, attention, innovation, and even critical thinking, are drained, privatized, and withdrawn from the commons (e.g. Gorz, 2010; Moulier-Boutang, 2011), and the growing demand for creativity in the workforce, is typically regarded by critical theorists as the reason for socio-pathological tendencies: "This kind of pimping of the creative force is what has been transforming the planet into a gigantic marketplace, expanding at an exponential rate, either by including its inhabitants as hyperactive zombies or by excluding them as human trash" (Rolnik, 2011, p. 29).

Is the creative activist contributing to this development or escaping the shackles of our instrumental monoculture? This question points toward how I will synthesize tactical ways of dealing with the *uncontinuity of capitalisms* and the dialectic tension between structure and agent. On one hand, knowledge economy seems to result in a cynical commodification of non-economic dimensions of our lives and a normalization of the original, that goes with capital's move from the material to the immaterial, private, and most intimate of all places, our unconsciousness, the place where creativity rests and the last stronghold of innocence. On the other hand, the cynical instrumentalization of the critical potential that lies within the creative radicals of our still somewhat unspoiled imagination might prove to be the best remaining hope of creating a better place for all of us.

Thus, based on my *structurally pragmatic but agent optimistic perspective* I combine a critical understanding of how creativity today is incorporated and tamed by capitalism with a confident belief in the emancipatory potential of creative critique, namely through its ability to break with existing norms and create new ones – be it indignation, a practical idea, or a whole new way of co-existing. Historically seen, this combination, as I have shown, demarks a tension between the 20th-century belief, coined by the infamous saying 'we are all artists', and the 21st-century business demand and crisis mantra that we all have to be innovative.

Superflex is a political art group of social entrepreneurs who experiment with new forms of collaborations that defy our conventional understanding of what an organization is. Superflex works with what they call 'tools' or 'projects', which function like conceptual social interventions. They are in many ways organized as a company since they copy the market, which is often the object of their critique. This setup also offers the group more flexibility than the obvious alternatives. As they say: The NGO is bound by specific agendas. (...) But with the creative elements one has the freedom to pose critical questions and suggest possible solutions to a given problem while maintaining an uncertain outlook.

In August 1997, Superflex developed a sustainable biogas mini facility in cooperation with engineers from Tanzania (http://superflex.net/tools/supergas/). The device can cover the need of a poor African family and runs solely on excrement of the family in question as well as the excrement of their animals. Both the partnering NGOs and the art foundation that supports the work were confused about the project's intentions due to problems of categorization. But the point was exactly to question how we in the Western world project and export our own definition of progress in a different cultural context. In cooperation with local NGOs, the device has now been introduced in several countries, including Tanzania, Cambodia, and Thailand. In cooperation with practical engineers the creative ideas became a real experiment and so what at first glance seemed like a silly idea was then developed into a real project that could lead to new and more sustainable solutions.

In *The New Spirit of Capitalism* (2005) Ève Chiapello and Luc Boltanski distinguish between artistic and social critique in their historical analysis of how the critical and creative energy of the 1960s was channeled into a new public management regime of the 1990s. The artistic critique is based on and demands freedom, autonomy, and authenticity. The social critique is based on and calls for solidarity, security, and equality – and is not least rooted in the traditional workers' movement. In *The New Spirit of Capitalism*, a modern classic for disillusioned leftist academics, the two types of critiques 'are most often developed and embodied by different groups' and are 'incompatible' (Boltanski & Chiapello in Lazzarato, 2011, p. 41). Analytically the division makes sense, but it is both politically and theoretically problematic. Many of today's creative activists, as demonstrated later, bridge this dichotomy as categories are blurring and the gap between the practical, pluralistic, and contingent critique and the theoretical normatively universalistic critique is closing – in a world where what works is increasingly understood as what is good and right.

In *The Rebel Sell* (2006) Joseph Heath and Andrew Potter present a related explanation with regard to why and how counter-culture becomes mainstream and eventually turns into consumer culture – or how the rebel yell is turned into something to sell. The premise here is that such a turn is a sign of failure. Many of the leading creative activists are cynical or pragmatic enough to view such mechanisms as an unavoidable and necessary evil if you want to be able to reach your long-term goals. Selective facilitation as a reason for the demobilization of social movements as understood in a cyclical perspective (to be elaborated on in Chapter 3) is one example of how the discussion of the differences between cooptation and recuperation become evident throughout the book.

In my critical analysis of how creativity is instrumentalized in the critical practices of activists, my aim is not to reject the legitimacy of those practices, but rather to understand the meaning of them. Just like Kant's critique of the various capacities of reason, creativity is not just criticized, but is also somewhat actualized in the procedure of critically differentiating between the elements that it consists of. Confining the democratic potentiality of these activists' creative activities is therefore also a way of emphasizing whatever potential these actions contain.

Tentative definition

For now the creative activist can be regarded as being creative in two senses of the word: firstly, by *creating* a space for the revitalization of the political imagination and secondly, by doing so in *inventive* ways.[2] The latter is necessary because of the increasing weight of entertainment and headlines in the political public sphere, which is related to factors such as globalization, the mediatization of politics, the personalization of politics, the sharing political economy, communication as organization, new and changing forms of capitalisms, as well as differences in institutional inclusiveness across regions, etc. (Bennett and Segerberg, 2013). As Stephen Duncombe and Steve Lambert teach at the School for Creative Activism (http://artisticactivism.org/our-rationale/#):

The first rule of activism is to know the terrain and use it to your advantage and the current political topography is one of symbols and signs, images and expressions. This is the avant-garde of activism today. From small community organizations to international NGOs, visionary activists are looking to broaden their base of appeal and the reach of their message by employing culture alongside more traditional organizing practices.

This kind of activism is not dogmatic but seeks to challenge habitual ways of thinking about a given societal situation – be it small or large. One may also define it negatively – in terms of what it is not. It is not the conventional civil society's NGO or mass demonstration, but something in-between. It is neither corporate innovation nor aggressive manifestation, but rather an inspired synthesis. It is not public newspaper columns or political art but something that involves both, in a social format. It is inventive ways of rousing non-automatic reflection in involved citizens, provoked politicians, or the captured public at large. This is also what makes it difficult to delimitate, categorize, and pin down.

On October 30, 2010 a *Rally to Restore Sanity and/or Fear* staged by Jon Stewart and Stephen Colbert, both popular satire news hosts on *The Daily Show*, gathered around 200,000 people at Washington National Mall – an event that was followed by millions of viewers. This raises the question: is the ability of a couple of comedians to gather that many people in a protest an expression of a shift in the critical topography? To make sense of this event it must be understood both as a conscious critical strategy designed to cope with the increased demand of the political public sphere to entertain and communicate in headlines, as well as a symptom of that same societal condition. Attention is one of the most precious resources in an information age – and punch lines give 'presence' to Stewart and Colbert's arguments. But is this the solution or part of the problem? The two are naturally intertwined, but whereas the first calls for an optimistic analysis of the potential for this sort of activism to offer diagnostic critique and reflection through provocation, the second necessitates that we view such critics as principal creators of systemic transformative conservation and thus the continuous survival of capitalism – in other words, as victims or accomplices, rather than answers to the current tactical questions of the left.

Two readings of these kinds of happenings will therefore be pursued in order to account for the ambivalence of the contemporary state of critique in its most flamboyant form. The *Rally to Restore Sanity and/or*

Fear went from being a joke that seemed unlikely to become anything more than that to a serious manifestation making truth claims about the state of the union. Stewart and Colbert used the non-rational discourse of comedy to promote reality (Ginsberg, 2011): "Parodic polyglossia, satirical specificity, and contextual clash are comic-frame strategies of incongruity that permit a communicator to be multivoiced, to deflate abstractions and mystifications, and to symbolically span a variety of situations" (Waisanen, 2009). Stewart and Colbert's comic strategies are more than just techniques for creating entertainment – they are tools for rhetorical criticism with socio-political application, reminding or instructing their audiences about moral democratic possibilities.

This transition is tricky because it jeopardizes the most important thing creative activists have going for them, which is the ambiguity of their message. This in itself is why their critical talk shows work best on a meta-level for commenting on news broadcasters, not as a substitute for classical journalism. Likewise creative activism should not only or always be understood as an alternative in its own right, but rather as a supplement to more traditional forms of participation. With regard to the rally, the uncertainty of whether the organizers were serious or not seems to have rescued it in the end. What I will later describe as the cynical appearance and the ironic tone left the crowd and the broader public imagining whether sanity really can be restored and if so, what it might take to do so. They force us to see issues from more than one angle, creating 'shocks' of insight, as incongruity and comic framing create expansive grounds for inventive communication.

Why did David beat Goliath? Because he was inventive in using what he had to his advantage. Since there was an imbalance in resources (size and power), he had to be resourceful (Gladwell, 2013; Ganz, 2010b). When 18 handpicked student participants (who usually have regular and important jobs in which they are able to apply creative activist tactics in one way or another) were asked at the School for Creative Activism how they would describe *what* they do, they said that they try to "teach," "inspire," "mirror the world as it really is," "facilitate dialogue," "mediate," "change reality – for a little while at least," "create the future."[3] When asked *why* they do it, they replied that: "You cannot legislate away child abuse or sexism. You have to change hearts and minds," and that: "This is the most effective way of changing peoples' consciousness."

KONY 2012. Within just a few days of its release, the Invisible Children's documentary about Joseph Kony, the rebel leader of the Lord's Resistance Army in Uganda, attracted more than 50 million views on YouTube and Vimeo, generating hundreds of thousands of dollars in donations on the first day alone. It spread like wildfire on Twitter and Facebook at a pace rarely seen before – and especially not for a half-hour film about a distant conflict in central Africa (Kron & Goodman, March 8, 2012: "How the Kony video went Viral," *New York Times*).

How did this video attract so much attention? It uses a whole range of the tricks and tools found in the modern activist's toolbox (http://www.invisiblechildren.com/). The cynical use of these also created a heated debate about the political role and actual impact of social media and met heavy criticism, with foreign NGOs and Ugandan officials alike accusing the viral media campaign of being imperialistic, simplistic, manipulative, and militant. KONY 2012 touches upon many of the moral dilemmas that creative activists face. Where do we draw the line between commercial guerilla marketing and viral activist PR? Does the end justify the means?

Tentatively I define 'creative activism' as civic, project-driven, and nonviolent forms of democratic participation where critical perspectives on a societal issue or a political system are communicated when, where, and in ways that no one else can or will. They do so in creative ways through temporal interventions such as strategic happenings, transformative events, and manufactured spectacles characterized by a cynical approach, an ironic attitude and/or an imaginary quest in order to provoke reflection in the individual spectator and the public sphere at large. They facilitate dialogue between traditional divides and actors, and when successful, provide an alternative space for action. So we cannot simply view these spontaneous outbursts of desire and strategically designed campaigns in their individual manifestations – rather, we must view them as part of an ongoing attempt to facilitate democratic experiments that allow the subject to continuously reclaim and reinvent its autonomy through a politics of playful subversion. As such, creative activism can be regarded both as a product of and a reaction to the dominant political rationale and the mediatized public in which it thrives.

The conceptualizations around happenings, events, and spectacles are distinct but interlinked. A *happening* can be defined as "a form of theater" that has a "non-verbal character" and employs "a structure that could be called insular or compartmented" (Michael Kirby in Sandford, 1995, pp. 1–25). According to theorists such as William H. Sewell, *events* are defined as a subclass of the happening. I too recognize the power of eventful temporality in the cause of history as events have the ability to "transform structures largely by constituting and empowering new groups of actors or by re-empowering existing groups in new ways"

(Sewell, 1996, p. 271). Events in this perspective can "become turning points (...) concentrated moments of political and cultural creativity when the logic of historical development is reconfigured by human action but by no means abolished" (McAdam & Sewell, 2001, p. 102). As David Hess and Brian Martin conclude (2006, p. 249), "a transformative event is a crucial turning point for a social movement that dramatically increases or decreases the level of mobilization." In fact it seems that the history of each movement and of contentious politics in each country always includes what Donatella Della Porta (2011) calls 'eventful protests'. As noted, Guy Debord uses the spectacle not only to diagnose society but also as a way to fight back. Stephen Duncombe, who is inspired by the writings of Bertolt Brecht, defines the *spectacles* that the creative activists manufacture as a certain way of making an argument:

> Not through appeals to reason, rationality, and self-evident truth, but instead through story and myth, fears and desire, imagination and fantasy. It realizes what reality cannot represent. It is the animation of an abstraction, a transformation from ideal expression. Spectacle is a dream on display. (2007, p. 30)

The risk of the Sewell methodology applied too mechanically is to miss how and when structurally rich but non-eventful processes have a profound impact on history. Change is triggered suddenly but happens slowly. It is therefore important analytically to distinguish between *eventful histories* (the primary focus of this book) and *events in history* as Charles Tilly (e.g. 2008) for example has dealt with. In the larger schemes of change and development Aristide Zolberg's "moments of madness" (1972) are tempered into more permanent tools of society's critical repertoire

Cracks

Creative activists can be said to operate in the cracks. The weakness in any kind of armor is always the cracks in it – whether it is the cracks in a dam holding back the water that keeps pushing to find a way to its natural repository or the cracks in the cement on our sidewalks that allow weeds and wildflowers to grow. As Leonard Cohen sings: "There's a crack, a crack in everything / That's how the light gets in." Or in less poetic terms: "The task of revealing the cracks in contemporary hegemonies and working to see things differently is central to the project of bringing into being a world of more equity and diversity" (McKinnon,

Gibson, & Malam, 2008, p. 279). Pragmatic critique clearly admits the existence of hegemonic visions of reality, "but maintains that they must be based on some form of legitimation and it is within the cracks in this legitimation that the possibility of critique is formed" (Rebughini, 2010, p. 471). It is in the cracks of the politicians' polished surface, in our seemingly coherent ideologies, in the political system, and in our belief systems that the creative activist works. This is where she finds weakness and uses it to mock a rival. But it is also within these cracks that she sees an invitation to change the minds of those who leave room for mistakes and are open to new ways of looking at things. "We create these frameworks, we operate within them, they begin to break down (...) and then we're looking for where the fractures are, where the constituents are for renewal" (Marshal Ganz interview). In line with this metaphor, creative artists can be said to 'crack a hole in the wall' (break down barriers) or 'crack a window open' (create opportunity) – often just by cracking a joke.

Creative activism works in the cracks of polished surfaces. In the cracks that we are all scared to fall into. In the cracks that prove that we are humans – imperfect beings. In the cracks that reasonable doubt luckily creates in our foundational beliefs. All of these cracks represent a space below the surface, a space in-between known terrain. Or – to relate it to terms within the aesthetic domain – a social interstice, a space of potentiality where relational art produces inter-subjective encounters that spur existential reflection.[4] In 2011 activists were occupying everything – public squares, parks, and buildings. It was even called the 'Occupy movement'. Creative activism occupies 'the space in-between'. It can be a physical space or a political position. It can be an idea's point of departure or a temporary hub where opinions meet. What these spaces have in common is that they are all perceived as 'no-places' (to begin with) – a literal meaning of utopia – since they 'exist' only when they are mapped, and they are not mapped until they are occupied by someone. As Louis Marin writes, "utopic discourse occupies the historically empty space" and works as a discourse that stages an imaginary solution to the contradiction that it situates itself within (1984, p. xiii). In this sense the creative activist is a first mover because she creates a new space and with it a new reality.

When the land for the temporary Roskilde Festival is occupied for one week every summer it becomes Denmark's fourth most populated city. Its new More Than Music initiative is an example of how such new realities are created. This part of the festival works like an urban simulator where artists, activists, and 30,000 volunteers, through the active involvement of the audience, co-create ecological, experimental, efficient, just, and beautiful sketches for the city of tomorrow in their sociological laboratory (Danielsen, 2012).

There seem to be three overall parameters by which it can be measured. These fall within the communicative, the organizational, and the cooperative specter of progressive politics. Characteristic for creative forms of activism is that it occupies the space in-between the dichotomies of the binary logic of conventional political measurement. Creative activism is neither irrational arts nor pragmatic politics. It communicates in a media-friendly symbolic language that uses cynical humor and ironic critique and can therefore be placed in-between those two.

The creative activist is not as cryptic as Pablo Picasso's *Guernica* and not as (seemingly) straightforward as politicians when they rationally lay out their reasons for going to war. The creative activist communicates in symbols, images, and narratives that are both familiar and uncertain as they use humor and drama to get their message across or accelerate those of others. It is not a painting on a wall and not a man on a pedestal. It is a social sculpture, an inventive campaign, and a provocative experiment that borrows from both worlds and then creates a new space.

On the organizational scale the creative activist also positions herself in-between known positions. She is not defined by her involvement in impulsive mass riots but nor does she follow the communally decided membership protocol of the local organization either. She most often operates in temporary, single-issue, project-organized cadres of activists where she facilitates self-organization of the participants – those who cannot be labeled as spontaneous masses and not (yet) members of an institutionalized movement, although recent developments in Spain (Podemos), Greece (Syriza), and Denmark (Alternativet) are examples of how those lines (again) are beginning to blur.

According to the cooperative parameter, the creative activist is not content with resistance for the sake of rebellion alone. She does not merely identify in opposition. This does not mean however that she chooses to cooperate with the private sector or join forces with the establishment in order to make a difference. Creative activism is critique in action *and* a variant of pre-figurative politics. This means that it not only criticizes, it also experiments with forms and practices that propose an alternative possible future society based on consensus decision-making, an expressive political style, anti-authoritarian lifestyles, ethical consumption, and a rejection of rigid ideologies and organizational forms. Is Beppe Grillo to be placed left or right on the traditional party political spectrum in Italy? Where do we place the young people on Taksim Square? And what role does ideology play in Kiev and Bangkok? In line with my definition of critique, "a unified political strategy is replaced by a pluralistic flowering of autonomous projects, practices, communities, and institutions" (Blair, 2012). As they learn to 'manufacture dissent' by employing a commercially inspired language of association from popular culture and its ability to speak to the irrational and emotional within us, reality and fantasy begin to coexist and intermingle. Reality needs fantasy to render it desirable, just as fantasy needs reality to make it believable.

Stephen Duncombe (2007, p. 17), founder of the School for Creative Activism, envisions a restoration of people's ability to dream:

> Dreams the public can mold and shape themselves. They will be active: Spectacles that work only if people help create them. They will be open ended: setting stages to ask questions and leaving silences to formulate answers. And they will be transparent: dreams that one knows are dreams but which still have power to attract and inspire. And, finally, the spectacles we create will not cover over or replace reality and truth but perform and amplify it.

Duncombe argues that these techniques should be implemented. I will show how they are already at work in the happenings, events, and spectacles analyzed. The underlying premise is that while illusion may be a necessary part of political life, delusion need not be. Jacques Rancière and other like-minded political philosophers have also emphasized how fiction, not in opposition to reality but as an addition to the perception of it, challenges daily routines through surreal narratives. To paraphrase Rancière, the revolution starts when the workers stop resting at night to be ready for another day at work, and start dreaming instead (Rancière, 1991).

Private–public collaboration, user-driven innovation, and socially experimental networks that operate in-between the state, the market, and the civil society have a lot to learn from the discursive autonomy of creative activists. Political parties, NGOs, labor unions, and private companies are starting to look to these new social actors for inspiration. That begs the question: Are these 'technologies' inherently good? There is certainly reason to be skeptical about the temporal nature of playful activity as a catalyst for emancipative real politics today and to ask, if not, whether totalitarianism is inherent in *aesthetico-politics*:

> The use of signs and symbols, and the aesthetico-politics demonstrated by the Nazi regime are excellent examples of the way in

which a subjective politico-aesthetic experience becomes instead the mobilization of a political movement towards totalitarianism; where the playful aesthetico-politics meant to re-politicize human society through the continuous practice of critique, self-reflection and prefigurative interventions, becomes instead a totalitarian, particular experience of the divine object of truth. (Ølgaard, 2015, p. 140)

The use of creative activist techniques by totalitarian regimes and Madison Avenue begs us, in fact it makes it incumbent on us, to reflect on what constitutes ethical democratic persuasion as opposed to manipulative propaganda. The range of creative activism's format and ideological base is wide – from the (uninvited) Santa Claus army (Solvognen) giving presents away at a department store during the holidays to remind capitalist society of the true spirit of Christmas, to Pepper-Spray-Cop memes created and shared to reveal and ridicule harsh police practice, to the Islamic State's iconic video *Flames of War* produced to mythologize religious struggle in the mediatized battlefield of war.

As I will show, creative activism uses mirroring techniques to try to get us to see alternatives, real or not, and reflect the world around us in beautiful, distorted, and surprising ways. This trend is therefore not only interesting as an expression of the perpetual reinvention of the modern progressive vanguard, it also tells us something about the political mainstream. That is why the study of these practices will also be used to make critical diagnoses of society itself.

This book is a large-scale study of creative activism that does not celebrate these new social actors as bearers of better societal alternatives, but rather explores how they facilitate the cultivation of such alternatives.

Interdisciplinary approach

Empirically I use both quantitative and qualitative data to support my claims and explore my hypotheses. The sources range from multilevel regression analyses of statistical data from, for example, the European Social Survey and World Value Studies to the sampling of data from distributed questionnaires, participatory observation in mass demonstrations, strategic interventions, and strategic organization building from the perspective of the board members. They also include case studies, informal talks, activist workshops, and interviews with leading activists and renowned scholars in the field. Numerous primary and secondary sources have informed this study, but a series of key datasets and interviews make up the core of my empirical analyses. Hundreds of cases have been analyzed. Only a small fraction of these will be used throughout the book as illustrative historical and present-day examples of trends and patterns from around the world in order to break the monotony of the textual linear format and remind the reader what is at stake (for more see e.g. actipedia.org – an open access community-generated wiki to document, share, and inspire creative activism).

Is today's creative activism a diagnostic symptom of a pathological societal development, or does it constitute a democratic potential as a strategic reaction to these developments? This question has stayed with me from the very beginning of my research because it touches on the dialectical tensions between citizen and society, agent and structure, and the fundamental normative ambivalence towards the experimental practices in question. The latter results in a parallel split in my analytical gaze, which now flickers between an optimistic belief in the ability of alternative voices to broaden the public debate and take some of us in an unexpected direction, and a skeptical view of those agents and their actual effect on which path we choose to take – which is why I am also concerned with identifying the contradictions, obstacles, and risks faced in the development of new types of collective action. This critical approach derives from a conviction (shared by Gerbaudo, 2012) that only by also "unearthing negative elements can we hope to gain a better understanding of contemporary protest culture and thereby aid activists in their development of new forms of communication and organization."

Throughout this book I combine an interest in moments of opening, when hegemonic understandings are ruptured and suppressed injustices disclosed, with an interest in moments of closure, when new understandings, forged through struggle and argument, galvanize public efforts to change.

With a balanced and sober scientific approach to this culturally hot political phenomenon I will generate a new interdisciplinary theoretical framework and apply it in my analysis of the practices in question, map patterns of participation, develop an anchored typology of activism, and discuss the moral implications and political relevance of what the creative activist does today – all with the purpose of clarifying how provoked moments of disruption or clarity can trigger resistance and move the social. This book thereby connects the dots – from triggering, one-off operations, to political campaigns, social movements, and conventional party politics.

Much has been written about artistic activism throughout the years, but no sustained study has yet really managed to establish this political research field or convincingly identified the new social actors operating in it. This book does so by contextualizing current creative activism in the larger collection of left-liberal activist practices and practitioners. Through its theoretical framework, the book also takes activism out of its ghetto by offering a new and broader perspective on topics that link up to wider discussions of citizenship, civil society, and participatory democracy.

The book is structured into four parts. Part I is about identifying the phenomenon in question. I have already given a preliminary definition of creative activism, even though the book can be read as one long attempt to do exactly that. Chapter 2 questions whether this really is a new phenomenon and also clarifies how the conditions have changed. Part II questions the field in which this type of activism usually unfolds – both practically and analytically. This means outlining and questioning traditional theoretical approaches and positioning the creative activist within and beyond that framework. Chapter 3 therefore focuses on how first movers can set in motion circular cycles of contention. Chapter 4 deals with paradoxes of participation related to psychological incentives and structural conditions. Where Part II is about understanding the terrain, Part III is about using it to our advantage and creating a new theoretical framework through an exploration of critical practice – standing on the shoulders of those who have gone before us. Chapter 5 thus supplements traditional theories of movement, citizenship, and art with ambiguity through the concepts of cynicism, irony, and utopia. Chapter 6 sketches the contours of a new critical theory of reflection using the mirror as a metaphor to show how creative activists' finest role is to get people to see the world and themselves from a new angle. Part IV deals with new trends and future dilemmas related to professionalization, cooptation, and the possibility of measuring the actual effect of these change makers' trouble-making. Chapter 7 discusses how states operate as facilitators of new types of conversations, social businesses crowding the activist space, and how new types of NGO partnerships all challenge the creative activist to rethink his organization, communication, and (non)ideological foundation. Finally, Chapter 8 considers more appropriate ways to measure the impact and value of these kinds of practices by distinguishing between effect and affect. On this basis our theories of change are revisited.

2
Creative Activism Today

Creative activism can now be defined as a kind of meta activism that facilitates the engagement of active citizens in temporary, strategically manufactured, transformative interventions in order to change society for the better by communicating conflicts and/or solutions where no one else can or will in order to provoke reflection (and consequent behavioral changes) in an attempt to revitalize the political imagination. In this chapter I will discuss why creative activism on one hand must be understood as variations of an already known repertoire, but on the other how it also needs to be reviewed as a new phenomenon owing to the changed conditions under which it operates. I then describe the political circuit that creative activists are part of and use it both to outline the broader field and to narrow down my focus:

> The infamous photograph from 1968 by Eddie Adams of the murder of a Vietcong by the Saigon Police Chief is modified so that the Coca-Cola label blows the brains out (google viet cong coca cola). Semiotic sabotage of Coca Cola's iconographic imagery is meant to undermine the brand and raise the issue of the company's claimed labor repression schemes and the changing forms of American colonialism throughout history.

Détournement as a technique (known from Guy Debord and The Situationists) "appropriates and alters an existing media artifact, one that the intended audience is already familiar with, in order to give it a new subversive meaning" (Zack Malitz in Boyd, 2012, p. 29). When it works best memes are created that help a rallying cry go viral because it is 'sticky' and communicates complex critique in an easy way. According to *Adbusters*, a Canadian magazine and a leading proponent of counterculture 'subverts' create cognitive dissonance by mimicking the look and feel of the targeted ad, when viewers suddenly realize they have been duped. These modern murals are meant to cut through the hype and glitz of our mediated reality and momentarily reveal a deeper truth within. Memes, such as *Casually Pepper Spray Everything Cop*, are playful political reconfiguration of the known into something else – and thus an example of an activist technique that captures the essence of the questions I am asking here.

> Memes transform the context of the original image in order to emphasize the act it depicts. And it does so through humor, which demonstrates to us how comic appropriation promises to criticize indirectly by drawing readers' attention to the absurdity of the act. (Ølgaard, 2015, p. 135)

So what's new about this phenomenon?

Jesus, Gandhi, and Martin Luther King used parables and narratives to capture the attention of their audience. They used dilemma actions to infringe those in power, and they staged performances to amplify reality and to question its legitimacy. Subcomandante Marcos used an air force consisting of paper airplanes to carry messages and poems for the enemy soldiers as a peaceful but very effective way to promote Zapatista and their cause. The Provos, the Situationists, the 77 movement, and Solvognen were challenging the dominant hegemony through their culture jamming and artistic interventions. The creative activists of today clearly stand on the shoulders of those before them. But the conditions have changed.

Globalization, diversification, individualization, virtualization, the increasing mediatization and aestheticization of politics, and the spread of cognitive capitalism have crucial spatial and temporal consequences for mobilization and thus necessitate a revision of the role and the why's and the how's of creative activism. The first rule of guerilla warfare is to know your terrain and use it to your advantage. The political terrain is changing, and today people sympathize, organize, and participate in ways that are different from what they used to do. Social activism has got a creative new edge that blurs the boundaries between artist and activist, pop art and political pranks, guerilla marketing and activist artistry as they seem to occupy the space in-between.

The principles, strategies, and tactics applied by creative activists are many (see Boyd et al., 2012), and include innovative manoeuvres such as flash mobs, subvertisement, hacktivism, urban guerilla gardening, identity correction, forum theater, infiltrating media-jacking, prefigurative interventions etc. As my approach is a phenomenological one, I am concerned with the strategic principles behind the various kinds of tactics. I will be looking at other types of examples too, but all of them share the aim of creating temporary autonomous zones (Bey, 2011) through the social production of space (Lefebvre, 1991). Creative activism is not violent. It is not your occasional demonstrator marching to the beat. It is not NGO lobbying, nor is it the everyday maker or the active citizen who takes the initiative to improve her housing co-operative's environmental footprint. Its goals, communication, and organization are different.

As pointed out, creative types of activism are not an entirely new phenomenon as they have taken place throughout history in one form or another. As Stephen Duncombe and Steve Lambert argue on their Center for Artistic Activism's website, "From Jesus' parables to the Tea Party's protests, working artfully makes activism effective." There is an art to every practice. And "While Martin Luther King Jr. is remembered for his example of moral courage, social movement historian Doug McAdam's assessment of King's 'genius for strategic dramaturgy' probably better explains the success of his campaigns" (we will take a closer look at the American civil rights movement later). In the 20th century the periods that most vividly testify to this tendency have always been characterized by crisis – e.g. Russia in the 1910s, USA and Germany in the 1930s, and around the world in the 1970s. These were times when spectacular and defining movements challenged the boundaries of art, science, and politics in original ways. Situationist International, the Art Workers Coalition in New York, the Artist Placement Group, which originated in London, and the 1977 movement in Italy are historically influential European examples of how social movements experimented with the political potential of art (see Bolt, 2005; Cuninghame, 2007). The transient, interdisciplinary, and hybrid nature of performance art allowed for public participation while the openness and immediacy of the medium was a hub of media attention. These periods represent modes of coping with the people's frustration and the avant-garde's demand for politically engaged artistic activism at the time.

A historical consciousness of these period examples and others like them is significant because an analysis of previous attempts to transcend conventional opposition bears witness to the difficulties of balancing between critique, recuperation, and cooptation. Furthermore they often function as implicit or explicit reference points for current creative activists. Critics of the 'newness' of new social movements (e.g. Plotke, 1990; Tarrow, 1991) have pointed out how new forms of cultural resistance have gradually developed from conventional political life, which is why their novelty is overstated by theorists in the field. Karl-Werner Brand (1990) suggests that so-called 'new' critical phenomena are always responses to crises of culture, and therefore merely the latest manifestation of a cyclical pattern that should be seen as a well-known and rather conservative reaction to the perpetual rebirth of modernity. For example, the idea that personal revelation through art can be a political tool has ensured that creative elements of social movements play a key strategic role in mobilizing members and sustaining momentum. So, this type of activism is not entirely new as it can be seen as a revitalization that take place through a reorganization of earlier movement practices.

But what *is* new about today's creative activism are the changed conditions for the immanent and potentially emancipatory critique at the heart of this type of engagement. However, perhaps we can speak of a depression-like crisis in today's western societies similar to the periods just mentioned? The number of stress-related and existential depressions are growing rapidly in the western world; the socio-economic base of the political parties is vanishing as membership of political parties has simultaneously steadily declined since the beginning of the 1990s (Gundelach & Siune, 1992; Putnam, 1995; Whiteley, 2009). Representative democracy as we know it is in crisis; the global gap between rich and poor has never been bigger; and the ecological balance is in jeopardy – just to name a few of the political challenges that the liberal democracy of capitalism is facing. The disappointment takes many pathological *and* resourceful forms.[1] Let us briefly touch upon some of these developments as they condition the way we participate as active citizens in our community and operate as part of our democracy in new ways.

Globalization, understood as an increased flow of information, people, and finances that politically and culturally intertwines countries and communities, has had a fundamental impact on how agents of contentious politics mobilize across borders. Scholars are rightfully starting to ask questions such as "How is globalization impacting on new democratic thinking and what, in turn, is the impact of social movement participation on globalization?" (Pearce, 2007, p. 465; Fominaya, 2014). This change does not only mean that we now see an increase in what one might call global activist nomads and a spread in rapid diffusion mechanisms (della Porta & Mattoni, 2014), it has also resulted in what Ulrich Beck calls a 'cosmopolitical consciousness' (Beck, 2006). Globalization has influenced the political opportunity structure, the mobilization strategies, the organization, and the attitude of the political activist in a number of ways. As the nation state has been both a target for claims made by, and a frame for, social movements since the late 18th century, so is globalization today both the object and the main dispositioning factor of defiant critics – including creative activists – "given a ramifying human rights regime, on the one hand, and spiraling networks of global governance, on the other" (Fraser, 2008, p. 5). With globalization, new and alternative public spheres arise that demand of the activist a facilitation of deep democratic dialogues across cultures independently of nationally defined state institutions – since:

> Civility now has to be entrenched globally before it can be guaranteed nationally and locally, but the guarantors of civility in the old national state, a legal system, rights, a judiciary, police, political representation and administration under the law, have no global equivalents. Democratic behavior then has to be lodged at a deeper level than in institutions alone. (Albrow et al., 2008, p. 4)

The United Nations describes participatory democracy as a process in which "anyone can enter the debate that they are most interested in, through advocacy, protest, and in other ways" (Annan (UN), 2004, p. 25, paragraph 13). This definition is however modified later on as it acknowledges that there are practical constraints: "If the United Nations brought everyone relevant into each debate, it would have endless meetings without conclusions" (Annan (UN), 2004, p. 27, paragraph 23). According to the first paragraph it seems that creative activists of all sorts agree since their actions try to honor such an understanding of democracy by giving ordinary citizens a voice. But alternative political summits, for example, stress the associational diversity of civil society as the basis for a deliberative democracy, and one that also provides a fertile contrast to the monolithic citizen–state relationship of representative democracy. With regard to the second paragraph, it can be concluded that seemingly 'endless meetings without conclusions' already seem to be the reality of the current UN climate summits in/despite its current form. Better decisions for the world's climate might be taken if civil society gets more involved.

The technological advances of the past decades are another example of a development that conditions the way in which we engage with the political public sphere in new ways. These advances are closely related to the power relations between the media and politicians, and indicate an important shift. Our new forms of communication means a change in the way activists are able to coordinate internally and also how they mobilize and profile themselves externally. The use of viral media in the Arab Spring and the Occupy movement in the US in the Autumn of 2011 are relevant examples of how crucial these new possibilities are. Straight after Egyptian President Hosni Mubarak decided to step down, American President Barack Obama commented on the increasing importance of fast and coordinated communication for the movements:

> Above all, we saw a new generation emerge – A generation that uses their own creativity, talent, and technology to call for a government that represented their hopes and not their fears. (Obama, 2011)

In a broader perspective:

> More value can be gotten out of voluntary participation than anyone previously imagined, thanks to improvement in our ability to connect with one another and improvements in our imagination of what is possible from such participation. (Shirky, 2010 p. 161)

In a wider popular context Gladwell (2010) points out that activism through social media does not produce the structure needed to mobilize effectively. The argument is that social networks like Twitter and Facebook involve weak ties rather than strong ties (Granovetter, 1973), and that these weak ties do not lead to high-risk activism. In line with this type of argument, Van Deth (2013) claims that newer forms of online engagement do not provide sufficient links between citizens and the political system. Other scholars disagree with the assumption that new forms of engagement are ineffective (Bennet & Segerberg, 2012; Gonzalez-Bailon, Borge-Holthoefer, & Moreno, 2013). They claim that the horizontal nature of online mobilization and coordination will strengthen civic networks over time.

During the course of the 18th century literacy, the printing press as well as new forms of association – when the state became a frame for collective contentious action – marked a shift from a traditional form of collective action to a modern repertoire (elaborated on in the following chapter). Moving up to the 1960s, Boltanski and Chiapello (2005) identify four sources of indignation in the critique of capitalism. These are: (1) a demand for emancipation; (2) a protest against non-authenticity;

(3) an opposition to egoism; and (4) a reaction to suffering. The first two can be classified as *artistic critique* and originally took shape in the bohemian milieu of the 19th century. This critique targeted the uniformity of mass society and the commercialization of human relations. It is romantic in the sense that it elevates merits such as spontaneity, autonomy, creativity, and authenticity, but it does not glorify the days that were. Freedom rather than equality serves as an ideal for the 'artistic critique'. The latter two sources of indignation can be classified as *social critique*, which is rooted in the traditional workers' movement. Here the focus is on the exploitation of the poor, and therefore the importance of solidarity is stressed as a fundamental principle. By proposing a change in ownership of means of production, progressive possibilities of emancipation were pursued by the social critique.

Today new communication technologies, the mediatization of politics, the public sphere, and globalization all mark a shift to an era where new forms of cognitive capitalism constitute a new order – one that the new types of activism seem to mirror. Whereas the disciplinary state or the exploiting business director, for example, constituted tangible adversaries for the leftist critique in western capitalist liberal democracies in the past, transformational adjustment means that we are now left with a less concrete adversary (Jensen, 2009). In so-called 'knowledge societies' where the neo-liberal management discourse has become a predominant ideology, it is revealed how power mechanisms are still in play, and it has therefore become one of the main roles for the creative activists of the 21st century. Where it seems difficult to disrupt the elites and offer radically new and attractive alternatives, new forms of activism sometimes seem content to expose unjust power relations and stimulate the political imagination. Moreover, the increase in the living standards of the growing middle class means that many of the former centers of mobilization, such as trade unions, organized social movements and political parties, do not seem adequate for the younger generation, which has witnessed how the radicalization of the great ideologies of the 20th century has failed. They are religiously eclectic, juggle identities, and are political drifters (Castells, 2004). Therefore, because of these changed conditions creative activism must also be understood as – at least in part – a new phenomenon.

The crucial point regarding these changes is that they are interlinked and in a subtle way complement each other in forming both the constraints and the possibilities of the new millennium's democratic participation. As Della Porta and Diani (1999, p. 192) write: "Recent transformations in both the distribution of power at the national and

Facilitating political participation

As new forms of participation challenge our conventional analytical categories, so must we, as researchers, adjust our analytical apparatus to their experimental practices – even if this means 'brokering' between traditionally separated disciplines. The overall way in which the changes just explained have affected the political landscape means that one of the creative activist's most important roles becomes that of a facilitator.

Today, process facilitation is widely used as a form of leadership group-tool for improving communication. Facilitation is in the broadest sense about making it easier for a group of people to do what they want to do – together (Ravn, 2011).

In the business and organization literature, a facilitator is typically defined as an individual who enables groups to work together and help them achieve synergy through collaboration (Doyle in Kaner, 2007, p. xiii). The facilitator thus often functions as a mediator of interests, helping parties to create value or meaning for its participants. The facilitator may direct attention to specific topics, contribute with specific relevant input, or set up particular frames for dialogue and reflection. A facilitator contributes with both structure and process in order to enable groups to make high-quality decisions (Bens, 2000, p. 5). The facilitator in a corporate context should encourage full participation, promote mutual understanding, and cultivate shared responsibility (Kaner, 2007, p. 32). A training facilitator does not have to be a subject expert. Her strength is in creating an environment – or situations – where posing the right questions helps unfold hidden potential, resolve suppressed conflicts, or reach an acceptable compromise.

It has not always been like this. When reading the most influential literature on facilitation, it becomes clear that practical handbooks and theories on facilitation, some of which are referenced above, are inspired by democratic theory, especially those on deliberative democracy (e.g. Hogan, 2002). It seems that the facilitating consultants of recent decades have turned the more theoretical abstractions about (and to some extent effectively so) principles of public democratic participatory mechanisms in society at large into practical handbooks that are only useful for small-scale groups in the private corporate sector of capitalism.[2] As opposed to efficiency, I argue that certain activists today are consciously utilizing the same language and practical techniques to create an inclusive space with its own intrinsic democratic values. Puppeteer and legendary activist organizer David Solnit, also key coordinator at The Battle in Seattle, explains his own work to me as follows:

> A core problem in society, as I see it, is that you have a top-down hierarchy where the lead institutions take power away from the people and make decisions for them. Any movement that wants to create change has to build into its practice a directly democratic participation of the people. When I make theater it is essentially the same. An organizer is someone who doesn't just do stuff themselves, but help other people do stuff. So, I facilitate other people's participation and also train and share skills with them in the hope that they become organizers themselves and you know, have the ability to help other people make puppets, run meetings, or shut down a bank. (Solnit in interview with Harrebye, 2011)

These activists thus reclaim the normative principles of deliberative democracy by applying the practical techniques developed by management consultants in the 1990s. Just as theories of deliberative democracy were turned into literature on meeting facilitation (from dialogue helpful to society to staff meetings useful to the company), so I will demonstrate how creative activists today apply the techniques of facilitators in a political context, politicizing them once again.

The Yes Men is an iconic group within this milieu. Their new initiative, The Yes Lab, is an example of the professionalization of the facilitating practices of creative activists. Bichlbaum, one of The Yes Men, explains this approach to me:

> A group will typically come to us and say that they want to go after a particular target, or they have a particular campaign goal. We will then brainstorm with them. Sometimes they come to us with an idea and all they need is some advice on how to carry it out. (Bichlbaum in interview with Harrebye, 2011)

As the facilitators are supposed to, the creative activists try to intervene in a way that adds to the group of participants' own creativity. As Andrew Boyd, the man behind campaigns such as The Billionaires for Bush, clarifies:

> We create a structure, a messaging framework, a set of tools, a kind of campaign momentum, a tone and sensibility, a central creative

organizing concept, that people can then be inspired by, learn from, take pieces from, and apply in their own way in their own communities. (Boyd in interview with Harrebye, 2011)

As opposed to what the direction-giving models seem to suggest, activists need to be good at enabling the participation of others. The facilitating task of creative activists thus also becomes a leadership task of both coaching and guidance, which in different ways are related to the role of a facilitator – or as Marshall Ganz describes:

> Leadership is enabling others to achieve their purpose under conditions of uncertainty. In other words, leadership is a mobilization of collective efforts to achieve a common purpose (...) Building a social movement is a demanding leadership challenge as commitment motivational structures work better than control and demand structures in such voluntary organizations. In other words, leadership as coaching as opposed to giving directions has better prospects in those circumstances. (Ganz in interview with Harrebye, 2011)

Mediating civil society

The prevailing view within civil society research stresses how the possibility for different loci of democratic learning, political reflexivity, and governance depends on the utility of the institutional mechanisms and broader institutional configuration. This angle on civic participation coincides with the move from models of 'government' towards modes of 'governance'. According to this perspective, decentralization processes are promoted, and strong state power replaced by innovative forms of horizontal collaboration between state actors and civil society. Consequently, networks emerge and become an increasingly significant mode of coordinating active citizens.

Such mediating perspectives between the private and the public sphere are especially fruitful when analyzing creative types of activists who deliberately play with the diplomatic grey zones between politicians, corporations, the media, and the everyday maker. As Martin Rosengaard, one of the directors of Wooloo (their New Life festival will be dealt with later on), says: "We operate as chameleons in a nomadic discourse across disciplines" (Harrebye, 2010, in interview with Rosengaard), thereby also challenging the typological stereotypes of activists. In my analysis, I imagine the creative activist as an intermediary or a translator between the cacophony of critical voices and hopeful aspirations in the private sphere – and the government, the financial institutions, and the media of the regulatory sphere (Janoski, forthcoming). The creative activist's facilitation of active citizens' participation is an experimental attempt at such mediation.

More direct forms of democracy place the democratic process itself at the center of the citizenship debate. With the 'deliberative turn' citizens are primarily viewed as neighbors bound together by shared concerns in the search for common solutions to common conflicts (Dryzek, 2000, p. v). They are the everyday makers of change. In most modern democracies it is still the case that:

> A compound notion of citizenship is at work: territory and birth are the condition of citizenship, whereas contract (the basis of governmental legitimacy), blood (the sense of a natural culture), and common activity (practical politics as a process) give it its concrete character. (Barber, 1984, p. 219)

The facilitating activist does not necessarily work vertically *or* horizontally. Rather she does *both* in a circular or dialectic manner by adopting the role of civic mediator between the private and the public spheres (vertically) *and* as a self-reflective agent in her own environment (horizontally). The debate of active citizenship is thus closely linked to the civil society discourse as 'citizenship' concerns the relationship of state and citizen, especially when it comes to rights and obligations. A theory of civil society provides the context or 'mediating institutions' between the citizen and the state (Saunders, 1993, pp. 78–88 in Janoski, 1998, p. 12). It is my point that creative activists of today, given what they see as a democratic deficit, take it upon themselves to function as these mediating institutions.

The People's Supermarket is a food co-operative set up in London that operates for the benefit of its members and the community. It is inspired in part by the legendary Park Slope Food Coop in Brooklyn, New York (www.foodcoop.com). Today many are popping up around the world:

> Our vision is to create a commercially sustainable, social enterprise that achieves its growth and profitability targets whilst operating within values based on community development and cohesion. Our intent is to offer an alternative food buying network by connecting an urban community with the local farming community. (www.thepeoplessupermarket.org)

Members pay a £25 annual fee and work four hours in the store every four weeks for 20% discounts on their grocery shopping. A four-episode documentary series follows Arthur Potts Dawson's experiment and shows his creative but sometimes hopeless attempts to overcome the challenges that you face when you are up against market forces and trying to do things differently. As an example the Supermarket was minimizing waste by creating prepared dishes from food close to its expiration date – a less radical version of the principles behind 'dumpster diving', originally done out of necessity – today practiced mainly by an increasing number of so-called 'freegans'.

The intensified interest in organized civil society and its impact on active civic participation and cultural identity has become a key issue on the political agenda (Edwards, 2004; Boje, 2010). However, a paradox that many activists are frustrated with, is that while active citizens and their autonomous organizations are often asked to contribute to fill the 'democratic deficit' in different ways, for example by participating in hand-picked climate summit events, they are at the same time not taken seriously and often mistrusted by public institutions (Moro, 2004; anonymous interviews; European Charter of Active Citizenship). These challenges have been ascribed to limitations of representative forms of democracy in capturing the heterogeneity, complex interests, and identities in contemporary complex societies (Janoski, 1998; Delanty, 2005; Alexander, 2006). However, the difficulty of realizing such processes remains – if they are genuinely to involve citizens in strategic decision-making for the community. This is why the creative activist operates as a facilitator trying to create a space that allows for a reconfiguration of the political imagination. In an interview with John Jordan about his role as an activist facilitator, he acknowledges that "the times where it's most successful is in a sense when we become invisible, as authors, (...) because in the end politics is about enabling the potentiality of people to feel that they have a creative agency in the world."

Field and focus

The field that we will explore in this book consists of a web of complex yet interconnected elements. Overall, the most fundamental ones are: (1) the structures and circumstances that condition agency (such as the media, the political system and its (more or less) democratic institutions, pop culture, and lifestyle as it is molded by modern capitalist society); (2) the creative activist as a change agent; and (3 & 4) the people that they hope to influence (directly viewers, listeners, and participants;

and indirectly the broader political public, which again, to close the circle, will feed back into the societal system that conditions the active citizen's ability to engage meaningfully). The political circuit that the creative activist is a part of is causally complex and includes many factors, some of which will be looked at in this book.

What follows is a discussion of how I work with the activist as an agent who is conditioned by the reality in which she operates (structure/agent relation), and subsequently clarify how the activist as an acting agent is communicating with and influencing the broader participating audience (agent/participant relation).

Changes that take place as a result of social mobilization and pressure on politicians are (almost) always a combination of a set of broad environmental shifts. Such shifts create disruption in established regimes and can lead to intelligent bottom-up pressure that expands, examines, and exploits the cracks in the system that are making those in power more vulnerable to challenges and the people more open and resonant to change. So the structural conditions are paramount for our understanding of why, when, and how people suddenly mobilize and get their demands met. But these structural openings are only significant if there are some experienced resourceful activists who can understand the political topography and use it and its resources to their advantage. The bottom-up perspective allows us to see why David is (sometimes) able to beat Goliath (Ganz, 2010).

Let us briefly consider one of the best-known examples in the field, namely the American civil rights movement. The Jim Crow era of a de facto caste system that upheld the "separate but equal" doctrine ran from 1876 when Rutherford B. Hayes negotiated a presidency for the South's control of racial matters. In the 1930s cracks in the system began to appear after resistance had been hard to mobilize (McAdam, 1999, Ch. 5). The cotton industry plummeted, which led to a migration of millions of Afro-Americans from the south to electorally key northern states – where they could vote. The black vote put pressure on the politicians who now, at least in their communication, had to open up to civil right reforms.

Just like the financial crisis helped open the door for Obama, the Great Depression in the 1930s also helped Franklin D. Roosevelt achieve office in 1932 after the Republicans had dominated American politics for three decades. Roosevelt never really addressed civil rights, as he didn't want to distance the party's old segregationist *Dixiecrats* who he badly needed, but he did introduce other progressive policies, which led the way for the reforms to come. These are some of the overall domestic changes that helped undermine the racial regime in the United States at the time. The foreign political perspective is no less relevant. In 1945 Harry S. Truman takes over as President after Roosevelt. Within a year he issued the first executive order in favor of civil right reforms since reconstruction. Why did Truman, a southern democrat himself, renationalize race with this much at stake? Well, in the ideological struggle with the Soviet Union, American racism became a real hindrance when seeking allies and influence around the world. So, in that sense, The Cold War helped create a context, both nationally and internationally, in which the civil rights movement enjoyed enormous leverage.

As argued previously, successful movements normally reflect a combination of favorable environmental changes and the creative efforts of activists to recognize, exploit, and expand the political opportunities afforded them by these broader environmental shifts (McAdam, 2010). Before the Second World War Roosevelt managed to place new liberal members in the Supreme Court, which meant a shift in its traditionally conservative ideological profile. The National Association for the Advancement of Colored People (NAACP) recognized that this was happening and began to systematically exploit the situation by carefully selecting cases that gradually undermined the legal underpinnings of Jim Crow. So the well-known case of *Brown vs. Board of Education* in 1954 was the culmination of years of campaigning – and by no means a sudden coincidence. Sometimes the absence of a clear leadership becomes the strength of the broad and flat movement. These are often described as spontaneous and self-organizing networks. But even those that may seem improvised most often have a strategic leadership who understands how to exploit critical points of intervention – the dynamics of contentious politics.

The Jim Crow system was strongest in the South so the activists had to mobilize there in order to be able to morally persuade the broader public of their just cause. Their media campaign had to communicate to the federal level. They staged public confrontations with the system in a way that resonated well with the broader public. The media covered how white men in uniform beat up peaceful black men and women, something that created an outrage domestically as well as abroad. Consider for example the Montgomery bus boycott initiated by Rosa Parks in 1955, the Greensboro sit-ins initiated by a handful of students in Woolworth in 1960 (Wolff, 1970), the first group of Freedom Riders in 1961 (Morris, 1984), the march against Washington in 1963 (where Dr King gave his 'I have a dream speech'), and the confrontation on the Edmund Pettus Bridge, Selma, Alabama in 1965 where people protested for their right to vote and are trampled by police officers on open camera. All of these are examples of how activists with needle-stick operations and the precision of acupuncture created sympathy in the population and thus added to a rising pressure on an otherwise reluctant government who would then – and only then – intervene in support of the movement and make change happen.

Let us compare the campaign in Albany, Georgia (1962) with the one in Birmingham, Alabama (1963). In Albany, Martin Luther King and his people organized community-wide activities that would educate the public, mobilize people, and garner much-needed attention. But the sheriff in Albany, Laurie Pritchett, seemingly understood this dynamic and was able to keep the Ku Klux Klan calm and avoid police violence when demonstrators were detained. Despite years of effort the movement never really made any headlines. Dr King later explained how the movement would subsequently and consciously choose to campaign in Birmingham, partly because of Bull Connor, the commissioner of public safety there, who was known to be a particularly hot-tempered racist – the perfect enemy so to speak, especially if you were chasing headlines. Just a few days into the campaign, although Connor had been warned by Pritchett, he let the dogs loose and turned on the fire hoses (Morris, 1984). Pictures went around the world at a particularly critical stage in the Cold War. John F. Kennedy had to intervene and the Congress was forced to deliver reforms, which they proceeded to do in the years that followed.

The world has changed. The American civil rights movement had a hierarchical organization, one leader, and clear demands. Occupy World Street fifty years later operated with a flat structure, a deliberate lack of leaders, and with no clear purpose. But the fundamental dynamics of contention were the same. When in 2015 a three-year-old Syrian boy, Aylan Kurdi, washed up on the Turkish beach in the midst of the worst European refugee crisis since the Second World War, the iconic picture of it went viral, changed the conversation, and ultimately politicians had to come together. It is just like the picture of a well-dressed high school senior, Walter Gadsden, being attacked by a police dog did when taken in Birmingham, Alabama, on May 3, 1963.

Small events and single acts can start an *avalanche* or create a *spiral* that sets others in motion – and in a revolutionary setting it sometimes spins out of control. The relationship between agent and structure is one that I will touch upon throughout the book, but let me here start by leaning against/on Anthony Giddens's *theory of structuration*. This theory suggests that social practice becomes the experience through which we as theoreticians are able to transcend the tensions and false dichotomies that sometimes seem to exist in academic debates between whether to focus on one or the other. Without giving primacy to either objective structures or subjective agents, Giddens proposes that in the examination of social systems structure, modality, and interactive dynamics are essential, and neither micro- nor macro-focused analyses are in and by themselves sufficient when trying to make sense of the productive relation between structures (rules and resources) and agents (groups or individuals). As Giddens says in an attempt to explain the duality of structure (Giddens, 1979, p. 5): "Structure is both medium and outcome of reproduction of practices. Structure enters simultaneously into the constitution of the agent and social practices, and 'exists' in the generating moments of this constitution."

I do not systematically use Giddens's concepts or designs in my analyses but I do agree with the dynamic reciprocity that he insists on, at least when it comes to structure-determined or agent-focused approaches. I call my point of departure for a *structurally pragmatic but agent optimistic perspective* when dealing with context-specific analytical questions of this matter with regard to creative activists. I hereby highlight that creative activists are conditioned by their socio-political environment, that they are in fact to some extent a product of their time. On the other hand, I do believe that they have the ability to fight back and create pockets of resistance where they are able to transcend the delimitation of historic socialization. It is the realization that structural change is needed and the belief that single individuals can change the course of time that has led me to write this book. This also helps explain and justify my focus on episodes, rather than periods, on small cadres of activists rather than larger social movements, on moments of disruption rather than institutional reform processes.

As Margaret Mead wrote, we must "never doubt that a small group of thoughtful, committed citizens can change the world; indeed, it's the only thing that ever has." Creative activists should not, and do not, only demonstrate against something, but also demonstrate how things can be different.

David Graeber, who became one of the favorite ideologists of the Occupy movement, finds the word protest problematic because "it sounds as though you've already lost" (Kliman, 2012). Andrew Kliman's critique of Graeber – and this is where it becomes relevant for how we read the theory of structuration and variants of it – is that he ignores or does not recognize that one side *has* already 'lost'. To emphasize his point Kliman quotes Marx, who in the *18th Brumaire of Louis Bonaparte* says that, "Human beings make their own history, but they do not make it as they please; they do not make it under self-selected circumstances, but under circumstances that already exist." I work from a compromise between these two positions, because while I have come to believe that all activists take into account the circumstances under which they work (cf. the first rule of activism), I also know now that the activists that I investigate to a certain extent are occupied with the creation of a space, a pause, a temporary platform (cf. L.H.M. Lings's notion of the creation of a third space and the Dao of world politics), where the limitations of current political and structural circumstances are less important. They operate in the cracks that allow us to see through and beyond 'the loss' that Kliman cannot see beyond. Finally, there is a huge difference between the various cadres of activists studied, which is also why it is necessary to adopt a flexible and non-dogmatic approach that will allow me to consider the multiplicity of actors within an ideologically relatively coherent field. This enables me to consider each case individually. But in principle I do believe in the ability to transcend one's materially and culturally conditioned political circumstances – at least in theory. To which extent that is possible in terms of the pragmatics of party politics is another matter, because total and sudden revolutionary breaks with the functioning system in place only result in chaos because of the complexity of said system.

Enough for now about how my analytical subject is conditioned. I also want to clarify how I work with the relationship between the creative activist, her participants and audience. In this dynamic political field, that is the more informal politics of active citizens taking place in the civil society, I have chosen to focus on the creative activist. This could have been done in different ways, but although I do consider organizational changes and socio-psychological profiles, I will concentrate on the intentions and the strategies of these change agents – and as an expression of that, also on their actions. In doing so, I consider both the structural conditions, as before mentioned, and the way their actions are meant to influence their audience. A certain closely related strand of research is interested in the production rationalities of what Christian Borch (2012) would call 'body-to-body formations related to the political anatomy of crowds'. From an aesthetic perspective these researchers look at imitations, crowd members, and how desire affects the masses. For example, when Kristine Samson writes about the shift from the functional to the performative city through analyses of Distortion and OWS she examines pre-cognitive and non-reflexive interaction (as defined by Nigel Thrift, 2008), as they emerge spontaneously. Such researchers are also interested in how spatial representation stimulates the political imagination, but contrary to them I look at the creative activist as the director behind the show, the conductor of the music being played so that the dancing can take place. I believe that their belief in the spontaneous, organic, and leaderless movements, and its unintended events' possibility to mobilize masses, at best ignores the central planning factors and at worst romanticizes the revolutionary potential of festive events. Furthermore where they are interested in the affections of the individuals who make up the crowd I am more preoccupied with the individual reflection that follows. Where their approach is based on an aesthetic approach to art and performance, I take a more normative approach to a political field where activists do not work with static institutionalized sculptures created by an artist, but evolving social sculptures created by the multitude, but often staged by the creative activist. Still, as Jacques Rancière has argued (2006), the aesthetic experience has a political effect as

> It is a multiplicity of folds and gaps in the fabric of common experience that change the cartography of the perceptible, the thinkable, and the feasible. As such, it allows for new modes of political construction of common objects and new possibilities of collective enunciation.

But instead of focusing exclusively on the emotions that Reclaim the Streets generates when you are dancing in the middle of a frenzied mass of like-minded people, I question how such events have the ability through their occupations of the public space to make people reflect on the way we use our cities. The move from emotion to reflection is a crucial one, especially since my interest group, the activists, is ultimately interested in conscious action-oriented change.

Another related but distinct possible route that I could have taken but chose not to (except from necessary references and useful inspiration when overlaps between the fields are too great to ignore), is the more art-theoretically inspired philosophical sociology, which is concerned with the interface between aesthetics (in its broadest form – see Nielsen and Simonsen, 2008, pp. 8–9) and politics. Overall it makes sense to distinguish between three types of aesthetic interventions in the political realm (cf. Nielsen and Simonsen, 2008): the depoliticizing aestheticizing of the political, the polarizing aestheticizing of the political, and artistic interventions in political discourse. Where the first two are problematic, the latter has potential insofar as it also manages to challenge the status quo, if it can do so without becoming dogmatic, and if it can interact with political discourse without losing its own autonomous expression, one that has the intention and sometimes the ability to open rather than closing the reflexive space within us and between us. The aesthetic move marks an epistemological turn for political resistance that becomes a premise for my work as it recognizes Rancière's observation that politics today "revolves around what is seen and what can be said about it, around who has the ability to see and the talent to speak" (Rancière, 2004, p. 13). Thus, to "enter into political exchange, it becomes necessary to invent the scene upon which words may be audible, in which objects may be visible, and individuals themselves may be recognized" (Rancière & Panagia, 2000, p. 115).

After a brief outline of the key components of my field and their dynamics, I delimit myself from a more extensive analysis of the structural conditions of today's activists and choose not to work with the more lust-oriented aspects of how crowds are spontaneously aroused by themselves. Nor do I take an art-historical approach to the aesthetic elements of theories of the avant-garde (cf. Stephensen, 2008).

To demonstrate that I do acknowledge the significance of identity politics, which is closely related to the research conducted into social imitations, not least in this particular type of participation, consider the following witness-bearing from the Luk Lejren event (close the camp event) – a march to an asylum center north of Copenhagen that was meant to end up cutting open the fence that surrounds the center and freeing the people living there. The crowd consisted of a civil disobedience part (mostly youngsters) and other, civilians, who were just there to demonstrate their discontent with the immigration laws (grandparents and women with baby-strollers), but somehow the two crowds intermingled and suddenly the police had surrounded the horde and started throwing tear gas. Everyone either ran or threw themselves on the ground to escape the gas as it tends to form a cloud that hovers half a meter above the ground. Lying there, my colleague Kasper Søndergaard got eye contact with a young girl close by, who was struggling to breathe. Should he help her? Would she be able to calm herself or would she panic? The girl did not run for cover nor cry to him for help. Instead, and much to my astonishment, she reached for a camera, extended her arm as far as she could, pointed the camera back on to herself, and captured the moment with a click. Her 'selfie' probably secured her a swarm of appraising comments on Facebook the next day.

Part II
Mapping the Field – Using the Terrain to Your Advantage

3
First Movers and Circular Cycles of Contention

Before dealing with the nuts and bolts of activism, let us take a look at the machinery of social movements in order to better understand how such movements work – as they are made up of activists. In this chapter I therefore present a systematic overview of the major theories of social movements. I map out the most relevant theoretical models and concepts, and position myself within this landscape. I also position myself in history as I argue how societal developments and the consequent changes in organization, strategy, and purpose of activists mean that theories about new social movements and the alter-globalization movements, which in a developmental historical sense followed, must be supplemented by theories more adapted to analyze today's creative forms of activism. The subsequent reconfiguration of the phases that social movements go through, from rise to fall, includes an explanation of why the trigger term is useful in the analysis of creative types of activism.

In my view social movements consist of groups of people who share a collective identity centered on social solidarity (internally and in a certain way often with the surrounding society), a common identifiable cause, and ideas that are maintained and advocated over time. This minimum definition reconfigures Sidney Tarrow's four empirical properties of social movements: collective challenge, common purpose, social solidarity, and sustained interaction (Tarrow, 1998, pp. 4–7). Now, this definition does not coincide with my tentative definition of creative activism, but, as I have already made clear, social and political movements still form the basis for most other forms of activism. So-called 'new' forms of participation are best understood as reconfigurations of already known repertoires – hence the relevance of this particular exercise. Furthermore activists make up social movements – and single events in a sequence may end up becoming a campaign.

Mario Diani argues in *The Concept of Social Movement* (2011) that most serious approaches agree that social movements are made up of networks of informal interactions between diverse actors, including individuals, organizations, and groups. These groups are bound by shared beliefs and ties of solidarity that make their participants attach a common meaning to specific collective events. They are often involved in political and/or cultural conflicts that arise as a result of social change. In short, three basic components of social movements are hereby identified: networks of relations between a plurality of actors, collective identity, and conflictual issues.

It should be mentioned that in literature on social movements there is an over-representation of what one might call left-wing cases. But liberal conservative movements (e.g. the Tea Party movement), right extremist movements (e.g. Ku Klux Klan), and religious fundamentalist movements (e.g. al-Qaeda) also fit the listed criteria.

You cannot become a formal member of a social movement. It has no official leader who can be held accountable. It does not make any (real) money either. Social movements are emotional movements. Uprisings and participation do not begin with a program or a political strategy. It might come later, though, when the movement turns into something else, and when leadership is constituted and ideological narratives are constructed. The decisive factor is this transition from emotion to action.

The contentious collective action that social movements have become known for can be brief or sustained, dramatic or repeated routines, institutionalized or disruptive. As I have just defined, social movements are distinct from activism. The movement involves many different kinds of agents, some of which are full-time institutionalized organizers, some who just privately identify with the cause and live their lives accordingly. The activist is a pro-active citizen who is often defined by her struggle for a single issue or against concrete policies. This does not mean that she is not or cannot be studied as a part of a social movement. It means that she herself as well as the politician, journalist, or scholar addressing her, often confine their association and analysis to the activity in question. This also means that often the investigative focus is on strategies and tactics – and what the use and development of these say about the circumstances and the rationality of the activists in question.

Theories on social movements are thus relevant for our work with a certain type of activist because they constitute an analytical framework in which concrete activities can be placed. They make it possible to place the phenomenon, that we look at, in the larger scheme of things. Most importantly they, together with the theoretical concepts already introduced, offer analytical concepts and perspectives that I translate and use as supportive pillars in my own readings of today's activist landscape. Furthermore, to clarify the link between the agent and the movement, activists will be understood much like the drivers of what Thomas Rochon describes as 'critical communities'. To Rochon these should be studied "as the originators of new value perspectives and the social movement as the source of pressure that brings these ideas to the attention of social and political institutions" (1998, p. 22).

There is an art to every practice – social protest is no exception

When we distinguish between theories of social movements, we often do so based on where they can be placed on various measurement scales: are they general theories that can be applied to most situations, or specific in terms of the historic period and the geographic or social space they cover? Are they grand unifying theories or narrow theories that deal with just one specific element of the dynamics of social movements? Do they operate at a macro or a micro level? Do they look at the structures that condition the movement or the agents who make them up – and are these agents rational actors or culturally embedded emotional subjects? Despite what the authors and followers of a given theory believe, theories seem to develop and adapt to the changing field of politics – as they should.

An iconic image from the 1968 Olympics in Mexico City portrays a Black Power salute meant as a rejection of racism and oppression (google the picture). Through their hijacking of the event and the media these US athletes (Tommie Smith and John Carlos) were able to redirect attention from a celebration of physical ability to a question of human dignity. Sophisticated media-jacking uses the target's own story against them by employing political jiu-jitsu style techniques to reframe an issue.

Let me start with a movement's repertoire. The repertoire changes over time, as movements search for tactical advantages and adjust to the environment in which they operate. Charles Tilly defined the repertoire of contention as "the ways that people act together in pursuit of shared interests" (Tilly, 1995, p. 41). What has been called the 'traditional repertoire' (Tarrow, 1998, Ch. 2–4) usually responded to immediate abuses and expressed the claims of ordinary people directly, locally, and narrowly. In conflicts over things such as land and beliefs, the disputes were brief and unorganized. Burning down a farm stays an isolated incident if no one sees it or hears it. From the 18th century on, the spread of literacy combined with the expansion of the printing press and new forms of association made it possible for people who were otherwise disconnected by social and geographic divides to become aware of each other's challenges, hopes, and actions against those in power. The spread of information (which with the internet has entered a whole new phase) was in this way a decisive factor for the birth of the national social movement as it enabled the creation of connective structures among larger numbers of people and made the diffusion of their messages into new publics possible. It also meant a broadening of claims and wider geographic reach. Paradoxically, as the nation state continued to expand its domain allowing for these broad movements to arise, the target of protesters shifted from private and local actors to national centers of decision-making. Likewise globalization today does not only feed into but also enables new types of networks, actions, and ideological superstructure. "The new repertoire was cosmopolitan rather than parochial; autonomous rather than dependent on inherited rituals or occasions; and modular rather than particular" (Tarrow, 1998, p. 37). Examples of this new repertoire are the boycott, mass petitions, the urban insurrection, and the barricade.

However, it can be problematic to place different forms of protest and participation in an evolutionary chronological frame. It might be useful on a heuristic level but should not be applied as a historically absolute or irreversible form of modeling.

The durability of innovations in the repertoire of contention depends partly on strategic modularity and adaptability, and partly on its symbolic resonance. Consider for example the repertoire of contention used at one time or another by the temperance movement: "From its origins in the 1830s to the passage of the Eighteenth Amendment, temperance utilized a broad repertoire of social movement organizing techniques and pressure tactics, ranging from education and proselytizing efforts in the schools and churches, to invoking legal restraints on the sale of liquor, to supporting candidates and lobbying, to mounting public demonstrations, to confrontational tactics, like invading taverns and staging public breaking of whiskey bottles" (Tarrow, 2012, p. 57).

Nineteenth-century scholars viewed social movements as the result of anomie, a lack of morally regulating norms, and social disorganization, from epidemics and the collective unconscious to hysterical imitation and totalitarian unification. Whether social mobilization leads to chaos or conservative backlash depends to a large extent on how they are organized. The unionization of unorganized masses, or the disciplining of passionate crowds, eventually made way for the political popular folk-parties as we know them – for better and worse – and today, it can be argued, that it may have become a way to pacify the consumer. The French Revolution is the prime example of extremism, deprivation, and violence. From time to time those kinds of readings reemerge with respect to militia movements, violent suburban uprisings, peaceful mass demonstrations gone bad, etc. At the beginning of the 20th century, scholars began to view social movements as both part of, and initiators of, civilizing processes that are important to the development of modern democracy, a just legal system, a vibrant civil society, and a legitimate political system. However, clearly not all movements serve that function.

The mob, the multitude, the crowd may be said to make up the backbone of the 20th century's sociological encyclopedia, where every reference to and analysis of the socially politically mobilized collective carry normative atonements in their definitional maneuvers (Borch, 2012). Mass culture has had immense impact on our political and scientific discourse because the social and the political, power, identity, and social order, are so thoroughly intertwined.

Karl Marx can be regarded as one of the first theorists of social movements. His point of departure is concerned with how the development of the structures of production creates an inequality that leads to class division. This division inevitably results in a class-consciousness that, according to Marx, is necessary to revolutionize society. Marxist theorists have later elaborated on why and how such resources are needed in order to engage in collective action, the importance of politics, and the cultural dimensions of it – see Lenin in his writings on the necessity of a professional movement organization (Lenin, 1960–70) and Antonio Gramsci through his writings on cultural hegemony and the need to build consensus within one's own ranks (Gramsci, 1992). Hardt and Negri have done it with their notions of Empire and the multitude (2000). Pro- and post-marxists, such as Manuel Castells and Alberto Melucci, have had a major influence on political and cultural versions of *new social movement theories* (Buechler, 1995).

As opposed to what some refer to as Marx's mechanistic and deterministic class perception, collective behavior theorists had no preferred social actor. Theorists such as Smelser (1962) and Turner and Killian (1972) did however share the functionalistic view that societal dysfunctions produce collective behavior. In the 1960s, dissatisfaction with the collective behavior approach spread as scholars began to acknowledge that grievances alone cannot explain mobilization. As a reaction, theories of personal incentives based on the idea of rational choice (Olson, 1965) were developed.

Resource mobilization theories that focused on the organization of professional movements were developed parallel to these and gained momentum through the 1970s (McCarthy & Zald, 1977; Jenkins, 1983). In its most elementary form this mobilization theory stresses that the more resources you have, the more likely you are to mobilize people and have your demands met. These resources can be material (e.g. money), human (e.g. volunteers), social-organizational (e.g. established networks), cultural (strategic tools), and moral (e.g. legitimacy) – and can be attained through aggregation, self-production, appropriation/ cooptation, or protection (Edwards & McCarthy, 2004, pp. 131–136). It is important to keep in mind that different movements require distinctive resources and acquire them in very different ways. Consider for example the difference between Greenpeace and Anonymous. Or Hare Krishna and Indignados. Resource mobilization theory has proven its relevance, but as with the other theories, it tends to make most sense when supplemented by other theories in the field.

With regard to the dialectic dynamics between structure and agent, one of the most influential theories within the field of social movements remains to be mentioned, namely political opportunity theory. Charles Tilly (1978) built upon Eisinger's work (1973) to offer a comprehensive theory of the conditioning influence of a variable of political factors for the tactical choice that activists make in an attempt to optimize their strategic chances of success. In his comparative longitudinal studies, the state plays a key role in the political opportunity structure. McAdam builds on Tilly, and offers a political process theory that shows how external circumstances often provide sufficient openness to allow for mobilization (1982). Tarrow's political process approach attempts to synthesize existing research by arguing that people engage and create new opportunities by widening the cycles of contention when patterns of political opportunities and constraints change.

> Contentious politics is produced when political opportunities broaden, when they demonstrate the potential for alliances, and when they reveal opponents' vulnerability. Contention crystallizes into a social movement when it taps embedded social networks and connective structures, and produces collective action frames and supportive identities able to sustain contention with powerful opponents.

By mounting familiar forms of contention, movements become focal points that transform external opportunities into resources. Repertoires of contention, social networks, and cultural frames lower the cost of bringing people into collective action, induce confidence that they are not alone, and give broader meaning to their claims. Together, these factors trigger the dynamic processes that have made social movements historically central to political and social change. (Tarrow, 1998, p. 23)

The key recognition in the political opportunity perspective is that activists' prospects for advancing particular claims, mobilizing supporters, and making an impact are context-dependent. However, one of the things that the theory has been criticized for is that its concepts are "in danger of becoming a sponge that soaks up every aspect of the social movement environment" (Gamson & Meyer, 1996, p. 275).

By political opportunities I will be referring to the dimensions of the political struggle that encourage people to participate. By political constraints I am referring to factors that may discourage people from getting engaged in the struggle for what they believe in. When doing so it is important to consider the relative weight of issue-specific versus general openings in the polity (Meyer & Minkoff, 2004, p. 1464). Furthermore, "only by separating the analysis of opportunity for policy reform from those for political mobilization can we begin to make sense of the relationship between activism and public policy" (Meyer, 2004, p. 138). In my case this also means an openness towards the possibility of creating one's own opportunity (cf. the *structurally pragmatic but agent optimistic perspective*). In Tarrow's structural argument there is a somewhat circular reasoning to be found in the mechanistic relation between the agent and the system that does not really allow for this possibility.

As I have shown, explanations – also within the social movement literature – have a tendency to be filtered by a dualistic kind of thinking such as the agent/structure divide. McAdam, McCarthy, and Zald's work (1996) is an example of how theorists have tried to integrate major developments in the field of social movement theory over a couple of decades in order to provide a more unifying basis of analysis. This conceptual framework intends to explain the emergence, development, and outcome of collective action and social movements by addressing three interrelated factors: (1) political opportunity structures, (2) mobilizing structures (formal and informal forms of insurgency organization), and (3) framing processes (collective interpretation, attribution, and social construction that mediate between opportunity and action) – relevant when dividing cycles of contentions into phases (as we will be doing later).

Now, "If the collective behavior paradigm's emphasis on grievances recalled Marx, and resource mobilisation's focus on leadership was parallel to Lenin, the cultural aspect of recent social movement studies is resonant of Gramsci" (Tarrow, 1998, p. 17). From structural factors the focus in this strand of theory is on the *framing* of collective action:

> Social movement leaders tell new public stories: A story of self, a story of us, and a story of now. The story of self communicates the values that call one to action. A story of us communicates the values shared by those in action. A story of now communicates an urgent challenge to those values that demand action now. (Ganz, 2010, p. 523)

The conceptual influences came from social psychology (e.g. Erving Goffman's concept of framing as 'schemata of interpretation', 1974), post-structuralism (e.g. Michel Foucault's concept of discourse, 1972), and social constructionism (e.g. Benedict Anderson's concept of imagined communities, 1991). The emphasis on collective identity formation was reinforced by the identity politics sparked in the 1960s and further instrumentalized by new social movements (NSM) a couple of decades later. As the girl with the camera underneath the thick cloud of tear gas shows, identity still – or perhaps now more than ever – plays a role when deciding who to back, what to participate in, and when to quit.

The idea of 'new social movements' was first articulated by Alain Touraine (1981) and signaled the arrival of new participants with new motivating themes. Theories of NSM have identified that such themes also recur in the practices of the new creative activists. This is of course the case because new social movements themselves gained momentum in the decades leading up to the milestones (e.g. the fall of the Berlin Wall, entering a new millennium, and the collapse of Lehman Brothers), after which, I claim, project-organized groups of creative activists have increasingly supplemented traditional movements.

The themes in question (in addition to the conceptual influences just mentioned), include underscoring symbolic action (Cohen, 1985; Melucci, 1989); stressing processes that promote autonomy rather than strategies to obtain influence or power (Habermas, 1984–87; Rucht, 1988); focuses on struggles over recognition and representation rather than traditional redistribution (Inglehart, 1990; Dalton & Kuechler, 1990; Fraser, 2008); problematizing the often fragile process of constructing collective identities instead of assuming that they are just structurally determined (Klandermans, 1992; Hunt, Benford, & Snow, 1994; Johnston, Larana, & Gusfield, 1994); recognizing a variety of temporary networks rather than assuming centralized organization as a prerequisite for successful mobilization (Melucci, 1989; Gusfield, 1994; Mueller, 1994); and insisting on a historical specific social formation as the structural backdrop for contemporary forms of collective action as a response to the inadequacies of Marxist theories to explain these.[1] These are the central themes that theories on new social movements have contributed.[2]

We note 'frames' as a crucial factor contributing to the relevance and impact of creative activists in particular, since a social movement frame is "an interpretive schemata that simplifies and condenses the 'world out there' selectively punctuating and encoding objects, situations, events, experiences, and sequences of actions within one's present or past environment" (David A. Snow and Robert D. Benford in Thornton, 2002, p. 663).

Another example of an attempt to foster a theoretical synthesis that would overcome theoretical division in this field is the book called *Dynamics of Contention* (2001). It was written by the founding fathers Doug McAdam, Charles Tilly, and Sidney Tarrow in an effort to forge a complex that challenges what they perceive as being a rather static and structural understanding of social movements, and instead suggest some analytical tools that may better capture the dynamic processes that characterize, not only social movements, but also protests, revolutions, and broad nationalization and democratization processes.

Their analytical apparatus consists of three parts and each part can be applied on three different levels: mechanisms, processes, and episodes. Phenomena such as the French Revolution or the democratic movement in Tiananmen Square are examples of what they call episodes. Episodes consist of at least two robust processes – for example radicalization and/or coalition formation. The Danish cartoon crisis in 2005–06 can be analyzed as such an episode (Olesen, 2007). Here a scale-shift process can be identified as the incident went from being primarily a national concern to becoming a global matter during January and February of 2006. This shift was mainly driven by two mechanisms: diffusion (the spread of information through mass media, mobile phones, and internet) and intermediation (in this case active attempt of the official Danish Islamic community to include actors outside Denmark).

The work inspired by this approach insists on placing social movements in the broader arena of contentious politics. As do I. In Tarrow's later reflections (2012) he qualifies the argument by showing how contentious actors (most often) are neither outside of nor completely within politics, but rather occupy the uncertain territory in-between absolute opposition and integration into policy – which can be read as a response to critical analyses from the likes of Boltanski and Chiapello, and Heath and Potter.

The creative activists are not strangers at the gate (cf. Tarrow, 2012), but rather political party crashers – provocateurs and facilitators in the midst. As we are moving towards a closer linkage between explanations focusing on structural preconditions of contention (such as state building or capitalism) to the ones stressing internal processes (such as resource mobilization and framing) it is important for the continuous development of the theoretical social movement field that we continue to forge useful analytical tools that can help us understand the ever evolving political terrain of new social actors and clarify dynamic mechanisms that move societies forward. The mechanism of mirroring and the contours of a theory of reflection meant to further explore this mechanism is this book's contribution to that toolbox.

As Flacks (2003) has pointed out, the ambition to create a coherent field of academic study may sometimes endanger the particular value of single and sometimes competing theories, which is also why I have felt the need to present more than one of the most relevant theories here as I believe each of them have something to offer.

In 2013 a new attempt to bridge the historical and theoretical gap between the US and the European social movement traditions was made in an ambitious transatlantic network collaboration (collected in an anthology) aimed at interdisciplinary innovation and understanding of the fast and fluid changing dynamics of contention (Stekelenburg, Roggeband, & Klandermans, 2013).

A number of historical milestones mark some of the changes that make theories of new social movements necessary, but are not sufficient to understand today's movements and more project-organized networks: the fall of the Berlin Wall in 1989 ushered in a new world order; in 1999 The Battle in Seattle announced the coming of what would become known as the (anti) globalization movement; and Lehman Brothers' collapse in 2008 led to the financial crisis and the global social movement, which since 2011 has erupted worldwide – characterized by their global network, by how their digital communication platforms complement and coordinate their physical occupations of central city squares, by their open and sometimes unclear ideological standpoint, and by their temporary character.

Even local and national movements gain international attention when they challenge regimes or change the way we do things in our everyday lives. They inspire beyond borders and cultures. Globalization is in many ways what moves the social today, not least through new communication technologies – the internet wave in the 1990s and the social media frenzy in the following decade. In the traditional media (newspapers, TV, and radio) some of the uprisings in recent years have been called Facebook and Twitter revolutions. The Facebook page "We are all Khaled Said" is one example of the significance of social media in the mobilization and coordination of the Egyptian Revolution. Traditionally, literature on political protest has been preoccupied with the role of organizations for effective mobilization. Bennett and Segerberg (2013) identify this approach as the *collective action* paradigm. They (and others, e.g. Shirky, 2011) argue that this logic is being replaced by another, namely *connective action*. It is true that these platforms play an increasingly critical role, but instead of a replacement of the physical manifestation, it is rather the case that online (often weak ties, low risk) activism supplements offline (often strong ties, high risk) activism. In *Tweets and Streets* (2012) Paolo Gerbauso explains how activists through social media become *choreographers of assemblies* as the city square develops as a trending place and venue of a magnetic gathering – not in contrast to online participation, not in spite of it but because of it.

Social movements exert counter power – and the mass media is to a high degree controlled by governments and corporate interests. Communicative networking today happens largely on social media, wireless platforms, and through mobile phones. Which is why independent amateur and activist journalists also continue to play a bigger and bigger role as counterpart and collaborator to the more established mainstream media. Take the random bystander's recordings of the police's attack on Rodney King in 1991, for instance, or Wikileaks' leak in 2010 of the so-called Collateral Murder video procured by Bradley Manning. But because of the need to gather in public spaces where people can see, hear, feel, and smell each other – and become visible to all other citizens – they also still occupy city squares and symbolic buildings:

> In our society, the public space of the social movements is constructed as a hybrid space between the Internet social networks and the occupied urban space: Connecting cyberspace and urban space in relentless interaction, constituting technologically and culturally, instant communities of transformative practice. (Castells, 2012, p. 10)

Historically social movements have depended on the existence of specific communication mechanisms such as hearsay rumors, sermons, pamphlets, and manifestos. Today multi-modular digital networks, with the horizontal communicative organization they enable, are both cheap and accessible – and the fastest and most autonomous and interactive means of information and coordination in history. New media technology thus constitutes a resource that can help open up the political opportunity structure – globally as well. Diffusion mechanisms highlight this point. They have tactical value when protest repertoires are shared and learned (e.g. CANVAS, which sprang from the Otpor movement in Serbia and which travels around and trains rebels in repressive regimes all over the world), and moral value when battles are won and induce hope (take the Apartheid movement's struggle in South Africa).

Overall we can (inspired by Rucht, 2004) distinguish between four different approaches in which political activists relate to the media: adaptation (Greenpeace cooperates with the existing media and operates on their premises) – and then the more critical approaches: distancing oneself from them, attacking them, or creating one's own alternative media outlets.

In an interview with Deva Woodly I asked: "what differentiates the movement's communicative challenges from other political actors such as the political party?" Woodly clarified that "movements are always there to disrupt the status quo, to change it. So the ethical and strategic constraints on the ways that they communicate are different than the political spin-doctors."

Alternative independent media outlets such as Pacifica Radio 1949, Adbusters, Wikileaks, Twitter, or personal blogs are not run by corporations or the state, but in different ways provide platforms that have the ability to challenge the stereotypes and caricatures that only too often fuel our fears and hatred. Such outlets break the monopolies and the censoring that too often hides the wonderful and heartbreaking realities – whether it is a Palestinean child or an Israeli grandmother, a young man from Iraq or a teenage girl from the US. The power of independent media provides a forum for these people to speak for themselves or see things in a light that Russian State Broadcasting, Fox News, or Al Jazeera would never cast (see Amy Goodman online on Democracy Now). These autonomous platforms increasingly make up the channels through which creative activists vent and communicate. But more importantly they enable others to do the same (see Milan, 2013).

One can easily get the impression that the new possibilities of this mediatized public is an absolute blessing. But the democratic implications are ambiguous and/or yet uncertain. Distance and cliquish alternatives can create a fragmented public and isolated echo chambers, which for example can become problematic in relation to radical movements like al-Qaeda (global), English Defence League (national), and militant radicals (often locally anchored factions). The traditional journalistic virtues and the possibility to ensure that they are upheld are also threatened – not least if pictures, scandals, and emotions prohibit broad and more principled discussions.

For these reasons the creative activist plays a central role in how we stimulate the political imagination, provoke reflection, and translate frustration into action – not only in movements but also in civil society organizations, unions, and social businesses. As previously mentioned, in a way they always have:

> Fools, clowns and carnivals have always played a subversive role, while art, culture and creative protest tactics have for centuries served as fuel and foundation for successful social movements. It's hard to imagine the labor movement of the 1930's without murals and creative street actions, the U.S. civil rights movement without song, or the youth upheavals of the late 1960's without guerilla theater, Situationist slogans or giant puppets floating above a rally. (Boyd et al., 2012, s. 1)

But since creative activism historically can be seen as the latest renewed indicative trend in the milieu of these years, I will point towards new conceptual frameworks that better capture the democratic undercurrents of our time. We do so by standing on the shoulders of the theoretical giants within their field. Some of those that are most important to my work have been juxtaposed above. All activists, including the new creative ones, have a history of contentious forms of protest that disposition their repertoire. This is why social movement theories also offer meaningful insights when it comes to analyzing the developmental dynamics of new experimental groups on the cutting edge of new forms of critique. But again, the global character of today's movements (Fominaya, 2014), progressive forms of action (Duncombe, 2007; Boyd et al., 2012), communication networks (Castells, 2012), facilitation techniques (Harrebye, 2015), diffusion mechanisms in times of crisis (Della Porta & Mattoni, 2014), changing claims (Fraser, 2008), global injustice symbols (Olesen, 2015), relations between political parties and social movements, modes of coordination, and identity networks (Stekelenburg, Roggeband, & Klandermans, 2013) call for new theories, analyses, and ways of working together that dare to break out of the silos in which universities, NGOs, political parties, unions, social businesses, and the movements themselves until now have been allowed to linger. In the future we must cooperate across these divides if we are to gain a better understanding of why, when, and how change happens from below. Creative and analytical practice are not two parallel tracks, but complementarily suggest ways of dealing with a world in constant movement.

Following this historical outline of how social movements have acted and developed, and how theories about them have changed accordingly, I will now examine the phases that social movements typically go through. From the triggers of insurgency to the decline of an organized movement, creative activists play their part in the lifecycle of most movements.

Main phases in cycles of contention

Above we outlined the historical development of social movements and the parallel development of theories that have helped us understand them better. Now we move on to consider the cyclical perspective, which will challenge some of the developmental theses and premises of the former. In doing so, I simultaneously use the theories presented above. For example, I approach the issue of mobilization from both a structural angle, one that considers the influence of windows of opportunities, and from a strategic angle, which takes into account the dynamics of an evolving repertoire and power.

Sidney Tarrow defines a cycle of contention as:

> A phase of heightened conflict across the social system: with a rapid diffusion of collective action from more mobilized to less mobilized sectors; a rapid pace of innovation in the forms of contention; the creation of new or transformed collective action frames; a combination of organized and unorganized participation; and sequences of intensified information flow and interaction between challengers and authorities. (Tarrow, 1998, p. 142)

Tarrow then characterizes these cycles as creative periods of intensified activity. He therefore operates with cycles of contention in a linear historical manner (Figure 5.1, p. 74). In his later work (2012) he explains how such cycles are characterized by heightened conflict, broad sectoral and geographic diffusion, the appearance of new organizations and the appropriations of old ones, new frames of meaning, and new forms of collective action. Here we will rather view the different phases that movements go through (large-scale over a longer period), campaigns (intermediate-scale during a fixed period), or activities (small-scale project, organized needle-stick operation) as circular cycles. The reason is that a circular movement insinuates the recurring nature of many social phenomena, such as fashion, bad decisions, national pride, crises, enlightenment, and movements – they rise and fall only to reemerge in a new form, with a different slogan or a new antagonist. The circle may spiral in different directions depending on the effects it has had on policy, the political culture, or our individual habits.

The main phases and turning points that these cycles consist of are as follows: the grumbling phase, trigger points, the mobilization phase, critical tipping points, phases of demobilization, and impact, which may occur prior to or long after the decline of a movement.

I will prioritize the role of triggers since it seems to me that creative activists often act as first movers. The following section will therefore examine how we may understand the triggers that move us from the realm of closed private complaining into open public debate as active listeners, passive participants, or engaged activists. They do however also serve a specific purpose in the other stages that movements go through – they are for example often used to sustain interest from the media and potential members through their alternative ways of circumventing traditional trench warfare, which is why I will also briefly touch upon the rise and fall of movements. Questions of measurement when it comes to the impacts of movements and the democratic value of activists will be taken up in the final chapter of the book.

*

Grumbling takes place in the phase before dissatisfaction is openly expressed. We shake our heads when we watch the news. We agree with our friends about what we think needs to change. We complain about the new company policy with our colleagues during lunch. Veiled complaints take place in this stage as a way of communicating dissatisfaction without taking any open responsibility for this dissent. News coverage also means that many rebellions and sudden movements come as a shock to the wider public, since the mainstream media has a tendency to cover spectacular episodes, dramatic events, and obvious rupture.

In James C. Scott's book *Domination and the Art of Resistance* (1990), what he refers to as 'hidden transcripts' are used to understand the cultural patterns and interdependent dynamics of domination and subordination. Even though his empirical data leans heavily on his work with colonial slavery, Scott's micro-sociological, anthropologically based theory is useful because it categorizes different types of clandestine forms of resistance and thus illustrates how power relations and sociopsychological structures of domination (relations of domination are in a Foucauldian sense always implying resistance and vice versa) keep us in a stage of *apparent* approval – until bottled-up frustration is triggered. The practices of resistance that the hidden transcripts reveal include speech acts, anonymous attacks, shunning, folk songs, poaching, deliberately not doing one's work properly, gossiping, etc. When the stewardess today chews ice cubes and aggressively flushes the toilet (Willig, 2009, pp. 29–30; Hochschild, 1983) it is an expression of the same necessity to ventilate and to do so covertly. To Scott, everyday forms of class struggle take place over the boundaries of and on the frontiers between the public and the 'hidden transcripts': "The public transcript is, to put it crudely, the self-portrait of dominant elites as they would have themselves seen" (Scott, 1990, p. 18) – in Part III we will explore how what I call the mirroring surface coding of capitalism projects a flattering image of itself while being the dominant mirror with which we can identify.

When a teacher leaves the classroom, the changed behavior of the students speaks of the kind of power that she holds. When the TV is turned off, the unrest that we feel is an expression of the hypnotizing power that the shimmering flash of this cultural hegemony has on us.

Scott's theory allows us to distinguish between four varieties of political discourse: the first one is the *accommodating strategy*. Slaves, for example, used the flattering self-image of elites (not to be mistaken for their practices) to appeal for small improvements in their daily lives (e.g. better food). In doing so they found representation in the prevailing ideological rhetoric without seeming the least rebellious (think of Lars von Trier's pop-provoking typology in the film *Mandalay*). This is how most of us operate in our daily lives. We adjust, fit in, and make the most of it. (cf. Rucht's previously mentioned first type of media relation)

In the second form of political discourse, used under the radar of the rich and the powerful, what Scott calls 'subordinates' gather outside the intimidating gaze of power where a dissonant political culture is possible. 'Offstage' (to use Goffman's wording), the mask is dropped and the feelings of resentment that are held back in the workplace or in the public space are let loose: "Discretion in the face of power requires that a part of the 'self' that would reply or strike back must lie low. It is this self that finds expression in the safer realm of the hidden transcript" (Scott, 1990, p. 114). Today this takes place on internet platforms, for example, where one can anonymously ventilate frustration with like-minded people (e.g. Starbucks employees, see Du Plessis, 2014).

Scott's third realm is a politics of disguise and anonymity. Strategically, it lies between the first two as it takes place in public view, but in a way that shields the identity of the actor or conceals the actual message so that it is lost for the slave owner, the manager, or the politician, but hits home with those on the same page. Folktales, rumor, gossip, songs, rituals, jokes, and all kinds of subcultural codes are examples of such practices: "The inventiveness and originality of these fantasies lie in the artfulness with which they reverse and negate a particular domination" (Scott, 1990, p. 44). In line with this perspective, creative activists often communicate in dubious terms, with intentional irony, and through dilemma actions (as Gandhi did in his Salt March). What Carol Humphrey calls 'evocative transcripts' are ambiguous by design and "intended to elicit or evoke a particular interpretation beyond the surface meaning" (Humphrey in Thornton, 2002, p. 666). Again, the anonymity that the internet today allows for plays a huge role here (for better and worse), but offline resistance movements also use disguise as a deliberate and symbolic weapon. As the history of the mask shows (Thomassen & Riisgaard, forthcoming), the mask functions as a mirror – a symbolic expression of social representations of power. The anonymous front figure of the Zapatistas subcommandante Marcos has done so with great success. The world community becomes curious and the movement's leadership and openness melt together. Members of Anonymous, a web-based freedom fighter/cyber terror movement, carry a mask when they take to the streets – for both tactical and principle reasons.

Whereas the first three low-profile forms of resistance constitute the 'infrapolitics' of the subordinate, whether he is a slave or she is an ordinary citizen living in the 21st century, the fourth and most explosive realm of politics, as identified by Scott, is the rupture of the dividing layers of rejection, irony, and resentment between the hidden and the public transcript. In these moments of challenge hidden frustration and built-up indignation erupt into open defiance.

Under Pinochet's dictatorship politicians did not dare speak up and criticize the regime publicly until the day when in 1988 Richard Lagos broke the silence in a live interview on Chilean television. Lagos at some point looked straight into the camera, pointed his finger, and declared that he would not be seeking re-election:

"And now," Mr. Lagos said, still seeming to speak directly to General Pinochet, "you promise the country eight more years with torture, assassination and the violation of human rights. To me, it seems inadmissible that a Chilean is so ambitious for power as to pretend to hold it for twenty-five years." ... As the three interviewers tried repeatedly to interrupt, he brushed them aside, saying: "You'll have to excuse me. I speak for fifteen years of silence." (News report referenced in Scott, 1990, p. 207)

Creative activists can be said to publicly act out the secret fantasies of those who dare not or cannot for whatever reason do so in the midst of managing their everyday lives. In the interest of oneself and loved ones anger and dissatisfaction are kept under wraps and only practiced in the dark – until one finds a daring 'voice' (to use Albert Hirschman's term, 1970) on the public scene. First movers have the courage, the resources, and the credibility needed to turn fear into anger and a sense of togetherness into hope (cf. Gladwell's law of the few, 2000, taken up in the last chapter).

In December 2010 Mohamed Bouazizi was selling fruit in the streets of Tunis in order to support his four children. The 26-year-old university scholar could not obtain a permit to do so, but refused to be corrupted. The police confiscated everything he owned and physically humiliated him in public. Later that same day, Bouazizi tried to complain about the incident (which is said to be the culmination of months of harassment) to the authorities but was rejected and refused access. In desperation he poured a liter of gasoline over his body and set himself on fire in front of the City Hall. The event led to minor protests in towns around the country. Bouazizi died in the hospital a couple of weeks later, and an uprising quickly spread throughout the entire country and eventually most of the Middle East. Bouazizi did probably not mean for his act of defiance to start a revolution, but his self-emulation sparked a regional wildfire because it broke the concealment of the hidden transcript and incarnated what the majority of the population felt – and did so while the world was watching (Harrebye, *Politiken*, March 29, 2011).

Scott's analysis, and those similar (e.g. those made by Gramsci, Foucault, and Laclau & Mouffe), offers us a look beneath the placid surface that the public accommodation of the existing distribution of power, wealth, and status quo often presents. More importantly the understanding of how such critical 'offstage' social spaces are created and used will allow us to move from the individual resisting subject to the socialization of critical practices and discourses without missing the interconnectedness of the two. One can only do so if one recognizes that 'the political' must include the stages that come before what is openly declared as politics. Failing to do so, "is to focus on the visible coastline of politics and miss the continent that lies beyond" (Scott, 1990, p. 199).

From this vantage point infrapolitics may be thought of as a foundational form of politics. The disguised forms of resistance that Scott covers are, "one might say, the elementary forms of political life on which more elaborate, open institutional forms may be built and on which they are likely to depend for their vitality" (Scott, 1990, p. 200). The vitality of the social movement likewise depends on these fundamental elements.

Scott compares the hidden transcript to 'a body of water pressing against a dam'. As described, the occupation of the creative activist can be seen as scratching and widening of the cracks that exist in the dam, in the hope that watersheds of withheld animosity at some point start seeping and soon will pour through the openings. When the pressure rises and there are weaknesses in the retaining wall holding it back, poaching escalates into land invasion, the cursing of former President Bush in the local coffee shops is suddenly catalyzed into the public sphere when an Iraqi journalist throws his shoe at the President at a press conference in Baghdad, and when the dam is undermined the conscientious shopper begins to actually put her money where her mouth is and starts boycotting her regular products.

When it comes to explaining how current social movements arise or movements that have been in a state of hibernation suddenly gain momentum and grow, macro-level political process theory has emphasized how changes in political opportunity structures condition the possibility to mobilize people. Given the field and focus of this book, several major criticisms must be raised regarding the scope and explanatory range of such theories.

Firstly, the conceptualization of political opportunity is loose, and does not distinguish, for example, between opportunities for mobilization and opportunities for influence (cf. Meyer, 2004). The studies that test political opportunity hypotheses against other explanations have therefore also generated mixed results.

Secondly, the narrow focus on structural factors of the political process theory does not encompass the role that culture plays in various ways when it comes to a broader understanding of what politics (also) is and how its micro and the macro levels interact. This is where new social movement theory fills a void in explaining the increasing influence that culture, identity, and storytelling has on how to frame a cause and when to do it.

Thirdly, political process theory does not explain how and why activists, at the micro level, are able to capture people's imagination.

Contrary to Tarrow, who believes that "the outcomes of such waves of contention depend not on the justice of the cause or the persuasive power of any single movement" (1998, p. 7) but on the changes in political opportunity and the reactions of the people, the state, and elites to such waves history shows that single agents, cadres of activists, or single movements *can* be a decisive factor and trigger movements that change the world. Martin Luther King, Nelson Mandela, and Mahatma Gandhi are excellent examples of this. Rosa Parks on the bus in 1955 in Montgomery, the anonymous tank man in Tiananmen Square in 1989, and the standing man of Taksim Square in 2013 are minor examples of individuals who suddenly became symbols in liminal phases of rupture and possibility.

The structural conditions that tire the systemic creature are important, as I have already acknowledged. But the focus of this book is rather on the straw that breaks the camel's back. That is why the insurgent, the first mover, the activist avant-garde on the margins of the repertoire of contention is of particular interest here.

In the coverage of the mobilization of popular mass movements – Occupy Wall Street being a prime example of this – analysts are often surprised at just how quickly a seemingly indifferent community is catapulted into mass defiance. Part of the reason is that we have been lulled into a false sense of security because we are not aware of the gravity of the hidden transcripts from which the Occupy movement, for example, derived much of its energy. Acts of daring and defiance do perhaps seem improvised on the public scene (cf. research concerned with affection, imitation, and crowd psychology), but in fact they have been rehearsed and prepared for centuries in the hidden transcripts of private practices and folk culture. Creative activists often function as triggers of the dissatisfaction that is suppressed and therefore not always directed at those in power. The point of departure, therefore, is not that creative activists produce trouble, but that they provoke people to reflect on their grievances and react to a simmering sense of injustice.

*

Building on this theory that is relevant for analyzing creative activists as triggers of dissatisfaction, let us briefly consider how and when creative activists play a role in the rise and fall of movements. Clashes between early challengers and authorities reveal the weak points of the latter and the strengths of the former, inviting a broader spectrum of citizens to participate. As Hill and Rothchild say: "As protests and riots erupt among groups that have long histories of conflict, they stimulate other citizens in similar circumstances to reflect more often on their own background of grievances and mass action" (1992, p. 193).

The ability to trigger people to reflect, to take a stand, and participate in their community is not the same as the power to control or sustain collective action.

The literature on social movement dynamics includes several types of explanations as to why and how social movements mobilize support. For Tarrow mobilization phases begin when a new political opportunity is being taken advantage of. Such an opening, whether it be a local political scandal, a surprising election, or a global financial crisis, encourages the creation of a coalition between actors, who normally do not associate with each other, and thus begins the formation of new organizations or the empowerment of already existing ones. This becomes possible through the creation of new master frames, according to Tarrow (1998), as uniting narratives are then able to enhance the convergence between different challengers. Arising political opportunities also reinforce the instability in the elite – an instability that might have been the partial cause of the opening in the political landscape to begin with.

In post-industrial democracies the state often plays a key role in determining which direction the movement will take at this stage. Throughout the different phases of mobilization, new forms of participation are experimented with and diffused as a way of keeping the spirit alive among supporters and selling the message in public. So, with regard to the dynamics of movement mobilization there are both internal and external dimensions to consider – creative activism plays a tactical part in both cases.

In 1930, Mohandas Gandhi launched the Salt March campaign as part of the Indian independence struggle against British colonial occupation. Britain passed laws granting themselves control of salt production. This production was both a major source of tax income and a vital part of the people of India's everyday life. The British government was faced with a dilemma about how to respond to Gandhi's non-violent march. On one hand, if the British didn't do anything, they would jeopardize their monopoly on salt and lose authority in the eyes of the people. On the other hand, arresting Gandhi would make them look ridiculous, as he was actually just extracting salt from seawater – a simple task, basic for the everyday life of millions. Arresting Gandhi would make him a martyr. And it did. Along with about 80,000 Indians, Gandhi was put in jail. Acts of civil disobedience spread across the country and thousands joined the movement, which changed the world's perception of the British occupation. The dilemma action is a commonly used model when creative activists want to force the opponent to reveal the illegitimacy of their claims (Popovic et al., *Canvas Core Curriculum*, 2007, pp. 142–152).

Tactics that put the regime in a position where it has to do something ridiculous have been employed all over the world. An example of this was when public singing was outlawed in Chile as a reaction to low risk methods of dispersion, such as banging pots and pans and writing and singing critical songs. That was the beginning of the end for Pinochet.

*

A tipping point indicates the moment of critical mass, a threshold of change, the boiling point. In the context of social movement mobilization, momentum is not easily kept: "The problem with all movement alliances, but especially those with the parties, is how to keep commitment firm once the persuasive sound of the marching thousands have become a distant echo" (Rochon, 1988, p. 174). Over time, across geographical boundaries, and with multiple interests in play, social movements decline and wither away for a variety of reasons. Changes in political opportunity structure, repertoire exhaustion, repression, and frame transformation are all important factors in the demobilization of social movements.

Of special interest here, given the dynamics between critique and creativity as an innovative and productive force, is cooptation and recuperation as reasons for movement demobilization. The difference between the two and how activists try to balance between them will be a underlying theme throughout the book. Movements sometimes fade not because they fail, but because they succeed – at least in part. The cooptation or recuperation of movement themes into mainstream political and economic discourse is often a result of what Tarrow calls "selective facilitation" of movement demands. In a progressive's view, large parts of the environmental movement have laid the groundwork for a new commodifying politics (e.g. "green growth", which to many is a contradiction in terms) instead of challenging commodification itself. For a reformist pragmatic, the gradual improvement in women's rights is a victory, not a way for the men to stay in power. So, to put it simply, one's success criteria depend on where in-between a revolutionary and a reformist position you find yourself. As Rochon (1988, p. 109) points out, "the ideal movement strategy is one that is convincing with respect to political authorities, legitimate with respect to potential supporters, rewarding with respect to those already active in the movement, and novel in the eyes of the mass media". These, however, are far from always compatible demands.

*

Social movement theory is useful when analyzing the role that creative activism plays in today's critical topography because it contextualizes it. It does so both historically, where it builds on the existing repertoire of contention and in terms of the cyclical movements dynamics. Here it plays a numerically minor but strategically major role as a trigger and mobilizer through its ability to, in eventful protests, gain attention, create feelings of solidarity, get people thinking, and getting them engaged or consolidating organizational networks.

In order to capture the rapid developments of contemporary society – especially when it comes to a phenomenon that is characterized for better and worse by the flux that has always been the trademark of the avant-garde – the usually separated traditions and disciplinary approaches within the theoretical fields of participatory democracy, creative critique, and social movements need to be reconfigured into a conceptual framework that supports a more eclectic approach to the study of creative and project-organized cadres of activists.

There is a recurrent dynamic of ebb and flow in collective mobilization, and the victories that are sometimes obtained challenge the order of things and provoke counter-mobilization. But alongside these cyclical fluctuations two more stable tendencies, I agree with Della Porta and Diani (1999, p. 192), (still) appear to apply at least as far as western democracies are concerned. First is that acceptance of the ineffectiveness of political violence seems to be steadily growing over time while the application of creative nonviolent campaigns is increasing. Secondly (and relatedly), the tactical repertoire of movements, campaigners, and activists continues to broaden because of the cyclical nature of movements.

A basic prerequisite for any well-functioning participatory democracy is that its citizens participate in a non-violent manner. They can be critical, disobedient, and subversive, but they cannot be violent. If they are violent it is most often either because they are not democrats themselves or because they do not live in a democracy. Now, I know that there are those who would argue that many of the so-called liberal democracies are not really democratic, but they do live up to minimum standards and want to develop as a democracy. Either way new research shows that it makes more sense to resist in a civil and non-violent manner, regardless.

A variety of terms have been used to coin different forms of creative activism, such as culture jamming, propaganda, civil disobedience, campaigning, tactical media activism, etc. Each of these sub-categories displays an array of particular types of concrete actions. Common for all of them are that they are non-violent. Gene Sharp's political analysis of non-violent action as a method for applying power in conflict (e.g. 2005) has inspired struggles around the world just as his theoretical writings laid the foundation for a whole strand of pragmatic research on the strategic significance of subjects' (dis)obedience to the leaders. In *Why Civil Resistance Works: The Strategic Logic of Nonviolent Struggle* (2011), Erica Chenoweth and Maria J. Stephan use historical data to show that non-violent resistance campaigns between 1900 and 2006 clearly and consistently have been more likely to achieve full or partial success than their violent counterparts.

It is necessary, however, to clarify three key components of this survey before proceeding: What is a campaign? What is the difference between violent and non-violent campaigns? And, what counts as a success in this context? These authors have simplified a complex constellation of resistance methods – but with explicit criteria and interesting results. A campaign is defined as a series of observable, continual tactics in pursuit of a particular political objective. Campaigns are to be distinguished from random riots. Although many campaigns can be said to use both violent and non-violent means, Chenoweth and Stephan separate the list of campaigns that meet their criteria (see 2011, Ch. 1 and 2) into violent resistance, which includes campaigns where unconventional violent strategies, such as bombings, shootings, kidnappings, and sabotage, are used by non-state actors; and non-violent resistance, which is defined as non-institutionalized campaigns employing boycotts, strikes, protests, sit-ins, stay-aways, and other acts of civil disobedience – in accordance with Sharp's definition of non-violent resistance as "a technique of socio-political action for applying power in a conflict without the use of violence" (Sharp, 1999, p. 567).

To be considered successful in their study a campaign has to meet two conditions: (1) the full achievement of its stated goals (in their case studies, regime change, anti-occupation, or secession) within a year of the peak activities, and (2) a discernible effect on the outcome, such that the outcome was a direct result of the campaign's activities (Chenoweth & Stephan, 2011, p. 14) – to what extent this is at all possible will be discussed at the end of this chapter and the final chapter of the book.

The analysis of 323 violent and non-violent resistance campaigns shows that both the frequency *and* the success rate of non-violent campaigns have increased over time. The frequency of violent campaigns has likewise increased, but the success rate of these has declined. Non-violent campaigns are generally far better at attracting diverse and large participation that is sustainable over time relative to armed campaigns – and at accessing points of leverage within society, based on the composition of their membership and to undermine or collaborate with the pillars of support (media, military, police, political parties, or business communities – depending on the country), since a much wider variety of tactics are available. Instead of just attack or retreat you have a variety of creative methods of concentration and dispersion that are not easily repressed.

One of the key figures in their book displays the success rates by violent and non-violent campaigns by decade from 1940 to 2006 (Chenoweth & Stephan, 2011, Figure 1.3), and clearly illustrates how the discrepancy in the 1990s becomes even clearer as the success rate for non-violent campaigns in this decade is nearly twice as high as it is for violent campaigns. Since the millennium they are about six times as likely to succeed.

Why have the differences become clearer from around 1990? Firstly, it might have to do with the fact that both the US and USSR supported armed insurgencies all around the world during the Cold War. That is no longer the case, at least not to the same degree. Today, it seems there is an understanding that any sustainable system-change needs to be instigated by a 'home-grown' insurgency. Secondly, the demonstration effect seemed to kick in, meaning that when people see that non-violent civil resistance is systematically effective, which they have increasingly seen with the wider spread of information and communication technologies during the last couple of decades (starting with the internet in the early 1990s and increased with social media in the beginning of the 21st century), they start to believe that it might just work for them too. This mechanism was debated widely during the regional spread of insurgency in the Arab Spring – a debate that we will touch on again later in the book.

Creative activists constitute the vanguard in the continuous development of this repertoire. Analyses of practical creative critique are therefore important because they allow us to understand how this development takes place in a mediating civil society where they try to facilitate alternative dialogues with active citizens to reinvigorate participatory democracy through transformative events. The theoretical intersection of participatory democracy, critical theory, and social movement forms is the necessary prism that enables such analysis. But are they sufficient? Later on we will explore why more open and ambiguous concepts are also needed when explaining how we move the social.

4
Paradoxes of Participation

This chapter deals with the facilitating aspects of active citizenship. We will focus on explaining the variation in extra-parliamentary activities, such as signing petitions, demonstrating, displaying badge stickers, and boycotting products – based on data collected from 20 European countries. Secondly, a broader typology of activism will also be developed. The main questions dealt with here are primarily how feelings of dissatisfaction with the government and feelings of being a member of a discriminated group affect the level of extra-parliamentary participation. Furthermore we will look at how various welfare regimes condition the extent to which these groups chose to act. So we are back to the dynamics between societal structures and political agents, and I combine a critical tradition which suggests that political participation is motivated by a feeling of dissatisfaction with an institutional perspective where certain institutional conditions are seen as enablers for citizens to actively participate in political life.

The European Union is democratically challenged by citizens who feel alienated by its distanced bureaucracy and complex representative system. The financial crisis, which for a number of reasons hit Member States unequally, did not contribute to the democratic sense of unity. This chapter politically points towards the need to further stimulate an active critical civil society in order to both complement and improve procedural democracy. Consider how the energy of some movements has led to the establishment of political parties (e.g. Indignados, which channeled into Podemos in Spain; the sustained protests that channeled into Syriza in Greece; and the sense of political homelessness that has given rise to The Alternative in Denmark, just to mention a few), whereas others have dissolved into thin air. From a Gramscian perspective the former is necessary to gain any influence. In the final part of the book we will discuss how particular interventions and social movements can make sense and make change happen without necessarily playing on the established political field.

But participation is important to any vibrant democracy because active citizens ensure the legitimacy of elected representatives and enable the people to use the power they as citizens are guaranteed by right and have a shared responsibility to exercise and preserve as a community, nation, or union. But why not just vote and trust the representational democracy (if you are lucky enough to have it)? Because the ideals of free participation and an open public sphere where everyone can be heard cover structural inequalities and a set of subtle exclusion mechanisms just beneath the surface. But the active citizen, understood as a critical and socially responsible civilian, uses her capacity to influence politicians through various acts of participation, to influence public opinion through deliberation, to influence the market through their shopping habits, or to influence their local community through practical initiatives. Numerous scholars have argued that such forms of non-electoral political participation influence the democratic system in a positive manner (e.g. Smith, 2009), on accountability issues (e.g. Innes & Booher, 2004), knowledge-based decision-making possibilities (e.g. Fischer, 2000), and for reasons of justice through inclusion of minority voices (e.g. Fraser, 2003, 2008).

In the book *Modernization, Cultural Change, and Democracy* (2005) Ronald Inglehart and Christian Welzel use empirical data that covers 85% of the world's population to develop a theory of human development. Their cross-national data demonstrate that with a rise in socio-economic resources (e.g. education and income) people think less about survival and more about self-expression values (such as trust and free speech). This in turn leads to an effective democracy in which people participate (Inglehart & Welzel, 2005, p. 3). The underlying theme of this process is that the broadening of human choice, including ways in which the active citizen may participate in the political life of society, is essential to the development of a modern democracy. One might question the causal relationship and the normative premises of the analysis, but the correlation between the importance of the value of self-expression in a given country (for example, manifested in the signing of petitions, demonstrating, or selective boycotting) plays an even more crucial role in strengthening democracy than communitarian factors and other variables tested in the study by Inglehart and Welzel. Based on this comprehensive study we still need to ask whether a pro-democratic political culture is a precondition for the success of a democratic institutional system, or whether participation and values of self-expression are a consequence of living in a well-functioning formal democracy.

Linking theories of personal dissatisfaction and structural conditions

Previous research has used individual motivations to explain why certain individuals participate actively in society while other groups of citizens do not (e.g. Blumer, 1939; Smelser, 1962; Gurr, 1970). From rational choice to deprivation theory (cf. previous chapter) many scholars have put the individual at the center. Personal ideology and values were seen as another version of this motivational perspective (e.g. Flacks, 1967; Keniston, 1967). Individual attributes were analyzed in order to explain how these 'pushed' people to participate in various types of activism. By contrast, the rationalistic approaches of the 1970s such as resource mobilization theory started focusing on how the 'pull' of organizations and social networks encouraged people to get involved. Structural, not psychological, conditions were now emphasized as decisive factors in case analyses. Examining the role of social status by focusing on stratification variables, when explaining variations in participation, has qualified this approach.

Motivational approaches have re-emerged however in social movement literature, where more culturally oriented aspects of the mobilization question, such as identity, norms, and commitment, again began to nuance wholly structural interpretations (e.g. Morris & Mueller, 1992; Laraña, Johnston, & Gusfield, 1994; Johnston & Klandermans, 1995). In continuation of this others have claimed that a sense of civic duty is central to participating citizens (e.g. Schlozman, Verba, & Brady, 1995). The importance of these different factors is broadly recognized. But the absence of emotions, some have argued, is problematic since it is passion that at the end of the day engages people (Goodwin & Polletta, 2000, 2001). The exclusionary cognitive perspective that characterizes all the first approaches misses this critical element (cf. what some call the affective turn – e.g. Massumi, 2002; Thrift, 2004; Leys, 2015). A related line of thinking invoked by this missing link defines anger as the essential political emotion (Holmes, 2004, p. 123) and analyzes its mobilizing potential (Jasper, 2006; Thompson, 2006; Beyerlein & Ward, 2007).

When considering how these individual sentiments are conditioned by institutional structures and democratic culture, in the literature on social capital there has been a discussion about the extent to which the welfare state 'crowds out' social responsibilities and engagement in civil society. Supporters of the crowding-out hypothesis argue that social expenditures and comprehensive social programs crowd out informal relations and social networks, leading to a general decline of commitment to civil norms and participation (Offe, 1984; Wolfe, 1989; Etzioni, 1995; Fukuyama, 2000; Putnam, 2000). Others have rejected the crowding-out hypothesis and claim that well-developed welfare states based on the principle of universalism create the structural and cultural conditions for active participation (e.g. Rothstein). In their opinion the welfare state encourages people to participate in civil society by investing in voluntary organizations and by offering people financial resources and time to develop social capital. This indirect link between social capital and a participatory behavior also seems to be related to the more optimistic view of their potential to influence their own life-chances – an attitude that is characteristic for trusting people (Delhey & Newton, 2003). This approach is in line with Thomas Humphrey Marshall's conceptions of citizenship where welfare states that guarantee citizens' civil, political, and social rights enable everybody to participate in political life. If the welfare state is developed it then ensures the integration of individuals in society and hence encourages individuals to participate.

My principal argument here is that institutional arrangements in different (welfare) regimes not only have an impact on the overall level of political participation but also seem to influence the specific relationship between dissatisfaction and political participation differently. The institutional design of the welfare state influences the political opportunity structure, understood as the "features of regimes that affect the likely outcomes of actors' possible claims" (McAdam, Tilly, & Tarrow in Sohrabi-Haghighat & Mansouri, 2010, p. 29), since the more responsive the welfare state is to citizens' claims, the more citizens will engage in the political sphere. The argument is that in welfare states dominated by universal welfare programs, citizens are more likely to participate because it is relatively easy for marginalized groups to mobilize, organize political action, and build coalitions. Universal welfare programs enable and even encourage people with different social statuses to mobilize political action – including when they are dissatisfied. The underlying explanation is that recipients of universal welfare programs have learned that they deserve benefits and certain services, and that the political system is responsive when they express dissatisfaction with the services provided. Rothstein, Samanni, and Toerell (2010) developed a Quality of Government approach to explain the support and mobilization for the welfare state. This theory stresses the importance of trustworthy, impartial, and reasonably uncorrupted government institutions as a precondition for political mobilization for the welfare state. According to this perspective, a lack of civic engagement is most often caused by dysfunctional governmental institutions (Rothstein & Stolle, 2007).

Now let us take a look at how this sense of injustice triggers indignation and dissatisfaction, which in turn induces people to get involved. Here dissatisfaction is viewed as a less aggressive and more relatable political attitude than anger – one that can be both emotionally and cognitively motivated (Figure 4.1).

On the macro level we tested whether welfare regimes have an impact on the level of participation. Instead of taking several institutional

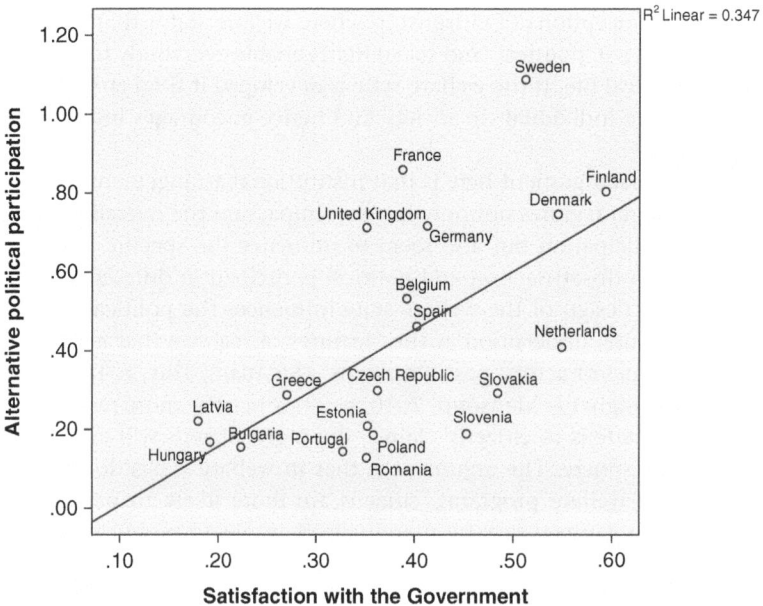

Figure 4.1 Cross-country comparison of the relationship between dissatisfaction and participation

Note: The figure is a condensed version of the multi-level regression analysis we made in the article printed in *Comparative European Politics* (see Harrebye and Ejrnæs, 2015). The data we used in this article comes from the European Social Survey (ESS) round 4, conducted in 2008. The sample includes 37,377 respondents from 20 EU countries.[1]

indicators such as corruption, social protection, years of democracy, and universalism versus means, we have grouped the European Union countries into five main groups, taking our point of departure in a broader version of Esping-Andersen's (1990) welfare state typology where we include Southern European and Eastern European countries in two separate country clusters. Table 4.1 summarizes some characteristic of the five country clusters when it comes to welfare provision and political institution.

In Sweden, France, Finland, Denmark, Germany, and the UK people tend to participate more than in the Post-communist and the Mediterranean countries, which have the lowest level of activity. So on a macro level, countries with a high level of satisfaction with the government are associated with a high level of extra-parliamentary participation.

I would like to combine the structurally conditioned approach on the macro level with the personal motivation perspective on the individual level, since, as will be demonstrated, analyzing one without the other makes for an inadequate explanation; let us see if the same correlation appears on the micro level (Figure 4.2).

Table 4.1 Country clusters

Country cluster	Key characteristics	Country
Continental	Insurance-based welfare Low to medium level of corruption High level of civil society voluntarism Long tradition of democracy	Belgium, Germany France, Netherlands
Mediterranean	Insurance/family-based welfare provision High to medium level of corruption Low level of civil society voluntarism Medium to short tradition of democracy	Spain, Greece, Portugal
Anglo-Saxon	Means-tested welfare provision Medium level of corruption Medium level of civil society voluntarism Long tradition of democracy	UK
Scandinavian	Universal welfare provision Low level of corruption High level of civil society voluntarism Long tradition of democracy	Denmark, Finland, Sweden
Post-communist	Insurance-based welfare provision High level of corruption Low level of civil society voluntarism Short tradition of democracy	Bulgaria, Czech Republic, Slovakia, Estonia, Hungary, Latvia, Poland, Romania, Slovenia

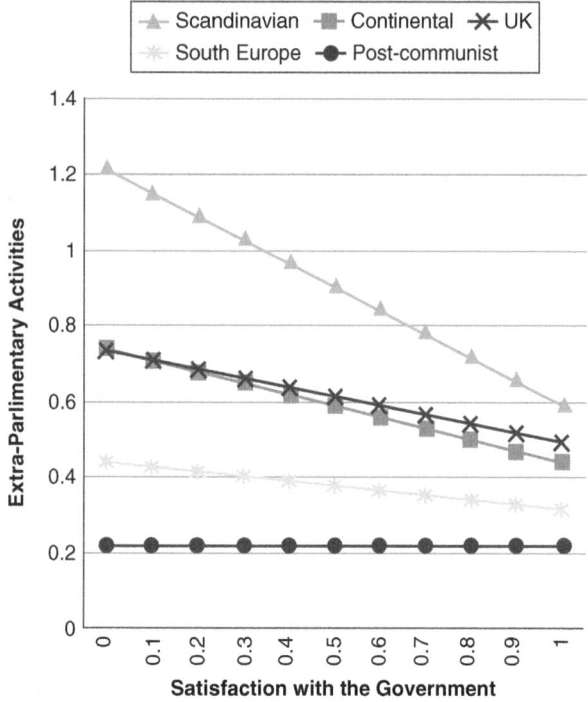

Figure 4.2 Relationship between dissatisfaction and participation on the individual level within different welfare state regimes

These results (surprisingly) show that the opposite bent appears when we look at the interaction effects. Where the cross-country comparison showed that countries with relatively satisfied citizens (e.g. Denmark) had a relatively high level of extra-parliamentary participation from those citizens, the micro-level analysis shows that within those countries it is (paradoxically) the dissatisfied citizens who participate the most. In Scandinavian countries the mean value of participation increases the more dissatisfied people are with their government.

The results are in line with most previous research in the field and confirm the hypothesis that in welfare states with a high degree of universalism and a high quality of governance, people express their dissatisfaction through extra-parliamentary activities that are civic, critical but lawful, while in countries with a poorly developed welfare state and a high level of corruption and lack of trust in political institutions the general level of such activity is relatively low. This indicates that the structural conditions for expressing dissatisfaction through extra-parliamentary activities are more favorable in Scandinavian and Continental countries than they are in Eastern and Southern European countries. The results could reflect the relative historically low level of corruption, a less clientelistic public philosophy, systems less prone to use violence against their citizens, and a long tradition of democracy – all of which provide better opportunities for citizens to participate in political life than in welfare states with a less developed civic culture.

In line with these findings, several studies have found a low general level of both conventional electoral participation and more protest-like activity in Eastern and Central European countries (Letki, 2003). One of the key explanations for the low level of political participation in these countries is the strong legacy of authoritarianism in the recent past. Lack of institutional and social trust, high levels of corruption, and inequalities in access to resources have been some of the key explanations for the political apathy of their civil society.

The results of our study thus indicate that in welfare regimes where political institutions are dysfunctional, dissatisfaction with the government does not seem to motivate people to participate in the political process, while dissatisfaction in Scandinavian countries, which have a long tradition for fair, non-corrupt, and responsive political institutions, seems to be an important motivation for engaging in civic participation.

The patterns of participation in Scandinavian countries can thus be seen as a result of the ability of these welfare states to stay in a close dialogue with civil society. This political architecture creates the conditions for a cocktail of structural and cultural welfare characterized by a high level of generalized trust between the state-system and citizens (Rothstein & Stolle, 2003). The point here is that voluntary activity works as complementary to the state, not as a substitute for it (Newton & Giebler, 2008).

These results suggest that critical active citizenship constitutes a potential for a democratic community because it has an invigorating reciprocal effect on the resonant character of universalistic institutions in line with the principles of deliberative democracy. People learn to participate by participating: "The structures and institutions that permit and encourage participation may form a mutually reinforcing system that encourages more participation" (Mascherini, Saltelli, and Vidoni, 2007). The investigated motivational factors of personal (dis)satisfaction and the structural conditions of the institutional political system seem to act as a mutually reinforcing system of cause and effect.

Thus, what leads to extra-parliamentary action is what we could call a *constructive reaction to dissatisfaction*. This oxymoronic social phenomenon captures what may at first sound like a paradox. But on looking more closely it turns out to be what many consider the driver and the watchdog of our modern democracy, namely the ability to combine a critical attitude with a constructive approach to your opponent – the system, the authorities, the society to which as a citizen belong. This balance is sought both within and outside the formal system of the welfare state, through both more conventional electoral modes of participation and extra-parliamentary activities.

Political actions such as signing petitions, demonstrating your beliefs and/or boycotting products only make sense for the citizen if she believes that the Government and/or state institutions actually listen and that improvements might occur as a consequence of one's critique. Disbelieving attitudes (no matter how legitimate they might be) often lead to more destructive forms of responses to dissatisfaction – opting out of the community, political apathy, or violent forms of protest. So, to spell things out, in well-functioning welfare states one tends to have a positive spiral where dissatisfaction leads to extra-parliamentary political participation, which then produces more good governance and hence an increase in satisfaction. In more corrupted regimes one tends to see a negative spiral where dissatisfaction leads to apathy, which then does not change things for the better, and only increases cynicism and mistrust between citizens and the political system.

Leafleting is one example of what extra-parliamentary participation can be as it is the bread and butter of many campaigns and NGOs. Most of the time, though, leaflets are not taken by passersby, not read, or not taken seriously. But campaigners can be creative to make leafleting catchy, interesting, and memorable.

In the 1980's activists opposed to U.S. military intervention in Central America dressed up as waiters and carried maps of Central America on serving trays, with little green plastic toy soldiers glued to the map. They would go up to people in the street and say, 'Excuse me, sir, did you order this war?' When the 'no' response invariably followed, they would present an itemized bill outlining the costs: 'Well, you paid for it!' Even if the person they addressed didn't take the leaflet, they'd get the message. (Lambert & Boyd in Boyd et al., 2012, pp. 8–9)

In a world where democratic institutions continue to move further away from the individual citizen, the importance of a locally vibrant civil society where dissatisfied groups can voice their critique and feel that they are heard becomes democratically significant. The (European) patterns of participation show how dissatisfaction motivates extra-parliamentary activities – provided that the right institutional conditions are in place. Responsive institutions matter in developing critical active citizens.

As the data behind these conclusions are from 2008 it would be interesting to see if and how the financial crisis might have altered the picture painted here. It seems, for example, that the proportional importance of institutional conditions drops exponentially when the level of dissatisfaction falls below a certain threshold under which the belief that your actions may make a difference does not outweigh the frustration that brings people to the streets when they cannot feed their children, are humiliated by the police, or have lost all faith in corrupt politicians. That tipping point is to be found somewhere between political cultural traditions, the belief that you can make a difference, and the sheer necessity to act.

A typology of activism

Activists, as we have established, engage socially in their community to change society for the better. They are, more than anybody, driven by dissatisfaction with the status quo, combined with skepticism towards the institutionalized political establishment. But this broad understanding of what activism is and can be entails that one must distinguish between many different types of activism.

Voting statistics cannot be relied on to provide a clear indication of people's democratic participation (e.g. Verba, Schlozman, & Brady, 1995, pp. 47–48). First we need to distinguish between electoral modes of participation and non-electoral modes. The former can include voting and party activity (Bäck, Teorell, & Westholm, 2011), certain forms of campaigning (Krishna, 2002), and certain kinds of membership and particular types of compliant activism through the traditional state (Hutcheson & Korosteleva, 2006). Non-electoral modes of participation include many different things, and are referred to as unconventional activism, particularistic activities, and untraditional forms of participation (Hutcheson & Korosteleva, 2006, p. 36), exemplified by direct action, contacting, demonstrations, and protest (Krishna, 2002, p. 442), and 'manifestations' understood as unconventional acts of participation (Bäck, Teorell, & Westholm, 2011, pp. 81–82).

In much of the referenced literature the latter kinds of participation are illustrated by the single participatory act that has functioned as our dependent variable (petitions, demonstrations, boycotts, and campaign support) when analyzing (European) patterns of participation. Some of the literature on the subject (e.g. Haddad, 2006; Maloney & Deth, 2010, pp. 12–13) works with a narrow definition of activist participation as volunteering in civic associations. This strictly organizational approach does not fit our purpose. We will rather open up the categories and make it explicit how they differ and/but overlap.

The media and politicians discursively precondition the possibilities of activists to engage in democratic dialogue in a multitude of actors and opinions. The second reason to distinguish between different types of activists is therefore that active citizens who are members of civil society want to be taken seriously in the broad public as such a multitude. This is a premise for understanding who the facilitating activists are and thus a prerequisite for the beginning of a constructive dialogue between the parties involved.

When developing a typology of the different groups of activists involved in the COP15 Copenhagen Climate Summit, I distinguished between corresponding regimes of practical reasoning when explaining *why* they do as they do morally – and *how* they do it strategically. The six kinds of activists participating in the summit were identified based on participatory observations, questionnaires, and interviews, while Table 4.2 is a condensed and adjusted version of a typology that I have developed elsewhere (see Harrebye, 2011).

The different forms of activism can be exemplified by active groups and citizens during the COP15.[2] The two groups of most interest here, however, are the creative facilitating activists and the everyday makers (the active citizen). The everyday maker is not to be confused with the ordinary citizen, as the former is more informed and politically conscious. As opposed to the majority of us, she embodies active citizenship in a daily effort to back good intentions with better actions.

A line can be drawn between the first three and the last three types of logic, as there is a fundamental distinction to be made between an antagonistic and a negotiable rationality. But the cooperation between creative activists and everyday makers seems to point towards a third option. Indeed, the cooperation between these particular groups, as we often witness at larger rallies and public hearings, is able to circumvent both the oppositional and the integrative environments since both types of activists are disinterested in what is perceived as the hollowness of the official negotiating system and the utopian martyrdom of uncompromising antagonists.

Table 4.2 Typology of activism

TYPES OF ACTIVISM	RADICAL	CONFRONTATIONAL	CREATIVE	PROFESSIONAL	OCCASIONAL	THE EVERYDAY MAKER (the active citizen)
FUNDAMENTAL LOGIC	VIOLENCE	DISCLOSURE	SYMBOLS	LOBBYISM	NUMBERS	DO-IT-YOURSELF
TYPICAL ACTIVITIES	MILITANT DEMONSTRATIONS	CIVIL DISOBEDIENCE	PUBLIC SPECTACLES	CAMPAIGNS AND MEETINGS	PEACEFUL DEMONSTRATIONS	LOCAL SOLUTION-ORIENTED PROJECTS
INTENDED GOALS	REVOLUTIONS	OPEN PROCEDURES	INDIVIDUAL REFLECTION	REFORMATION	MORE DIRECT DEMOCRACY	IMMEDIATE AND TANGIBLE RESULTS
SAYINGS	"War on capitalism" (Disruptive slogan)	"Join the summit now! We have a right to!" (Challenging slogan)	"What would mother earth say if she could speak at the summit?" (Critical questioning)	"Let's commit each other in writing to cut emissions in reality." (Campaign suggestion)	"Save our planet. There is no backup plan(et)" (Cause slogan)	"We are planting trees on Sunday. We're bringing coffee." (Note in cooperative)
DOMINATING PERCEPTION OF FRAMING AGENTS (police, politicians, and media)	TROUBLE MAKERS (very tense relationship)	CHALLENGERS (somewhat tense relationship)	ENTERTAINERS (uncertainty frames the relationship)	CANTANKEROUS EXPERTS (relationship is appreciated, but often ignored)	VOTERS (fairly respectful relationship)	HEROES (highly regarded, but rarely listened to)

Maybe the creative climate movement should be listened to as a critical jam session rather than a constitution of a new static genre in the activist repertoire with a clearly formulated manifesto:

> These varieties of action constitute a repertoire in something like the theatrical or musical sense of the word; but the repertoire in question resembles that of commedia dell'arte or jazz more than that of strictly classical ensemble: people know the general rules of performance more or less well and vary the performance to meet the purpose at hand. (Tilly, 1986, p. 390 in Della Porta & Diani, 2006, p. 185)

Social research has not yet clearly identified the reasons for and the potential of this particular kind of activism. So, the typology is used to distinguish between 'ideal' forms of activism, exemplified by concrete groups active during the COP15.[3] The difference is that the above typology is sensitive towards movements that fit more than one of the formalized types of logic. This is an important feature as many new activist project-based cells intentionally move in and out of theoretical categories and political labels.

Active citizenship

In this broad typological perspective, the activist is closely linked to the notion of active citizenship understood as a broad variety of participatory activities, including actions that hold governments accountable, voting, participation in the everyday life of the community, one-off issue politics, responsible consumption, and more traditional forms of membership in political parties and NGOs (Hoskins & Mascherini, 2009). Generally speaking, citizenship theories involve four components: rights, responsibilities, participation, and identity. But following Gerard Delanty, this framework no longer fundamentally constitutes a unitary model of citizenship in the 21st century as its components in contemporary research to a great extent have become separated from each other and taken up in other discourses.

> Rights have become embodied in discourses that extend far beyond the legal reach of the nation state; responsibility has shifted from a discourse of personal obligation focused on the state to a discourse of co-responsibility for nature and for future generations; participation is less focused on the national community than on others' spaces, which have been opened up as a result of subnational mobilization linked to globalization; and identity has become pluralized

to the extent that citizenship must now contend with reconciling the pursuit of equality with the recognition of difference. (Delanty, 2000, p. 132)

So, theorizing over active citizenship can be seen as a particular articulation of the debate over rights versus responsibilities and the development of civic virtues as they are understood in the tradition of civic republicanism. Most scholars agree that the active exercise of social rights and shared responsibilities associated with belonging to a community, society, or a nation state is at the heart of the concept of active citizenship. When I speak of active citizenship I refer to the emancipatory potential of participation as a part of a community in line with the principles of deliberative democracy. This understanding is not to be mistaken for the more liberal perspective represented by theoreticians such as Anthony Giddens, who argues that citizens in the social investment state must take more individual responsibility for themselves, as active citizens.

This brings me to the second reason why the defense for and implications of fostering an active citizenship are multifarious, normatively as well as politically, as the citizenship discourse more generally speaking can be seen as an expression of known theories of justice:

> Those on the left look for ways in which economic inequality erodes active citizenship; those on the right look for ways in which welfare policies aimed at reducing economic inequality erode civic virtue. (Kymlicka, 2002, pp. 318–319)

But the concept of citizenship, I argue, has the ability (in deliberation at least) to transcend the opposition between liberal individualism and communitarianism (Janoski, 1998; Delanty, 2000). Democracy depends not only on the justice of its basic institutions, but also on the qualities and attitudes of its citizens. As Habermas notes, the institutions of constitutional freedom are only worth as much as the population makes of them. Procedural–institutional mechanisms to balance self-interests are not enough. Some level of civic virtue and public-spiritedness is required (Macedo, 1990, pp. 138–139 in Kymlicka, 2002, p. 285; Galston, 1991, pp. 217 and 244).

The notion of active citizenship is often defined as the engagement of individuals in political and civic activities through democratic processes. This entails interactive participation. Such participation primarily comes about and is most efficiently channeled when it is facilitated by people who know what they are doing.

Designing active citizens

In the private home of Danish CEO Lars Bonde, the Peruvian shaman Francisca Angelica is performing a healing ritual for the dying Mother Earth. In a temporary pavilion in the City Hall Square (where the 'Coke – a bottle of hope' campaign is happening) a highly unusual live press conference is taking place where a number of random bystanders take a pledge to never again drink Coca-Cola until the company stops stealing water from communities around the world. What are these two meetings an expression of? The first is an example of how activists were coupled with local citizens during the climate summit. Francisca was actually living with Lars and his family. The latter is an example of how summit spectators were involved by creative activists, such as The Yes Men who were posing as Coca-Cola representatives to question the legitimacy of their commercial campaign. What they have in common is that Wooloo, as part of their New Life Copenhagen initiative, facilitated both incidents.[4] The facilitating approach creates dialogue. The challenging elements provoke people to reconsider ordinary practices, whether everyday habits or international summits. Both characteristics are essential for the understanding of a new particular kind of activism where participatory reflection often is a goal in itself.

The New Life festival does not involve any traditional exhibitions or physical works of art. Instead, participants are invited to live together in new ways with a particular purpose:

> Rather than traditional activism I would characterize the work that we do as social design or social architecture. Through the framing of specific social scenarios we allow people physically, not only through discourse, to experience and explore new ways of living together. (Kai Nielsen, in interview with Harrebye)

According to this political version of social design, architecture frames the way people interact in the city. Likewise Wooloo's 'social design' aims at creating a space where otherwise disconnected people can meet in a meaningful manner to exchange knowledge and interests. This experimental form of direct democracy is much in line with the deliberative principles of civic republicanism:

> Instead of asking people whether they want to join our party and handing them a flyer, like you see at most traditional demonstrations,

we practice handing out 'blank flyers' and ask people if they want to participate in filling them out with us. (Rosengaard, in interview with Harrebye)

Through their design of social networks, meetings between passionate professionals and volunteering citizens change attitudes in the civil soil that feeds the grassroots. The *social architects* thereby frame a social room through the physical allocation of intentions and curiosity. Furthermore, the goals are not pre-determined. No set agenda is interfering with the co-creative process. The meetings are framed, but it is up to the participants to decide what to make of them. Thus, many happenings were launched in cooperation with other internationally well-known artists, scientists, and activists on the basis of the New Life festival.[5]

They must therefore be understood as an expression of a cultural and more indirect political movement: 'Our creative approach to activism largely depends on the rules and the framing that we construct' (Kai Nielsen, in interview with Harrebye). In this respect it is a process-based endeavor that believes that answers will be provided if the correct and inspirational communicative and philosophical conditions are in place. In that sense one might think that a Habermasian ideal public sphere is pursued where dialogues free from domination undoubtedly lead to political change – if properly facilitated, of course. But New Life Copenhagen is not apolitical just because it is not attempting to occupy the formal polarized space of politics – rather:

> What is political is very much in the eye of the beholder, and what is regarded as legitimately political is policed by the state. To analyze politics and political participation, we need to rethink the claim that individuals who do not participate in politics in conventional, orthodox ways are politically apathetic. (Marsch et al., 2007, p. 23 in Bang, 2009, p. 129)

As opposed to the discipline's standardization of actions into a program of combined sequences, Wooloo's project entails combinatory improvisation (Jensen, 2009, Ch. 6). For this group in particular, clear alternatives are not necessarily formulated in political terms but suggested in poetic, provocative, or puzzling ways ranging from theatrical happenings to ironic media declarations, and alternative platforms for dialogue. This leaves the listener curious because of its aesthetic or intellectual edge and resonance in the absence of ideological doctrine. This meta-activism is thus facilitating active citizenship in struggles for justice – through ambiguous practices that leave the participant or spectator thinking and hopefully acting differently.

A dilemma arises, however, when creative activists like the Wooloo group on one hand have to relate to the established system to be able to apply for official funding and facilitate a dialogue across divides, while at the same time wanting to distance themselves from traditional 'party politics and related constraints'. They handle this dilemma by accepting the paradox and trying to maintain their balance on the edge of both the establishment and the resistance movements as agents of a mediating civil society.[6] The creative activists are critical without wanting to sabotage, and constructive without being submissive or compliant. When I asked renowned activist David Solnit how he deals with this dilemma when he is trying to organize and facilitate or control open participatory and more organic democratic campaigns, he simply did not accept the question's premise:

> I do not see a paradox (...) any kind of movement that wants to change the elitist society has to build into its practice direct democratic participation of the people.

The COP21 in Paris in 2015 was a whole new scene. The big carbon emission countries, China and the US, were now committed to change and/but the terror attacks on innocent civilians in Paris a couple of weeks earlier gave the French police the warrant needed to minimize public gathering and dissidents. That has only made activist interventions even more acutely needed and creative – marches, human chains, personal ribbon sculptures, thousands of shoes standing in place of protesters, healing ceremonies, climate games, the run for your life experiment, a series of interventions in cultural institutions around the world sponsored by oil, and "physical hubs for people creating, organizing or performing creative climate interventions throughout the city, as well as virtual home for activists far away" coming out of a nine-week Europe-wide artist-activist residency in the Catalan Pyrenees (see e.g. Bloch, 2015, Aronoff, 2015). The virtual march in Madrid, Spain against new so-called 'gag laws' (Boren, 2015) and the War On Smog performance in Chongqin, China (actipedia.org) are beautiful expressions of how repression sometimes leads to innovation of the expressive repertoire.

My analysis suggests that we should distinguish between overall antagonistic and negotiable rationalities. Creative activism represents an attempt to bridge the gap between these two rationalities *through* facilitating practices aimed at creating reflection through mirroring technologies. It is through such reflective qualities that we are able to step back from the apparent issues at stake and problematize the deep structures that underlie them. As Nancy Fraser (2008, p. 154) notes when formulating her politics of framing, 'The capacity to interrogate the frame, to make it an object of critique and political action, is yet another instance of reflexivity.' In the following chapters we will be pointing towards a theory of reflection that supplements Fraser's three-dimensional concept of justice and offers a new conceptual framework and analytical tools useful in our attempt to understand the emancipatory potential of new creative types of activism.

Part III
Exploring the Practice – New Theoretical Framework

5
The Ambivalence of Cynicism, Irony, and Utopia

In this chapter cynicism, irony, and utopia are proposed as analytical concepts that can supplement existing theoretical frameworks, and I will demonstrate how these alternative perspectives can be fruitfully applied to understand the reorganization of critique regardless of whether one views creative activism suspiciously as a societal symptom or more optimistically as a democratic potential.[1]

Political actors are always adapting to current events and conditioned by structural changes at the economic, social, and cultural level. The mobilization strategies of social movements are changing accordingly as the communicative tactics of creative activists seek to influence the participatory culture and the organization of active citizens. But the general attitude towards this development across political parties, in the population, and in terms of how it is portrayed in the media is ambiguous. So how do we best capture the normative ambivalence towards the culture jamming of today's creative activists? Is today's creative activism best understood as a diagnostic symptom of a pathological societal development or does it constitute a democratic potential as a strategic reaction to these developments?

It is firstly shown how cynicism, irony, and utopia characterize central features of creative activist practices, thus contributing to the development of a more adapted and applicable conceptual framework. To allow for a balanced evaluation of the qualities of these, Boltanski and Chiapello's critical view of the paradoxical effects of artistic activism in *The New Spirit of Capitalism* (2007) will also be considered. On this basis it is finally concluded why the ambiguity of the cynical, ironic, and utopian traits of today's creative activism calls for a revision of the grammar of activism, its culture, and its organization.

Despite a consciousness about the limited ability to generalize from a few cases, this chapter underscores the importance and the difficulties of developing a usable theoretical framework for the analysis of creative activism that can inform a greater variety of empirical investigations. Such theories are important due to the increasing relevance of this form of critique but difficult due to the efforts of these actors to complicate any attempt at simplified labeling. But if a new conceptual framework can help explain both the negative and the positive aspects of the particular cases included in this chapter, it may also be used to make tentative generalizations that hold across cases.

This question touches on the complicated relationship between citizen and society, agent and structure, and the fundamental normative ambivalence within and towards the experimental practices in question. My readings of the selected cases therefore shift between optimistic appraisals of the ability that alternative voices have to broaden the public debate and lead some of us in an unexpected direction, and skeptical views of those agents and their actual effect on which path we choose to take. The principles of my reflexive methodology are important when shifting back and forth between two normative interpretive frameworks and from one level of case analysis to another.

Challenging traditional theories

Now after having described and defined creative activism in various ways we can characterize it by three overall traits. First, these new social actors *strategically and consciously use the new media*, which is why the approach of traditional art theories is insufficient. Debates such as the one about the current conditions for art as an exercise dependent on commercial markets (e.g. Lind & Velthuis, 2012) are relevant for creative activism, because the line between art and activism admittedly can sometimes be rather thin – which is also why creative activism, as I use it, should not be understood as an exhaustive category. But these activists cannot just be labeled and analyzed as political artists, as art is often perceived as useless and for good reasons celebrated as such. In a narrow and technical sense, one should be wary of conflating activist art with political art, as doing so obscures critical differences in methodology, strategy, and activist goals. Creative activism seeks to have sociopolitical impact and to break free from the institutional framing of the art-world and its confinements of exclusive and privileged galleries, museums, and private collections. Creative activism wants to engage with and appear in the local streets of a globalized world – and on its own terms. Furthermore, the function of the classical political artist is to reflect the atrocities that were or abstractly commenting upon what is, but not necessarily co-creating a future that might be. Creative activists therefore differ from the political artist by practicing prefigurative politics that 'potentiates the re-programming of reality' (St John, 2008, p. 172) and to a large extent really being the change they want to see in the world.

Monthly Critical Mass bike rides take place in cities across the world and prefigure a carless future. The rules are simple: Gather after work on the last Friday of the month in a set location. There are no fixed routes. No one and everyone is in charge when it comes to the direction of the parade. Known rituals provide an overall script and an accepted symbolism created by creative meta-activists constitute a suitable format for self-organization. This celebratory swarm-like protest bodily illustrates the social dynamics of radical participatory culture.

Secondly, creative activism is *process- rather than result-oriented*, which is why the citizenship debate in itself cannot entirely capture what there is at stake for this group of activists and the active citizens that get involved. For the creative activist it is not always about claiming specific rights and enforcing specific responsibilities, as the citizenship discourse argues. It is more often about getting citizens to question what is right and wrong – and why. Creative activists prefer to pose questions and provoke reflection on the transformation of capitalism and to a certain degree avoid communicating cemented beliefs in their actions.

Thirdly, this kind of activism is *project-based*, which is why classical theories of social movements, such as collective behavior theory, rational choice theory, resource mobilization theory, and political opportunity theory are useful but inadequate *in themselves* when describing the mobilization and organization of these new protesters. As Jenny Pearce emphasizes when she raises the challenges of a future post-representational politics: "There have been organizational innovations among social movements toward more horizontal forms of decision making in recent years and resistance to bureaucratization and the emergence of unaccountable leaders" (2007, p. 471). These campaigners do not necessarily fight for a common cause or subscribe to a certain ideology, and are more often driven by eclectic engagement rather than by persistent critique in accordance with the generational change in political attachment mentioned earlier. Thus, these activists do not always match the basic empirical requirements for most definitions of social movements, such as a collective challenge, a common purpose, social solidarity, and sustained interaction (Tarrow, 1998).

Project organised social activism is not based on a stable political organization – with reference to party membership or a well-defined repertoire of protests such as strikes and mass demonstrations. Neither does it stress the importance of long-time planning and registration. The new form of critique is better expressed through creative events, contemporary groups on Facebook and spontaneous reaction, than on policy agendas and membership. (Sørensen, 2012)

So, in a way we do need to differentiate between more traditional forms of participation and new social actors who do not live up to the criteria of thematic consistency and ideological coherence. But the creative activists do also play a role *within* larger social movements as they often trigger sympathy, set an agenda in the media, boost morale, and mobilize members.

That being said, the artistic element of these practices may meaningfully be analyzed by scholars within the aesthetic field (e.g. Nielsen & Simonsen, 2008). Even though these actors are more about process than policy, their drive is often rooted in a sense of justice that institutionally links to the citizenship discourse of civil society with regard to the possibility of articulating their critique.

Finally, but not least, all activists, including the new creative ones, *have a history of contentious forms of protest* that disposition their repertoire. This is why the aforementioned social movement theories despite their inadequacies can also add or provide meaningful insights when it comes to analyzing the developmental dynamics of these groups on the edge of new forms of critique. Again, this is especially true for theories of *new* social movements that identify new forms of collective action in advanced industrial societies that stimulate a provocative and innovative reconceptualization of the meaning of social movements (Johnston, Larana, & Gusfield, 1994), and introduce themes that have formed the basis for the new creative activist (Buechler, 1995). These themes include underscoring symbolic action (Cohen, 1985; Melucci, 1989); stressing processes that promote autonomy rather than strategies to obtain influence or power (Habermas, 1984–87; Rucht, 1988); and focusing on struggles over recognition and representation rather than traditional redistribution (Inglehart, 1990; Dalton, Kuechler, & Burklin, 1990; Fraser, 2008).

Problematizing the often fragile process of constructing collective identities, instead of simply assuming that they are just structurally determined, is likewise something that NSM theorists do (Klandermans, 1992; Hunt, Benford, & Snow, 1994; Johnston, Larana, & Gusfield, 1994) and something the creative activists are very conscious of. Recognizing a variety of temporary networks rather than assuming centralized organization as a prerequisite for successful mobilization (Melucci, 1989; Gusfield, 1994; Mueller, 1994), and insisting on a historically specific social formation as the structural backdrop for contemporary forms of collective action as a response to the inadequacies of Marxism when it came to explaining these, are also important characteristics for the theorizing on NSMs that are relevant for the understanding of creative activism. So the claim here is that these traditional approaches can be useful and necessary, but are also insufficient *in and by themselves* when it comes to offering a richer conceptual palette for analyzing this new critical tendency. This chapter should therefore be read as a supplement to these theories, not as an alternative.

Having shown how traditional theories are relevant but not sufficient to capture the ambivalence of this phenomenon, creative activism can be defined as a practice that attempts to create a new political space in the attempt to revitalize the political imagination. It does so through innovative tactics such as flash mobs, subvertisement, hacktivism, urban guerilla gardening, identity correction, forum theater, infiltrating media-jacking, prefigurative interventions etc. (see Boyd, 2012). I am taking a phenomenological approach and am therefore mainly interested in the strategic principles behind the different kind of specific tactics. I will be looking at other types of examples that share the aim of creating temporary autonomous zones (Bey, 2011) through the social production of space (Lefebvre, 1991). Creative activism is not violent. It is not your occasional demonstrator marching to the beat. It is not the NGO lobbying nor is it the everyday maker/active citizen who takes the initiative to improve her housing co-operative's environmental footprint (cf. the typology of activism outlined earlier).

Creative types of activism are not an entirely new phenomenon as it is something that has taken place throughout history in one way or another, as discussed in the beginning of the book. The crucial point regarding changes that have conditioned the way in which we participate politically is that they are interlinked and in a subtle way complement each other in forming both the constraints and the possibilities of the new millennium's democratic participation. These changes include of course globalization, new communication technologies, intertwined crises, etc. As Della Porta and Diani (1999, p. 192) write: "Recent transformations in both the distribution of power at the national and the international level and in the structure of mass communication suggest that new repertoires will emerge." My aim in this chapter is to map out single but seemingly central parts of today's progressive repertoire. In order to capture and further investigate the characteristic features of this reorganization of critique I therefore propose irony, cynicism, and the utopian imaginary as philosophically embedded concepts, which may augment the aforementioned traditional approaches in this regard.

The cynical manner of creative activists

Etymologically cynicism refers to the beliefs of the ancient school of Greek philosophers known as the Cynics. In contrast to other philosophical movements, little is known about the axioms and doctrines the cynics relied on, but their philosophy was that the purpose of life is to live a life of virtue in agreement with nature. In his Berkeley lectures of 1983 the French philosopher Michel Foucault (2001) emphasized how the cynics used various methods to call into question what could be characterized as true or false knowledge in epistemological terms – which of course in a Foucauldian optic is inevitably linked to power. In these lectures Foucault lifts the critical concept out of the Kantian contract, where critical practice is reduced to questioning the limits of reason (cf. the chapter on critique, creativity, and capitalism). Foucault uses the cynical philosophers' practice as an example of the relationship between *parrhesia* (candid speech) and public life. More specifically he differentiates between three forms of praxis used by the cynical philosophers: critical preaching, scandalous behavior, and provocative dialogue. Today these critical practices take the forms of critical documentary films, which revolve around the borders of fiction, manipulation, and deadly serious humorous journalism, boundless theater-performing demonstrations. Through artistic provocation they stretch the boundaries of civil disobedience and performance installations, and interactive happenings, which take people by surprise and cause outrage through elements of surprise, cliquish satire, and unorthodox communication. Play may therefore, as some researchers have pointed out (e.g. Ølgaard, 2015), serve as a template for investigating the political potential of creative protest action specifically and the interplay between aesthetics, politics, and resistance in a broader sense.

Christian von Hornsleth's Village Project is an example of such a cynical happening, a 'social sculpture' as he calls it, which drummed up a heated debate about how development aid is enabling the conservation of unequal relationships between the North and the South, and therefore in effect doing the very opposite of what it is supposed to. In short Hornsleth got all the inhabitants in a village in Uganda to bear his last name in exchange for a goat. What he hoped to accomplish was a prosperous business for both parties. The Ugandan Government condemned Hornsleth, and the ensuing diplomatic crisis fused a heated debate in Denmark and neighboring countries. This type of creative activism breaks with what is perceived as false dichotomies, upheld to ensure the status quo. As opposed to an ideological critique, Hornsleth cynically disrupts the existing order by breaking barriers of respectable behavior. This triggers a cognitive dissonance and alerts our senses to what is at stake. This way he as a provocative creative activist cracks open the public debate in a different manner than more traditional activists and professional lobbyists are able to. By annoyingly challenging the way we usually view the world in ways that annoys us he wants us to take a second look. To repeat Theodor Adorno's famous saying, 'The splinter in our eye is the best magnifying-glass'. Hornsleth is an example of how radical attacks of cynicism often originate in an immanent critique within the hegemony by taking the values of ruling elites seriously, while claiming that the elite does not. "Not only is such an attack a legitimate critique by definition, but it always threatens to appeal to sincere members of the elite in a way that an attack from outside their values could not" (Scott, 1990, p. 106). Since critics do not actually share the principles and values that they are contesting, an ironic attitude and a utopian outlook are constantly lurking underneath the cynical façade.

When the legendary creative activists The Yes Men manipulate their way into business conferences and pose as top executives, they are parodying the business community in order to wake up their audiences to 'the danger of letting greed run the world'. In their first documentary, they characterize their tactic as 'identity correction.' In their second film, which is also documenting how they operate, Andy Bichlbaum pretends to be a Dow Chemical spokesperson and is invited on the BBC in that role. He announces that Dow will *finally* clean up the site of the largest industrial accident in history, the Bhopal catastrophe, for which they were responsible. The result was that while many people worldwide were celebrating, Dow's stock value lost two billion dollars. When asked about the hoax, The Yes Men answered that "We would not say it is a hoax. It is an honest representation of what Dow should be doing." They defended themselves by claiming that it "sometimes takes a lie to tell the truth." The doubling function of the parody allows people to 'relax' around power as we dare to laugh at the tragic but benign imitation (cf. Hariman, 2008).

The critical point, stripped of the otherwise satirical tone, is to be found on The Yes Men website, where it is stated that "We have created a market system that makes doing the right thing impossible, and the people who appear to be leading are actually following its pathological dictates." The quote begs the question however: might that be true for The (cynical) Yes Men as well? So in an interview with Bichlbaum I asked him "is there a danger that your kind of activism becomes more form than content? That it in some cases distorts or takes away attention from the content?" Bichlbaum defends himself: "Sure sometimes the media is paying too much attention to the form that our joke is taking instead of the point it is making. But most often they cannot do one without the other. That's the beauty of it." I pushed him a little further: "So how would you reply to the critique of this kind of activism and what some people see as the cynicism beneath your practices?" Bichlbaum shrugged his shoulders, leaned back and said: "We are not just making fun of people. We are laughing with a purpose."

The ironic attitude of creative activists

One trait that transpires through the history of theorizing irony is the implicit, perceptive distance within which the ironic critique is always embedded. As opposed to the spontaneous laugh, which has a latent universal reach, ironic wit has a constricted resonance only with likeminded people, even though others may sense the implicit critical premises of the irony. So humor in its historically most political form, irony, is about sharing an indirect and unformulated awareness of the contingency and transitory nature of our human existence.

When asking Srdja Popovic (the leading figure in the Serbian Otpor movement and co-founder of CANVAS) about the democratic potential of creative activism, he was quick to accentuate the tactical importance of it, since

> creativity and especially humor serves as a huge boost for the morale of the non-violent movements and is the best cure for fear (...) it is also building credibility, it attracts attention and it is thus capable of recruiting more people. (...) You *need* to look at the dynamics between fear and enthusiasm when you are targeting the pillars of support – whether they are politicians, the business community, media, or police.

Irony as opposed to humor, which is more conciliatory, is critically directed towards those who cannot see and share this existential insight, Henri Bergson notices (Andersen, 2008). As such irony captures some of the underlying attitude of creative activists and describes the way many of them communicate their messages.

The Danish philosopher Søren Kierkegaard holds Socrates to be the first renowned ironist owing to his ability to get the Sophists to reach their own conclusions simply by posing the right questions. Creative activists use irony in similar ways that require people to seek answers that are only indicated by their apparent absence, and thus try to transcend the limits that Bergson points at that have to do with who understands the irony and who it is directed at. To Kierkegaard, the subject of irony is 'negatively free'; "Irony is a determinant of existence, and nothing is more ridiculous than believing it is merely a form of expression (...) it is the infinity within him" (Kierkegaard, 1920–36, vol. 10, p. 181. Own translation). This kind of irony implies a special understanding about the true status of the world – one that can only be hinted at. "Irony can therefore always be used to critique worldly matters, not humor though, which is directed at one's own reality" (Malantschuk, 1968, p. 194. Own translation). But the creative activist does not just declare herself 'out' of the community. She questions the premises on which critique can be made and tempts us to try and change them.

The use of irony, parody, satire, sarcasm, puns, and mockery has a long history in the 'infrapolitics' of resistance (Scott, 1990), but in a contemporary perspective the experimental groups of the 1960s and 1970s (e.g. Situationist International, Kommune 1 in Germany, the Provos in Amsterdam, and the 1977 movement) seem to have had a direct influence on the political style of contemporary alter-globalist and anti-capitalist movements (see e.g. Cuninghame, 2007). Concretely, parody, understood as a subcategory of irony, is a commonly used technique by the groups in question as it has an effective critical function and helps us laugh at power and imagine alternatives (Critchley, 2007). "Parody is an act of duplication where the original is placed 'beside itself' and the copy is used as a joke" (Hariman, 2008, p. 249). In the case of the creative activist the joke reveals the powerful as vulnerable, the unchangeable as contingent, and the enchanting as dangerous. Robert Hariman points out how parody is essential for a healthy political and cultural debate as it forces people to see that which they would otherwise take for granted in a different light. Relatedly, Judith Butler uses drag artists as an example of how gender parodies open up traditional categories and make us question 'reality' as the parody always reveals that it is an "imitation without an origin" (Butler, 1990, p. 175). By highlighting the tenuous nature of what we take for granted, the ironic parody can yield a plurality of perspectives on any given matter. But parody can also be used to maintain routines and order in the workplace, for example, and thus act as a safety valve for the expression of dissent (O'Doherty, 2007). Therefore it can be said to be ambivalent in its relationship to power (e.g. Westwood, 2014). Still, by allowing the temporary suspension of normality, parody can reinvigorate discussions that have been numbed through repetition and by entrenched positions on either side of a stale debate (Kenny, 2009).

Sacha Baron Cohen's alter egos Ali G., Borat, Brüno, and Admiral General Aladeen are pop-cultural examples of parodies that leave the viewer in continuous/constant doubt about who is making fun of whom and why. When the fictitious Kazakh character Borat, in the mockumentary comedy film of the same name, travels the United States he interacts with and also interviews a series of unsuspecting Americans (feminists, racists, and random pedestrians) whose beliefs and/or prejudice are revealed, exaggerated, or ridiculed by Borat's deliberately naïve and provocative encounters with them. A troubling angle on a delicate matter is often followed by the relief of laughter or a smile of doubt when Cohen's characters bring unaware civilians into embarrassing situations – displaying insights of intercultural value.

The Daily Show with Jon Stewart does the same thing but draws on comedy and satire from recent news stories and political figures, and does so with a more explicit normative point of departure and party political sting. Cohen and Stewart's reluctance to speak within the boundaries of what is commonly perceived as polite conversation becomes a relief from the dominant hegemony of rational consensus. To modern creative activists comic strategies such as satire and parody play a vital role in public life by connecting aesthetic to rational–critical concerns.

Habermas (1989) does not include aesthetic matters from his writings on the ideal speech situation. His critics note that within his scheme "writing poems and telling jokes are secondary to authentic illocutionary acts" (Aune, 1994, p. 129). Stewart and Stephen Colbert combine poetic imagination with concerns for a better politics, and demonstrate that illusory boundaries do not need to be drawn between entertaining and rational approaches to deliberation. Børge Outze, founder and former chief editor of the Danish newspaper *Information* (which started out as an underground resistance tool during the Nazi invasion), lived and fought by the principle that "you shall not strike your victim with a stick, but throw him up in the air and let him fall down and hurt himself" (Nielsen & Lund, 2015). Cuninghame declares that "language is the site of political struggle and the derisory laughter born of irony is one of the most potent weapons a social movement has, humiliating the 'powerful' and inspiring the 'powerless'" (2007, p. 165).

Irony and humor both have a disarming effect on dialogue and conflict as it makes it harder for authorities (be they judges, politicians, the police, or journalists) to use simple force. By surprising the public one may also affect people who would have otherwise chosen not to watch and participate were they given a choice. The Clandestine Insurgent Rebels Clown Army (CIRCA, aka Smile Liberation Front) are famous for using clowning and other non-violent tactics to act against corporate globalization as one element in larger traditional demonstrations and civic activities that supplement formal political summits. There is a psychological strategic aspect to the joker as the clown persona that can be used to defuse tense situations and both represent the fool and a truth teller (the jester has been used for both purposes throughout history). "Instead of wearing an all-out assault on the castle, the prankster slips through the gates wearing a fool's outfit" (Art Tinnitus, *Beautiful Trouble*, 2012).

In Shakespearean plays, the importance of the fool is its wisdom-in-folly (Asimov, 1970). Exactly because the fool stands simultaneously on the inside and the outside of power, both alien and recognizable to society and their sovereign ruler, the clown-fool 'operates as anti-rulers' (Amoore & Hall, 2013). They offer to their spectators "sceptical, unencumbered viewpoints that scorn pride and challenge concepts such as logic ... and solution" (Janik, 1998, p. XIV). The clown-fool playfully appropriates situations and facilitates a new political interpretation (in Augusto Boal's writing, reflecting on his theatrical processes developing the heritage from Paulo Freire through the Theater of the Oppressed, and the facilitator is tellingly referred to as the joker). But most importantly, the seemingly innocent stories of the clown, trickster, and fool offered the subordinated groups a space where they could openly declare and idolize dissent. As Scott (1990, p. 166) puts it:

> The heavy disguise [these tales wear] must all but eliminate the pleasure it gives. While it is surely less satisfying than an open declaration ... [it] carves out a public, if provisional, space for the autonomous cultural expression of dissent.

As such, the clown, the trickster and the fool embody a unique social and historical persona that has been allowed to speak truth to power – even under domination (Amoore & Hall, 2013). As expressed by Mikhail Bakhtin:

> True open seriousness fears neither parody, nor irony, nor any other form of reduced laughter, for it is aware of being part of an uncompleted whole ... it does not deny seriousness but purifies and completes it. Laughter purifies from dogmatism, from the intolerant and the petrified; it liberates from fanaticism and pedantry, from fear and intimidation. (1984, pp. 122–23)

The carnivalesque as a political performance therefore becomes a resource of political action that uses ambiguity and humor to undermine the false seriousness of the self-interested (Bruner, 2005).

These ironic parodies have the ability to constitute what Butler (1990) calls a 'performative surprise' and displace norms through radical proliferation of conventional representation. By allowing the temporary suspension of 'politics as usual' parody can reinvigorate our political imagination by questioning our presuppositions.

In 2007, the Dutch TV channel BNN aired an unprecedented reality show that was meant to be exactly such a performative surprise – The Big Donor Show. The concept was that a woman with a deadly brain tumor should pick one person out of a group of people in need of a kidney and donate hers to save their life. The selection was to be based on a series of questions posed to each person in the group and their respective responses – much like a dating program. Even before the show was aired it created a heated debate in Holland and beyond. Both the ethical considerations related to organ donation as well as what is morally acceptable to show on TV were disputed. Despite complaints and attempts to sanction the show the authorities had to reject a juridical intervention as it would go against the channel's right to free broadcasting.

On June 1, 2007 the show was aired, with millions of viewers watching from all around the world. The ironic twist to an already spectacular, but maybe morally questionable agenda, was that it had all been a hoax. At the end of what was believed to be the first in a series of shows, the host announces – and this right before the alleged cancer patient is about to choose her recipient – that the entire program has been a show produced to raise awareness of the lack of organ donors in Holland. He admits that the cancer patient is not fatally ill at all but just a hired actor. The people who were competing to receive the kidney are, however, real patients from the Dutch waiting list.

This happening is interesting for several reasons: first, a TV network ironically enough operated as a creative activist. Researchers and politicians who had been quick to denounce the show and analyze its implications for future society were now forced to rephrase their initial diagnoses and so/to offer a meta-level reflection on the event. Two days after the show had aired 18,000 citizens in Holland had downloaded an organ donor form from the internet. In Denmark alone 700 citizens registered as donors the day after – fifteen times the average on a regular Saturday. Manipulation is used here not to trick the population out of something, but to trick them into viewing the world in a different way – if only just for a minute.

Now we have established why irony is central to the critical practices of creative activists. In the following cases it is revealed why these political actors believe that you sometimes need to take a trip to a place that does not exist in order to be able to revisit your own reality.

The utopian imagination of creative activism

Despite the popularity in the creative critical milieu of a new segment of spectacular leftist thinkers, including the creative deconstructions of Jacques Derrida, the nostalgic communism of Slavoj Žižek, and the radical democratic orientation of Jacques Rancière – one example being the philosophical references used by the members of Pussy Riot in court to justify their acts in Russia in August 2012 – most contemporary theorists of utopianism agree that its influence is in retreat. The spirit of utopianism – the sense that the future could transcend the past – has been claimed to be "stone dead" (Jacoby, 1999, p. xi). One might also argue that utopianism has not ended, but it is just no longer *called* utopianism and has an increasingly conservative character (e.g. market managerialism, cf. Parker, 2002), or that it has given way to the related popularity of dystopianism and the pseudo-utopias of turbo-capitalism, such as the belief – enhanced by advertisement – that the use of material products will bring us instant peace and happiness. In this chapter it is argued that a creative critical practice on the rise is an expression of how utopia is actually used in critical practices today.

Candy Chang's "I wish this was ____" fill-in-the-blank stickers that were posted on vacant buildings all over the city of New Orleans after Hurricane Katrina can be seen as a street level, small-scale example of this. "By asking people to write their own responses, Chang prompted everyday citizens to imagine what they would like for their community, and raised the critical question of whose interest are catered to when urban areas are developed" (Duncombe & Lambert, Ch. 2, 2016).

It is a widespread political demand that if you criticize the status quo you should also be able to present alternatives – if you want to be taken seriously. But to a number of critics, being taken seriously is not seen as a goal nor a quality in and by itself – quite the opposite, it sometimes seems. This of course limits their party political relevance but also allows them to say and do what many other actors on the political scene cannot. They act as if their most important responsibility is to expand our repertoire and involve the future in doing so – not necessarily through realistic proposals (sold by politicians), not through statistics that may give us a probable trajectory of how much the urban population will increase, say (projections made by academics) or through analyses of where the next economic crisis might occur (guesswork by journalists). Rather, these critics do so through artistic expressions of protest, through alternative narratives that suggest how the city may deal with future challenges in alternative ways, or in surreal distortions of how financial instability is developing. This is a practice that when at its best leaves us thinking 'what if?' and revitalizes our political imagination.

These activists work with utopia not as a fixed end that we should all strive for but rather as what Martin Parker defines as "statements of alternative organizations" (Parker, 2002, p. 2). Organization in this sense should be understood in the broadest term possible, meaning alternative forms of social order articulated, performed, or tested to cast a critical eye on the oppressions and unnecessary suffering of the present. So to Parker, utopian practices are about pointing towards possible alternatives, but they also have a critical purpose. Relatedly, Louis Marin (1984) approaches utopian practices at the categorical, schematic, and aesthetic levels and stresses their critical function. To Marin (1984, p. 274) "utopia is the form the unexpected takes." As such it is useful, but it cannot in this view become a political response that serves as a realizable project. Realizing utopia is not its function according to Marin. To him it is primarily "an ideological critique of the dominant ideology" (1984, p. xiv).

Without pursuing a lengthy discussion about the nature of ideology, it is worth stating that when judging critical comments made by creative activists, in whatever form they may take, it is important to take into account that they may be driven by a moral set of principles but the actual events rarely point towards a grand unifying ideologically based vision that has it all figured out. They should perhaps rather be understood as an investigation of alternative principles of organization and social order. I therefore, like Valérie Fournier (2002), use utopianism to emphasize movement over static visions of a better order as I focus on its critical, transgressive, and transformative functions rather than its form and content (as do Levitas, 1990; Sargisson, 1996; Harvey, 2000). It is exactly the decentralized and project-based nature of this multiplicity of activists' cadres, as well as the inconsistency of the movement, that make them effective vehicles for utopianism. So there is an almost anarchistic vein to this argument: "If utopianism is about establishing the conditions under which we can be free to decide our own affairs, we can develop alternatives, it is simply paradoxical to believe that this freedom can be achieved through centralized means" (Fournier, 2002, p. 208).

The Danish Roskilde Festival can be seen as a utopian example that challenges the existing hegemony of market managerial organization. With 130,000 inhabitants living in tents on what amounts to 215 football fields, the population is for this week more dense than Shanghai. Through its More Than Music initiative, which cooperates with a number of creative activists, artists, and social entrepreneurs each year, the festival wants to function as a social, ecological, and political laboratory – a co-creative urban simulator that functions like an open laboratory simulating the city that enables the testing of new ideas (Danielsen et al., 2012). The festival (as a phenomenon) can therefore be viewed as a temporary autonomous zone (TAZ).

Hakim Bey (aka Peter Lamborn Wilson) used this term to describe areas of momentary eruption that elude formal structures of (state) control where people can explore their own and each other's freed revolutionary energy and experiment with the creativity that springs from it. From pirate utopias to online autonomous movements today, temporary autonomous zones are created to co-create and let the political imagination run wild. At Roskilde Festival the urban simulator, unconstrained from the external juridical and internalized rules and regulations of the ordinary city, is created with 30,000 volunteers working in a rather flat organizational structure where any surplus is donated to charity. This would make you think that anarchism would reign. But in fact it is recognized as a very attractive and innovative workplace. Moreover, "In Denmark we have a long tradition of working across organizational boundaries. Roskilde Festival reinterprets this tradition in a radical way" (excerpt from *The Danish Leadership Canon* where Roskilde Festival is included alongside, among others, Lego and Mærsk). Thus the festival's curators, its volunteers, and its audience challenge conventional organizational theorems when it comes to size, ownership, and structure. Creative activists in general use the creation of temporary autonomous zones to challenge exactly these often politically restrictive parameters.

In another example, the a-temporality of utopian representation and the deliberately blurred boundaries between fantasy and reality characterize the work that The Yes Men do. A week after the historic presidential election that brought Barack Obama to the White House, The Yes Men were joined by hundreds of independent writers, artists, and activists in an elaborate project, six months in the making, to release a 'special edition' of *The New York Times* – in cities across the US. The paper (dated July 4 of next year) with headlines of the long-awaited news that: "Iraq War Ends." The edition, which had the same look and feel as the real deal, included stories describing what the future could hold, *if* Obama was forced to become the President he was elected to be (including his plans for national health care, the abolition of corporate lobbying, a maximum wage for CEOs and other stories, reprinted on The Yes Men's website). This happening was an active imagination of what could be and a utopian media practice that was intended to get people to stop and wonder instead of just registering the immediate bleakness of usual reporting. An example of such a political axiom, it is often stated that politics is the art of the possible. It also seems though, as Stephen Duncombe warns in his *Open Utopia* (2012, p. xlii) "that our imagination is constrained by the tyranny of the possible."

One of the trademarks of creative activism is the way in which it insists on exposing us to the impossible and thus forcing us, at the very least, to reflect on our axiomatic truths. Compromise is evidently an unavoidable part of politics and democracy, but the underlying logic of the utopian practice is that the practically possible should be a compromise with the impossible ideals and ideas of our collective dreams and deep creativity, which are too often suppressed by our realistic modesty. In a world increasingly influenced by branding and storytelling, it seems the creative activist is attempting to bridge the widening gap between truth and fiction, dreams and reality. They seem to be suggesting that imaginary practice does not have to be detached from practical solutions. In fact it is only when the creative imagination is channeled through practical action that the fantasy becomes a useful fiction. Duncombe (2007, p. 17) describes these fantasies as enacted dreams, but stresses that they must be "dreams the public can mold and shape themselves (...) and that will not cover over or replace reality and truth but perform and amplify it." Thomas More in his book *Utopia* (2007, originally published in 1516) first introduced the notion of utopia to the modern lexicon in the form of a literary paradox – signifying both *ou-topia* (no place) and *eu-topia* (the good place) – suggesting that the ideal world did not and maybe could not exist. More modern analyses focus on a more direct political application and relevance of utopia. Fredric Jameson (2004, p. 43), for example, argues how "utopia emerges at the moment of the suspension of the political." Likewise creative activism can be said to insist at a certain distance from political institutions, which encourages the play of fantasy around their possible reconstructions and restructurations of the world as we know it:

> As in Freud's analysis of dreams, there is the satisfaction of secondary elaboration or interminable over-determination; but there is also the implacable pressure of the unconscious wish or desire. Can we neglect that wish, without missing everything that gives utopia its vitality and its libidinal and existential claims on us? (Jameson, 2004, p. 46)

In this sense, the creative activist functions as a disturber of the censored hope, bringing images of the dream into broad daylight and awakening the public from the routines of their everyday life, inviting them into a world of disturbance and vision – the first as a critical necessity, the second as a future possibility. Seemingly the ironic element contains a critique of what is whereas the utopian element admits a sense of what could be. But, as I will argue below, the two cannot be easily allocated nor divided.

The Yes Men's fake *New York Times* and the festival's temporary city both include, although in different ways, the utopian model in their practices – The Yes Men by bringing the good news that we hope for in the future to our present day and Roskilde Festival by facilitating a co-creative playground that works as a laboratory for future urban development. Experimental organization is essential to both. Nonetheless, as I have stated above, the spirit of utopianism, the idea of positing and indeed pursuing an ideal form of collective life, is commonly said to be in decline: "Instead of championing a radical idea of a new society, the left ineluctably retreats to smaller ideas, seeking to expand the options within existing society" (Jacoby, 1999, p. 13). But creative activists,

I argue, represent a part of the left that has not (yet anyway) become so pragmatic. One of the reasons why political ideologists resign from utopian projects seems to be the fear of the link between the pursuit of radical utopias and totalitarianism, so closely linked with the collective memory of the horrors of the 20th century. But, as I have shown, these new activists do not have a *specific* utopia in mind. Instead they utilize utopian 'techniques' to revisit our own actual world through an other-worldly reference point. As noted, they are process- rather than result-oriented. This critical detour has several functions for the creative activist, the most important one being disruption. The United Victorian Workers and Operation First Casualty are both excellent examples of this (see Duncombe and Lambert, 2016, Ch. 2, for short, clear-cut analyses of these cases).

Karl Mannheim proposed that when the utopian element in thought passed over into conduct, it had the effect of "bursting the bonds of the existing order" (1968, p. 173). According to Mannheim there is a dialectical relationship between the notions of ideology and utopia. They both represent visions of the world that are incongruent with reality. But whereas ideology transcends reality for purposes of maintaining the existing order, the utopian function is one of disruption. Disruption can be regarded as the archetypical expression of challenging groups and has taken a variety of forms. In the 18th century it could be an attack on a wrongdoer's house, in the 19th century it took the form of barricades, while in the 20th century it could be the sit-ins and the sit-down strikes in the workplace. Today's opposition movements have become skilled at mounting symbolic and peaceful forms of disruption that avoid repression while maintaining contentious vigor – the feminist movement in general, the Zapatista movement in Mexico, and the environmental movement today are relevant examples of this possibility. To Parker, "the radicalism of the *eutopia* lies in its pointed alternatives to the present" (2002, p. 223). This seeks to demonstrate that there are other ways of thinking about how human beings might organize themselves. But according to Marin (1984, p. 279) there is also, apart from the suggestive and the critical aspect, an introspective aspect of these exercises since utopian practice is also about "coming to the awareness of its own process, a critical consciousness seeing itself in its own figures and emerging spaces for concepts and in their production." The activists in question attempt to create a social space (as mediation between the discursive and the event, cf. Ross, 1988) that allows for such reflection.

In the analyses above, I have accentuated a positive interpretation of the democratic potential of these new activists and the relevance of the ironic and the imaginative perspective in trying to understand them. I will now give way to a more skeptical view of this new tendency to capture the ambiguity of the phenomenon. The conceptual supplement to traditional theories suggested here does not however lose its relevance with this 'normative turn' from a positive to a more disparaging use of the concepts in question. In fact the point is exactly that the analytical applicability of the concepts is only strengthened by its analytical usefulness to both 'opponents' and 'allies'.

Critique of the creative critics

In Luc Boltanski and Ève Chiapello's modern classic *The New Spirit of Capitalism* (2005) a sociology of critique is developed to explain how different types of critique in a paradoxical way have and still are contributing unintentionally to the continuous reproduction and necessary transformation of capitalism. From this perspective the creative activist can be seen as an ideal example of the central network figure presented to personify the symptomatic tendency as she lives without job insurance and traditional long-term employment, and plans and jumps from project to project – *iceberg to iceberg* – in an attempt not to drown but to save the planet. In 1968 the artistic and the social critique blended when the student riots created the largest strike in world history. The existing capitalist order had to adjust and social improvements were made as a token of cooperation and necessity. The social critique faded out parallel to the decline of communism in the East and has since then been marginalized. The artistic critique flourished in the sense that it coincided with the development of capitalism. The artistic critique focused on bourgeois hypocrisy, consumer conformity, and bureaucracy, which in a sense can be said to have led the way for the abolition of clear classes as a base for social movements, the creation of new and more specialized markets, and less rules and regulations for merchants (Boltanski & Chiapello, 2005, Part II – 3).

I understand today's creative activism as somewhat of a reconciliation of the artistic and the social critique (Boltanski & Chiapello, 2005). It primarily operates as the former but also incorporates the sources of indignation of the latter. For Boltanski and Chiapello, critique can have three kinds of effects on capitalism: (1) it can have a delegitimizing effect on the existing system; (2) it can contribute to reinforcing the existing system; or (3) it can create confusion and thereby make the mechanisms of exploitation even less transparent. The creative activist, I argue, challenges this somewhat limited set of possible outcomes. But

Figure 5.1 Creative filter bubbles and ideological echo chambers
Source: By artist Thomas Thorhauge.

as their argument goes: "The history of the years following the events of May 1968 demonstrates the real but sometimes paradoxical impact of critique on capitalism" (Boltanski & Chiapello, 2005, p. 199). The contra values that were celebrated helped to create a new dynamic 'lean capitalism' characterized by its flexible organization of workers and a new management paradigm. From this perspective, creative activism can be seen as an important motor for capitalism, not as one of its most dangerous enemies. Through Boltanski and Chiapello's lens, the creative activist as a critical phenomenon serves as an example of how civil processes similar to decentralization, subcontracting, and commercialization of political interest groups have helped to break down traditional communities of solidarity and political social movements that have always been the condition for class consciousness and hence the potent formation of serious structural critique (Figure 5.1).

Think of the discussion we had earlier in the book about facilitation as a coopted co-creative management tool. Combined with the dynamics of the outlined 'infra politics' it is worth remembering the risk that "Those obliged by domination to act a mask will eventually find that their faces have grown to fit that mask" (Scott, 1990).

Visual culture denotes the perpetual interplay between looking and experiencing, and in this case disruption and production – in popular culture, art, news, film, internet, and advertisement. Ad-busting is a critical engagement with visual media partly indebted to the situationist's critique of the commodification of signs and symbols in late capitalist society that Guy Debord (2004) famously diagnosed as the Society of the Spectacle.

So, are these activists just representatives from and for a spoiled creative class? Many find it tempting to denounce the importance of these activities as juvenile attempts to pose as critics while dishonoring a hard-working community in their own selfish and temporary interest of finding a suitable identity. Creative activism may induce a debate in the public, but can it actually have a real effect and influence politicians?

It might rather become a singular outburst, an isolated space allowed to exist within the current condition of politics, where desires are allowed to manifest themselves momentarily as to prevent them from entering politics proper (Ølgaard, 2015, p. 141). The Russian thinker Anatoly Lunacharsky reminds us that maybe, the carnival is simply "a safety valve for passions that otherwise might erupt in revolution," which allows dissident voices to "let off steam in a harmless, temporary event" (Docker, 1994, p. 171).

In an interview Deva Woodly, a New School scholar of social movements, shares her concern about simply preaching to the choir:

> Movement is very much about persuasion. It is about not only developing your analysis in the smaller circles of concern, which tends to happen in more demographically or ideologically similar groups. If you really want to change the society that you live in you also have to communicate those concerns outside these groups. And you have to persuade people that what you are working for, what you are striving for, is worth pursuing together.

Michael Dutton's response to this fundamental activist dilemma is clear:

> The fact that we may not like the particular form dissent takes, or approve of it being offered for sale, does not alter the dissident nature of the act, nor the delegitimizing effect it has on the government (...) The process is productive in so far as it does not simply cater for a market, but actually produces it, by manufacturing desire. (1998, p. 6)

Based on the critical counter-position of Boltanski and Chiapello, the term 'creative activism' itself must be revisited. Creativity, understood as an unexpected transcendence of normality, often springs from necessity. In this case, the constraints of different forms of repression or the cooptation of critical elements have necessitated creative solutions to overcome and transcend the mainstream. In this positive interpretation creative activism has the audacity through facilitating actions to create a space for critical reflection. On the other hand, the term creativity, as an attribution of artistic critics, has been internalized by the capitalist system to a degree where it is noted as a desired quality in job listings from caretakers and librarians to account managers and CEOs – and most obviously exploited in the advertisement industry (e.g. de Waal Malefyt & Morais, 2010). As a side effect of the celebration of creativity it has been inflated to the extent where one may say that it has lost its critical autonomous potential (cf. discussion in Part I of the tensions between creativity, critique, and capitalism).

To sum up, creative activism should be interpreted as an attempt to invigorate civil sovereignty through culture jamming and experiments with the irrational sources of politics. One's interpretation of its relevance and success determines whether its creativity is ascribed the former or the latter attributes. Cynicism, irony, and utopia capture the ambiguity of this phenomenon – the public's ambivalence towards creative activism and creative activism's ambivalence towards public politics.

The ambivalence of creative activism

Based on this critical perspective, concepts used to highlight key features of creative activism, cynicism, irony, and utopia, must also be revisited. The aim of the creative activist, seen in the cynical light, seems to be the 'de-masking' of power and thus encouraging a change in the political dynamics. But in our modern, everyday use of the word, cynicism does not refer to ancient ways of challenging power in public, but rather points to a distrust of the world and the apparent motives of others. Today it should be understood as an emotional defense mechanism protecting the emotional hardliner from disappointment. In this sense of the word, the cynical features of the creative activist do not make her a proactive critic, but an unengaged pessimist. The disruptive behavior of the modern cynic may be able to disturb the daily routines of a resonant elite and a targeted groups of citizens, broaden the scope of conflict, and keep authorities off balance for a minute, but the practice, from a more skeptical standpoint, is also unstable and has difficulties sustaining the commitment to a cause or a movement over longer periods of time. In my interview with Andrew Boyd, the man behind the decade-long Billionaires for Bush campaign, he pinpoints the ambivalence of the cynical activist practices as follows:

> How to be cynical without being hopeless? If you can do that as an activist, people will respect that, because you are not just hitting them over the head with some beautiful vision of utopia, and you are not just being a bitter cynic either. If you can keep a faith alongside your faithlessness, and maintain that dialectic tension, people pick that up as they have both of those things competing within themselves as well (...) So yes, there is a cynical edge to the campaigns that I have been involved in, but they do not lead people to a cynical place. (Harrebye interview with Boyd)

Critics of the ironic activist see a selfish elitist preaching to the choir and arrogantly distancing herself from reality in the assurance of the possibility of a better world:

> For the ironic subject apparent reality has lost its legitimacy, it has become an incomplete form that bothers her everywhere. On the other hand, she does not withhold the future. All she knows is this – the current state of affairs does not match the idea. (Kierkegaard in Himmelstrup, 1964, p. 106. Own translation)

The activist has often been accused of being irresponsible because she has not always felt obliged to present coherent alternatives to the system she is criticizing. Portraying the ironic mass culture, which creative activists can be said to be part of, the Norwegian literary scholar John Erik Riley coins the unimpressed view as follows:

> The modern mass culture is exposed as an avant-gardism ripped of any real engagement and critique – one 'cool' radical tendency adapted to the neo-liberal need for new and unexpected turns in the market in an endless chain of caricatures. The experimental form comes from an irony that has turned against itself or against its original content – an irony without substance. (...) The result is a climate where it becomes impossible to find forms, which can challenge power because they all sooner or later become accepted and transformed into its own ideological contradiction. (Riley, 2000, p. 8)

With regard to utopia, while dreams may inspire us to imagine how things could be different, they may also blind people to reality and send them off into a pleasant doze of apathy – just like the dream of a divine heaven has been seen as an opium of the people. The dreams produced by creative activists are not just meant to entertain, though. They are real in the sense that they mirror reality differently than people are used to and thereby challenge the status quo. Skeptics have also pointed out the dangers of strategic aestheticization of communication and a slippery slope pointing towards the political propaganda of fascism directed at the collective and the calculated sales tactics of commercialism aimed at the individual consumer (pointed to in Part I).

So there is a normative ambivalence to the creative approach of the ironic and utopian activists, but there are fundamental differences that are necessary to keep in mind. Guerilla marketing and creative activism are both adversaries and sources of inspiration to each other. But the creative activist, I argue, is inherently different. The cause itself justifies her means. Furthermore, the happenings, stunts, pranks, and spectacles put on display are inclusive in that spectators become participants and co-creators of expression and meaning. They are transparent, meaning that they do not pretend to be reality, but in fact deliberately explicate its illusionary character, thus avoiding becoming a delusion.

Finally, the *'ethical* spectacle' is open-ended (Duncombe, 2007). It leaves room for interpretation and the freedom to make up your own mind without being told what to do. There might often be a specific agenda, but the main function is to broaden a given field of possibilities. As Patricia M. Thornton concludes in what seems to be a James C. Scott (1990) inspired analysis of the critical use of traditional doorway hangings (it is custom to hang small pieces of paper over say your neighbor's door with a poem or today a political statement that is supposed to have talismanic origin) and the body cultivation techniques of the practitioners of Falun gong (using their bodies as a metaphorical frame for critical, symbolic tattoos) and the way that these activities in China mask and evoke political meanings beneath a protective veil of ambiguity:

> In the face of repressive capacities, irony, ambiguity and double entendre represent adaptive strategies for contentious claim making. (...) (I)ndirection, imagery and allusion serve to create conceptual 'open spaces' within which collective identities may be forged and political agendas refined. (Thornton, 2002, p. 680)

Cynicism, irony, and imagination can not only be used to praise the potential of these cadres of activists, as has been demonstrated, they can also be used to question their reach. Either way the concepts have an explanatory strength when it comes to a balanced characterization of this contemporary phenomenon.

Based on the outlined arguments creative activism can be defined as an immanent form of critique – for better and worse. To begin with the latter, accepting the premises of whatever one is critiquing does not allow one to propose radical alternatives to the existing order. From this perspective the creative activist can never function as a coherent revolutionary leadership figure as she is limited to a fragmented critique and only able to punctuate space and time in specific and isolated temporary instances. The death of the grand narrative, in this view, only points to reformist adjustments of the system or the culture that you want to change. Taking a point of departure in the rationale of the regime one is critiquing does however enable one to illustrate the absurdity of the ideological rationality of that regime. From this standpoint the creative aspect of the broader repertoire of contention serves a specific purpose – one that may revitalize the political imagination of others and hence transcend the strictly immanent critique by capturing and redirecting the attention of the masses to the urgent problems of our world and stimulating the imagination of those who may have the resources to make a difference. In this way the immanent critique not only makes us question why things are the way they are, it also makes us wonder how things might be different. Creative activism thereby becomes more than mere critique, it also becomes a suggestive gesture pointing forward. In an interview with Ève Chiapello, about reformist versus revolutionary change, she is close to (and most unwillingly so) questioning her own critique of the artistic activists when explaining how "you may have a revolutionary purpose, but you *have* to change piece by piece and regulations by regulations."

Again, the optimists choose to believe in the democratic potential of the thought-provoking spectacle. The critics stress the limited representational legitimacy of the creative activists and the limited (if not counterproductive) effects of their efforts. My point is that this ambivalence needs to be analytically captured by ambiguous concepts. According to Marin the role that goals and norms play with regard to how you perceive utopian practices seems to underline just how important the central tension between *outopia* and *eutopia*, which is constitutive of the concept of utopia. The ambiguous concepts suggested here are useful for skeptics and supporters alike because they coin an attitude, which is characteristic of these activists, and this in a manner that captures both their weakness and their strength – and does so in a way that is analytically useful when explaining the logic, the organization, the strategy, and the resonance of the practice.

According to Fukuyama (1992, p. 46), "We cannot picture to ourselves a world that is essentially different from the present one, and at the same time better." The cultivation of possibilities by grassroots movements and the daring to imagine alternatives by creative activists is proof that some still try to change, if not the world, then at least the lives that we live. The argument of this book so far, then, has been that creative activism must be seen as a new critical practice due to changes in the conditions for contentious politics and subsequently developing characteristics of this type of participation. These changes have meant that traditional theoretical approaches, such as theories of art, citizenship, and social movements, are in themselves analytically insufficient if they are to capture the marching beat of today's new social actors. Cynicism, irony, and utopia, as this chapter has shown, are helpful applicable concepts, and thus a useful theoretical supplement, when trying to understand the creative activist – both as a symptom of and a strategy against the pathologies of capitalism.

Theories of social movements offer many insights into the dynamics of cycles of contention. They are for example often triggered by changes and openings in the political opportunity structure, and they decline because people tire of agitation, internal fraction, or because the movement transforms into more institutional forms, which makes it easier for the elite to repress and/or replicate it. One of the advantages of more creative coalitional campaigns or happenings led by small cadres of organizers mobilizing a much larger faction of sporadically active citizens is that they are better equipped to meet the challenges that come with critiquing conditions in constant and gradual change. Creative activism simply seems to be entertaining enough for a large and potentially powerful segment to take things seriously.

This strength also however seems to be the biggest problem for these groups, as they do not take the time to formulate a systematic structural critique capable of pointing in one direction, and thus end up serving as a coherent alternative to the existing order. Values in today's network society, which the artistic critique might help shape, are based on principles of temporality, flexibility, and elasticity – none of which are compatible with the stability and stubbornness that critical masses need to mobilize momentum. The cynic, ironic, and utopian features of creative activism are in a frustrating cyclical sense both a reason for and an effect of this predicament. As Boltanski and Chiapello note:

> The revival of critique accompanies – but always after some delay – the appearance of new kinds of protest mechanisms more attuned to the emerging forms of capitalism, in accordance with the principle that critique, in seeking to be effective, tends to become isomorphic with the objects it is applied to. (2005, p. 518)

The question is whether innovations in the margins of the repertoire of contention can break this cycle and crystallize into wholly new forms. I argue that it can.

6
Mirroring Counter Strategies

From broad social movements to sudden uprisings, social enterprises, smaller cadres of professional activists and everyday makers around the world are challenging the status quo. Nancy Fraser's latest theory of framing and Michel Foucault's concept of heterotopology form the theoretical basis from which I here show how creative activism in practice is an example of how counter-mirroring strategies today are used to circumvent what I characterize as the reflexive character of capitalism. The ambiguous social architecture of facilitating meta-activism depicted so far has been pointing towards these mirroring technologies aimed at creating an alternative reflection.

In this chapter, four types of tactics that overcome the inherent misrepresentation of capitalism are identified and a typology of tactical mirrors developed. The forging of such mirrors, as will be shown, constitutes an immanent critique and a utopian imaginary. By adding a fourth dimension to Fraser's three-dimensional conception of justice, this chapter finally points towards a new theory of reflection that has both critical diagnostic and politically constructive, suggestive potential.

Deadlines and headlines – beyond trench warfare

At a certain point during the American Civil War, soldiers had problems detaining the increasing number of captives. They simply did not have enough prison space. In the civil prisons a psychological detainee mechanism was therefore developed that could replace the purely physical ones. A line of charcoal on the ground made up these new prisons walls and marked the borders of the prisoners' maneuvering space. If they crossed this line they were shot. Hence the term 'deadline'.

Today the term does not signify a spatial line drawn in the sand, but a definite timeline for delivering our work. We meet the deadline. We do not cross it. Our private lives as well as our shared political public sphere are increasingly conditioned by such deadlines and the simplifications of the headline hegemony that seems to be a result of it.

In his critical theory of acceleration, Hartmut Rosa (2005), who can be said to belong to the fourth generation of the Frankfurt School, claims that democracy only works properly within a certain 'speed-frame' of social change and that the dynamics and the speed of socio-economic development alone threatens to undermine the proper functioning of democracy.

The French philosopher Michel Foucault analyzed how the logic of prisons can be seen as the starting point of modern political economy as we know it (Foucault, 1995). According to Foucault the institutional space helped to create the docile bodies that our society needed in order to develop as it did. Likewise, the simplification of human nature and societal complexity into catchy headlines has turned open philosophical questions into barricaded political positions, which have not been fruitful for discursive ethics of public deliberation. The question now is where and how critical techniques that are able to cross those deadlines and compete with those headlines are cultivated. Paola Rebughini (2010, p. 475) suggests that we should look at our daily routines:

> Over the past thirty years, research conducted into the 'new social movements' and on the more recent phase of critical mobilization against neo-liberal economic globalization has revealed that collective action that aspires to express a critique, to widen the space for democracy and individual freedom, often grows from networks that are initially formed in the area of local and daily life of the activists.

One of the students' tactics during the protests of 1996–97 against the Milošević regime in Serbia was to hold up huge mirrors in front of the chains of police officers blocking their way. The police were now confronted, not with the students, but with themselves. A typical analysis would view this situation as a practice meant to mock the officials and reveal the true nature of the system. In this chapter I suggest that it was rather meant to *reduce* the social distance between campaigners and the police force, by depicting them, the police, as 'victims', not bearers, of the regime – and thus an act of solidarity, not contempt. Fraternizing with the police was in fact a conscious strategy of the non-violent resistance movement Otpor (cf. CANVAS's formulation of Otpor's ten key principles). In communist dictatorships as well as in capitalist monopolies, mirrors in all shapes and sizes are used to open up a space and allow for alternative perspectives other than the usual. The Serbian mirrors functioned like a crack in the dam designed to hold back criticism.

Now, a distinction can be made between two different critical strategies. One necessitates a critical phraseology and often appeals to an intuitive feeling of what is wrong with a certain matter. This kind of critique manifests itself at all levels of our society – from gossip in the workplace to political public debates where it needs to adjust to the popular discourses of that time. The other form of critique entails an explicit normative fundament that considers the historical and structural conditions that shape our society. This kind of critique is referenced in the ideological manifests of political parties and debated in cliquish academic journals. In his book on the same subject, Rasmus Willig (2007, p. 11) concludes that: "While the one preserves the daily, normative order by virtue of its continual critical corrections, the other maintains a reflexive distance as a form of second order observation of the first" (own translation). But it is my assumption that there is a third way, a critical practice, which challenges the two aforementioned strategies and the institutional conditions that gave rise to them. Creative activists serve as principal examples of practitioners of a kind of critique that attempts to bridge the everyday critique of minor matters and the more fundamental structural critique.

Thus, it is argued, there *are* alternatives to the present-day ideological trench warfare, mirrored by the quarreling found in party politics. As practitioners of 'small politics,' creative activists, for example, are experimenting with a different approach to the weighing of political issues – as they have done so for years. Instead of having a clear idea about what the good life is and let that form the basis of a critique, which eventually might lead to reflection, the logic is reversed in these more experimental practices. Whether it is Ai Weiwei in China, The Yes Men in the US, or Pussy Riot in Russia, provoked reflection is meant to lead to critique, which might eventually result in the formulation of alternatives to today's perception, and offer a way of pursuing the good life.

The practices of this reverse logic are not methodologically arbitrary. In fact there is an explanation underlying the arguments of exclusion, interaction, and practice that has to do with the reflexive nature of modern capitalism, which seems to call for a counter-reflexive strategy through mirroring tactics. The creative activists who will be used as an example of groups consciously using these mirrors as critical 'devices' assume that the creation of pockets of imagination are necessary if we are to establish counter-hegemonic positions. These are useful when it comes to social innovation and deriving autonomous alternative suggestions about what constitutes the good life.[1] But let us first consider whether we can and should demand that critics must always have fixed solutions ready. The creative activist rarely does. Does that render her critique irrelevant or invalid?

The good life as a precondition for critique

We all know the situation: you have criticized someone or something and the opposing party poses the question: so what do you suggest we do instead? If you do not have an answer ready, such a question often ends up dismantling your initial critique. This is why spin-doctors make sure that their politicians always know the answer to that particular question. At times, they actually seem to switch to automatic pilot and follow ideological emergency procedures when that situation arises. The ethical question behind this more strategic political one is the following: do we always need to have an alternative to what we are criticizing to be entitled to put our critique forward?

One of the fundamental premises in newer critical theory is that a normative foundation is needed to be able to formulate a valid structural and diagnostic critique. Axel Honneth, a representative of the third generation of the Frankfurt School, advocates that, "if the idea of a 'struggle for recognition' is seen as a critical frame of interpretation for societal developmental processes, the normative view on these processes must be able to be legitimized theoretically" (Honneth, 2006, p. 220. Own translation).

Through a new reading of Hegel's philosophy of right Honneth argues that we must re-establish the connection between justice and self-realization as exemplified in Hegel's models of freedom, which together allow for the individual's ontogenetic *Bildungsprozess* (Honneth, 2000). In Hegel's analysis the critical diagnoses of society interact in a dialectic relationship to his ideas about the good life, which allows him to reveal the pathological tendencies of his time. This project is further systematized in Honneth's own work as he develops a methodological construction that allows him to formulate principles of justice and hence a normative foundation for a structural critique, developed parallel to his analyses of the pathologies of our society. This enables the rest of us to see where he is coming from (which is not always immediately clear). As opposed to Hegel, who tried to define an abstract horizon for his ethical values (Honneth, 2006, p. 229), Honneth stresses the necessity of a contextualization of the concrete struggles of recognition. His own writings are nevertheless about the formal condition for the good life (which are meant to allow for more empirical studies of struggles for recognition). His project is not only about human moral autonomy but also about the conditions for its self-realization as a whole, which is why he is placed somewhere between Kantian morality and Aristotelian ethics.

Those who try to practice what Honneth (only) teaches often stress how this exercise makes it possible to transcend devastating effects of self-criticism and the ineffectiveness of what the Polish sociologist Zygmunt Bauman refers to as a kind of 'camping site critique' which we have seized to question the fundamentals of our society (Bauman, 2006). "If the critique is supposed to measure up to the problems of society, maybe it should not be developed in the same tempo, but in a pace that allows alert and potential conceptual development of an alternative idea of the good life" (Willig, 2007, p. 58. Own translation). In other words, chasing deadlines might only result in critical headlines, but not a critique substantial enough to constitute a foundation for sustainable change. The question still remains, though – is a predefined idea about what constitutes the good life necessary to create such a foundation?

On February 12, 2012 three members of the Russian feminist punk rock collective performed an unauthorized musical 'punk-prayer' critical of the rerunning of Vladimir Putin for President and the patriarchs of the Orthodox Church in Russia for openly supporting him. The women were quickly interrupted but the filming of the event soon hit the YouTube hit list. The members of Pussy Riot were prosecuted with 'hooliganism motivated by religious hatred'. Some were imprisoned. The trial has been analyzed as a microcosm of the political tensions in the Post-Soviet region as the prosecutor referenced church regulations from the seventh century while the women on trial quoted postmodern philosophers. Pussy Riot managed to create an international debate about the relationship between those in power and the oppressed opposition and have received widespread public support from celebrities around the world.

When arguing against such a claim, it is important to consider (1) the implications of having to live up to such demands, (2) the advantages of not (always) doing it, and (3) distinguishing between different practical contexts in which such requirements may or may not apply.

What I will refer to as *the exclusion argument* (ad. 1) emphasizes who and what we leave out if we choose to set such standards. Firstly, those without a voice and the ability to formulate alternatives should be heard if we want an inclusive democratic public sphere, according to this argument. Honneth himself has actually argued so in his critique of Habermas (Honneth, 2003, Ch. 3), where he contends that the Habermasian theory systematically has to ignore those existing forms of societal critique that are not recognized by the hegemony of the dominant political public because the theory does not accurately or sufficiently consider the class-specific expression of morality or the condition under which it takes shape. The young immigrants' critique of police violence must be heard even if they use a language far from the *lingua franca* in the mainstream public sphere. The children's critique (crying or misbehavior) of the daycare system should be heard even if they cannot offer an alternative way of organizing it. If not, there is a danger that we end up excluding and thus suppressing certain groups of society based on elitist formal demands. The normative potential of different social classes cannot be measured from fixed collective conceptions of justice or moral forms of consciousness.

One question is whether we can always offer alternatives. Another, and equally relevant question, is whether we always should, even if we could. For example, we can criticize totalitarian states for their violations of human rights (in fact we should), without dictating how they should organize their society and live their lives (in fact we should not). One reason for this is that an ethnocentric and historically bound undercurrent always runs beneath the imagined formal universal principles of moral philosophy, this argument claims.

Furthermore, some things cannot yet be put into words. In these cases it is not a matter of individual or group abilities of expression. It is a matter of timing. Sometimes the source of one's frustration has not yet manifested itself in one's verbal consciousness. That does not mean that we do not have a gut feeling that something is wrong or cannot have a cloudy sense of what is emerging. Organizational theorist Otto Scharmer is one of those who most vividly talk about 'pre-sensing' (signifying the double meaning of being present in the moment and the potential of pre-sensing that which has not yet manifested itself in the world) as a way of freeing human collective creativity from the shackles of dogma. In his U-model, used on management courses and in organization development around the world, Scharmer stresses how the ability to transcend habitual ways of thinking and acting is an important element of good leadership: "When the future cannot be predicted by the trends and trajectories of the past, we must deal with situations as they evolve" (Scharmer, 2009, p. 61). Following this argument, critics often need to have the same courage to trust their inner voice telling them that things could be better – even if they still do not know how exactly. Artistic forms of expression rely on this belief to be true. The social movements from the 'Arab Spring' and Occupy Wall Street of the 'American Fall' in 2011 and onwards also relied on this courage.

In conclusion, the exclusion argument reminds us to consider who will be excluded because they cannot live up to the demands of new critical theory (and many others!), whether we always should attribute our beliefs even if we can, and what is excluded if we choose only to listen to that which we can rationally formulate and comprehend. The last point will be further developed below.

What I call *the interaction argument* (ad. 2) stresses curiosity, reflection, and innovation as democratic traits that do not easily coincide with the demand in question. As I hinted earlier, from the very beginning, human beings developed a culture where public opinions crash. They are delivered, but not always received, and rarely open-mindedly exchanged. This argument's point of departure is that we fight to be right, rather than exercising our right to listen and fight against the challenges that we face together.

According to Scharmer, "Any social entity or living system can operate from more than one inner place" (Scharmer, 2009, p. 118). In the development of his U-model he distinguishes between four different stages of consciousness as manifested in four different forms of listening and ways of interacting: downloading (where you focus on having your own beliefs confirmed), debating (where you are curious, but cannot help judging others), dialogue (the borders between you and them are broken if you can overcome the voice of cynicism and become truly empathetic), and pre-sensing (where you are open to the potential future by letting go of the old stubborn ways).

One might also culturally reinterpret this latter stage as a way of transcending the invisible deadlines of the headline hegemony. Whereas mainstream politics, as it unfolds in the media, tends to happen at the first two stages, some critics who are not confined to the claustrophobic open public and the squabbling of party politics – and who are not frightened by the demand for immediate alternatives even though they do not necessarily have any – seem to want to communicate on the two latter stages. Listening (in a certain way) also entails opening up for the possibility of seeing things in a new light, from a different angle, and maybe doing something that is not necessary consistent with one's beliefs. Questioning one's own beliefs or acting against them is the first crucial step towards change.

The Polish philosopher Leszek Kolakowski (1966) does not believe that we need to accept the awkward logical divalent illusion of ideological trench warfare. In a celebration of the inconsistency of human beings, which is based on free will, he argues that:

> Inconsistency comes from the secret consciousness of this World's contradictions. [...] Inconsistency as an individual human outlook comes from a reserve of uncertainty that has remained in our consciousness, a permanent feeling that one might be wrong, that the opponent might be right. (Kolakowski, 1966, p. 200)

If we have too firm an idea about what is right and wrong – what constitute the good life – we have a tendency not to listen to those who might disagree with us. 'Why should we? They are confused,' the argument often goes. This does not only make us reproduce social patterns of exclusion, but ultimately it makes us dumber – because voices of judgment and cynicism constrain us to an ideological echo chamber. Ultimately it may even at a societal level lead to totalitarianism as: "Complete consistency is practically equivalent to fanaticism" whereas "inconsistency is the source of tolerance" (Kolakowski, 1966, p. 199. Own translation). The point is that we can avoid the antinomies of life if we accept their inherent nature.

Common for theorists such as Scharmer and Kolakowski is that they are pointing in the same direction. They believe that virtues such as curiosity, openness, and humility should precede the temptation to decide on a final grand unifying belief system (be they scientific, religious, or ideological). In fact, doubt should continuously make us reflect about the choices and decisions we make. Theorists whose line of reasoning supports these types of counter-arguments all celebrate 'the benefit of the doubt' (which is somehow related to the Habermasian virtue of fallibilism).

What can be referred to as *the practitioner's argument* (ad. 3) differentiates 'small politics' from 'big politics' (Bauman, 1999, p. 2; Bang, 2009; Sørensen, 2012), and thus differs between those whose job it is to rightfully pose realistic alternatives to the status quo (typically agents of party politics) and those who (just) want us to reconsider our belief system, change the way we participate, and reflect upon the nature of our basic justice claims (typically cultural agents of civil society). The boundaries are blurred between the two, and many political actors operate in-between (e.g. corporations and lobbyists). So is this critique, of the normative premise for critical theory, then itself pointing forward? Yes, there are alternatives to the present-day ideological trench warfare, mirrored by the quarrelling of party politics as practitioners of 'small politics', creative activists, are experimenting with a different approach to the weighing of political issues – and have done so for years. Instead of having a clear idea about what the good life is and then let that form the basis of a critique, which eventually might lead to reflection, the logic is reversed in these more experimental practices. Here, provoked reflection is meant to lead to critique, which might eventually result in the formulation of alternatives to today's perception and way of pursuing the good life.

To return to the beginning, there are no guards about to shoot us if we cross the deadline today. We have internalized this function, and we discipline ourselves and each other within mental ideological penal complexes that try to make sure that we do not start to reflect on how we might do things completely differently or whether the truisms on which our moral and ideological beliefs rest actually hold up. These invisible borders are what keep us busy at work and content as passive citizens. The mirroring counter-tactics must be understood as communicative weapons in the struggle for autonomous reflection about what constitutes the good life.

Provocative thinkers such as Leszek Kolakowski (1966) and Otto Scharmer (2009) argue (although in very different ways) that we must continuously reflect on our convictions to avoid automatic conservatism and societal totalitarianism.

But before drawing the contours of a new theory of reflection the basic scales of justice must be considered.

Framing reflection

In the last decade, American critical theorist Nancy Fraser has worked on expanding her theory of social justice to include not two, but three core elements.[2]

Redistribution seeks to address injustice in the *economic* structure of society, including exploitation, economic marginalization, and deprivation, through the remedy of economic restructuring. *Recognition* seeks to address injustice in the *cultural* order of society – in the social patterns of interpretation, evaluation, and communication – including cultural domination, non-recognition, and disrespect, by pursuing cultural or symbolic change (Fraser & Honneth, 2003, p. 13). In *Scales of Justice* (2009), Fraser expands her understanding of justice to include *representation*, which seeks to address injustice in the *political* dimension of society. When interviewing Nancy Fraser about her shift of focus from the 'what' to the 'who' of justice, she motivates her change of thinking with society's collective move, saying that "there is not the same kind of agreement now, that the key issue is class, that the key problem is distribution, that the key arena is the nation state. That's why I am saying, there is a kind of dis-organization if you like, of the language of justice."

Fraser distinguishes between three types of representation: (1) *ordinary misrepresentation* occurs when politicians do not represent voters as promised. Such behavior has only added to the much-debated mistrust in politicians and the political system, which again has been one of the highlighted factors when explaining declining voter percentages and increasing interest in alternative political organizations. (2) The term *misframing* covers the challenges to representation raised by globalization and other tendencies that change the frames within which we are affected by and are able to participate in politics. When the nation state, the primary basis for representative democracy, is to a certain extent substituted by overarching institutions, such as the EU, the principle of 'parity of participation' is challenged.[3] This development has also resulted in new parallel international social movements and project-organized, cross-border, web-based forms of political protest that challenge the conventional institutionalized forms of participation. (3) What Fraser calls *meta-political misrepresentation* just begins to deal with *how* we can debate *who* gets to decide *what* we should do about the questions at hand. This endeavor must take place outside the already established polity and representative political system in order to make sense. The same applies to protesters. To be able to critically and fundamentally question any given system, procedure, or organization one has to step outside the frames set up by these, as protesters are basically thinking and acting 'outside the box.'

Analytically, we have gone through how this practice can be approached by differentiating between different kinds of activism, as explained with different social movement theories in hand – keeping the ambivalence of the alternative first move in mind. Here I propose a different lens as it is my thesis that they do so through the sculpturing of critical mirrors – inside and outside of the concrete and imaginary borders that make up our society, be they physical boundaries, legal regulations, social norms, or behavioral habits – headlines and deadlines.

As I have argued throughout the book, the participatory exclusion of the constitutional, the media, or the discursive framing has in recent years mobilized global movements and creative project activists all of whom are challenging the conventional participatory channels through alternative involvement. In continuation of the conceptual alliteration but more importantly because it coins and captures key elements of the current political climate, I therefore, in this chapter, reason that *reflection* should be added to Fraser's framework as a fourth element of justice.

My use of *reflection* focuses on pragmatic and strategic types of critique and has a double meaning. The mirroring aspect in these tactics refers to the possibility of seeing something, literally, from a different perspective than the ones usually offered to us in the hegemony of mainstream culture. The contemplative aspect refers to the potential of such tactics to provoke reflection in the individual, because it triggers questions about the truisms that form the foundation of the automatic defense mechanisms that enable us to maintain the coherent worldview that we feel is necessary to feel safe in a society full of ideological trench warfare and confrontational headlines. The mirrors used for/against the police by the Otpor movement were reflexive in both sense of the word: they 'allowed' the officers to see the situation from a different perspective (they saw themselves) and they consequently (may have) forced some of them to review the conflict and their own role in it.

Accordingly, I focus on how systemic mirroring mechanisms generate strategic attempts of resistance through the establishment of alternative (metaphorical) mirrors. The intention with these mirrors is to open up a temporary space for autonomous reflection. In that respect they, at least in principle, have an emancipatory quality to them. With this focus I delimit myself from the parts of sociology that deal with reflexivity as an existential component of what has been called late-, second-, fluid-, and reflexive modernity – not because it is irrelevant for my analysis of this activist phenomenon, but because it is not within the scope of this theoretical design process. In this sociological tradition reflexivity is perceived as an ambivalent and unavoidable condition for the individual, not a possible trigger for political action and change (Giddens, 1994, 1996; Beck, 1997; Ziehe, 1997; Beck & Beck-Gernsheim, 2002; Lash, 1994; and Bauman, 2006). From the position taken here, provoked instances of reflection (when performed as intended) allow for a break with/from the determining totality of society. To these sociologists society imposes constant decisions and creates individuals who question everything. Sure, we have the freedom to choose, but only from the options available to us. I am interested in how some people question the frame within which these options present themselves and how they try to offer a different menu altogether.

Now, having Fraser's basic scales of justice in place and initially briefly clarifying my use of reflection in relation to those, I will now describe the reflexive surface of capitalism and consider how it demands and conditions a certain type of creative, pragmatic critique through counter-mirroring tactics.

The reflexive surface of capitalism

Capitalism is closely interrelated to the concepts of critique and creativity that we dealt with at the beginning of the book. 'Capitalism' is a commonly used word by most of the activists that I have worked with. It is both a term they use to describe the type of society that most of them are opposing, and the frame within which they are struggling.

From an economic viewpoint I operate with a minimal definition of capitalism based on Boltanski and Chiapello, stressing an imperative to unlimited accumulation of capital by formally peaceful means (2005, p. 5). These authors suggest that people need a powerful moral reasoning for rallying to capitalism since wage earners have lost ownership of the fruits of their labor and the possibility of pursuing a working life free of subordination. Boltanski and Chiapello call the ideology that justifies engagement in capitalism the 'spirit of capitalism' – or in other words, "the set of beliefs associated with the capitalist order that helps justify this order and, by legitimating them, to sustain the forms of action and predispositions compatible with them" (2005, p. 10). Hence, I also consider the necessity of powerful moral reasoning to sustain the forms of action and predispositions compatible with capitalism (cf. competing justification regimes, Boltanski & Thévenot, 2006). The world (only) as mirrored by our capitalist society, I argue, functions as the foundation for such 'tests.'

In my use of the term I thus pay less attention to the principle of accumulation and focus more on the related multiplicity of a sociopolitical and cultural phenomena, a way of life, which together characterize the legitimized political rationality in most governments in the world today. So, when I use the word capitalism, I refer to the democratic implications of the economic logic that prevails in our increasingly instrumental ways of formulating the fundamental values that we praise in our societies. The societal model of late-capitalism has been sustainable so far because the moral practical interests of the social class of the wage earner to a large extent are compensated materially and redirected towards a privatized consumer attitude (Honneth, 2003, p. 52). I do however find it problematic to say that we have gone from one type of capitalism to another (say industrial capitalism to cognitive capitalism, or state-interventionist capitalism to global capitalism). Instead of one all-embracing capitalism, it seems more appropriate to talk about overlapping forms of capitalism that operate parallel to each other – even if they share fundamental traits. Using Ernst Bloch's term, there seems to be 'uncontinuity'[4] in the way that many 'eras' are present in the present – just as we today live in a historical situation marked by confused constellations of coexisting economic structures and sociocultural formations from different epochs. Facebook, making money on personal communication about lifestyle issues, has been listed on the stock exchange, but Ford Motor Company is still a major concern to legislators and harvests still influence investment cycles.

We are on our way to the future, but are in many ways still living in the past, which is why I believe we are witnessing material and mental logics that are conflicting in today's fast-moving capitalist societies. For example, we have set up our system so that we are ready to work as early and as much as possible, and we are doing so in the pursuit of security, recognition, and paid freedom. On the other hand, more and more of us get sick because we work way too much, never knowing when enough is enough, and long for an existence where we are free to do whatever we want. The uncontinuity of capitalism has become even clearer with increasing globalization where global and local, rich and poor, old and new coexist – and are moving even closer. Despite this multiplicity of capitalisms and the variety in which capitalism impinges in our lives, a set of basic laws and principles that can be challenged (e.g. Gibson-Graham, 2006) manifest themselves in our lives and society in different ways. I will thus be referring to capitalism as a system of interpretive mechanism through which we are more or less forced to see the world.

Creative activism uses innovative techniques in an attempt to create an alternative space for reflection. But what does this phenomenon tell us about the system it is often resisting, challenging, and operating within?

The critical practices of such agents can be seen as a reaction to the changed conditions of communication (e.g. Rheingold, 2005; O'Reilly & Battelle, 2009; Shirky, 2010) and the political opportunity structures as such (e.g. Meyer, 2004; Fraser, 2009 Harrebye, 2015b), but they can also be used to draw more fundamental conclusions about the self-referential mechanisms of the systemic culture that these kinds of activists are often fighting against (cf. Niklas Luhmann's concept of autopoiesis, 1995). Single-issue struggles are often particular expressions of more fundamental claims of justice, and most of today's progressive activists' project-based campaigns can be interpreted as practical critiques of capitalism.

But how do the creative activists view it? On a critical note, if we keep the multiplicity of capitalisms in mind, most activists seem to agree that financial speculation is problematic, but what is their take on the cognitive capitalism that they themselves are such an infiltrated part of? My entire analysis of their practices can be read as an answer to this question, and it refers back to my position on the theory of structuration with regards to the activists' possibility to transcend the frame of capitalism that they are working within.

But the question remains, how can today's contentious politics help us make a critical diagnosis of contemporary capitalism – not through their beliefs, but through our analysis of their way of fighting for what they believe?

In what might be referred to as the fourth generation of the Frankfurt School, as exemplified by Hartmut Rosa (2013) the dimension of *time* has been incorporated into the analysis of how our possibility to lead healthy lives, criticize, and develop society is conditioned by the technological acceleration, the acceleration of social change, and the acceleration of the pace of life (we will return to Rosa in the final chapter of the book). Here we shall focus on a particular *spatial* aspect of modern capitalism and depict a specific trait with inspiration from the first generation's Max Horkheimer and Theodor W. Adorno's *Dialectics of Enlightenment* (2007, originally published in 1994) where they analyze the all-pervasiveness of commoditizing social relations, the totalizing presence of cultural production, as well as how rational thought's inherent mono-cultivation suppresses alternative ways of thinking, the other, the unknown.

Like a glass-covered building, capitalism as a logical thing, an attitude, and an attraction shaping our societal model, can be said to be 'coded' in that it reflects its surroundings. Imagine an invisible layer of fluid mirror glazing that covers all things – the products that we buy, the pages in our magazines, the whiteboard in the classroom, our money, commercials, clothes, and the look in our eyes as we go to work. It attracts attention like thieves to diamonds and fish to spoon bait. However, like water on rubber and grease on Teflon, critique tends to bounce right off this surface coding of capitalism. It does not seem to stick. Instead it backfires. The mirror coding mirrors critique and returns it to sender – address unknown. This distinct 'quality' can be observed in all aspects of our lives where 'the new spirit of capitalism' (Boltanski & Chiapello, 1999) has molded our reality. When an employee goes down with stress it rarely leads to a critical reassessment of the company's culture or policies. Instead the diagnosed consultant is sent to a coach who suggests ways in which *she* can work with *herself* and get back in shape. The critique is turned back on to the individual herself. She is in a way responsible, not the company. The critique bounces off the surface of the capitalist enterprise and 'boomerangs' back to whoever formulated it in the first place. In his latest book, Rasmus Willig analyzes how the consequence of this phenomenon increasingly means that employees and citizens turn their critique inwards instead of out towards those in power or the structural conditions causing social pathologies (Willig, 2013). When the fast food industry is criticized for creating an unhealthy food culture, the critique is likewise turned around: 'If you think it is wrong, stop letting your children eat it' is the typical response. Again the structural critique is avoided by way of reflection, deflection, and redirection. If I argue that our way of life creates an unfair and unnecessary inequality in the world, capitalism's neo-liberal protagonists encourage me to give more to charity. When the climate change crisis is said to be the result of our capitalist lifestyle, the advice is to buy more green products, not re-evaluate our way of life. When capitalism was said to have cost millions of workers their jobs, their houses, and/or their pension in the aftermath of the financial crisis of 2008, the frontrunners of neo-liberalism argued either that it is a healthy part of the evolution of capitalism (cf. creative destruction), not a bad thing, or that we only had a crisis to begin with because capitalism was (too) regulated, not because it was not. The critic in this perspective may be depicted as a suspect starring into an interrogation mirror, not knowing if some sort of authority is lurking behind the one-way glass, only able to see her own image in an (allegedly) unlawful position.

In what renowned creative activist Andrew Boyd refers to as "the postmodern hall of mirrors" we are used to seeing the world as it is portrayed by the mirroring reflections of capitalism – mirrored indefinitely. In popular culture everything is a reference to something else. That is the tyranny of the signifier. Like an all-embracing echo chamber we hear our selves as the institutions, the language, and the images that capitalism repeatedly shouts back to us. It resonates with us – and we repeat it. What we consider to be good, beautiful, and worthwhile is accordingly a reflection of the values, images, and criteria we are daily bombarded with. When we look in the mirror to evaluate ourselves we see what we have been taught to see. "What guides us in this creation of territories (...) is an almost hypnotic identification with the images of the world broadcast by advertising and mass culture" (Rolnik, 2011, p. 28). Neuroscience's recent discovery of the mirroring neuron,[5] mimicking instincts, and psychological mirroring techniques[6] from cross-disciplinary angles oddly testifies to the human resonance when it comes to the productive and manipulative effects of mirroring. Freud, among others, pointed to the performative potential of mimicry. To him it is tantalizing to its audience exactly because it displayed and ridiculed the mechanic, deterministic aspects of human nature (Freud, 1938, pp. 776, 782–783). By pointing out these characteristics, one effectively unmasks and questions the very notion of human 'nature.' I therefore agree with Daniel Ølgaard (2015) that the aestheticization of political resistance does not necessarily "mark the total surrender to the totality of the political spectacle's seduction, but interrogates it by adding friction to its seemingly slippery surface."

But how has critical theory, in the broadest possible sense, analytically related to this reflexive nature of capitalism?

Analytically relating to capitalism

Global late-modern capitalist societies are substantially different from those Marx analyzed. The reflexive character described above makes it difficult for us to 'penetrate' the smooth surface of capitalism, practically as well as analytically, because of its ability to function as a mirror rather than a glass that we can see through or a brick wall that we can break through. Critical theorists Jürgen Habermas and Axel Honneth represent a different kind of critic who articulated the challenges of this predicament. Despite their differences they share this fundamental premise. Their position may be referred to as *a conscious outside stand*. From this position we *are* able to position ourselves outside the system – Habermas (1990) constructs a universal discourse ethics and Honneth (2006) formulates formal conditions for what constitutes the good life – but we must be aware that what we are witnessing when we investigate society is the reflection that capitalism (or we as parts in and of this totalitarian system) casts. Despite the insightful analyses that were made from this position, the belief that the critic can formulate an independent critique of the systemic manifestation of capitalism from the outside, based on universal principles and criteria, still seems problematic to some. While we often think we are (somewhat) objectively looking at capitalism, or more specifically the way it manifests itself in our society, such as advertisements, privatization of collective goods, or work-related stress, we are in fact seeing a reflection of ourselves – our shopping patterns, our choice to put our kids in a private school, or our career aspirations.

This has a number of implications, all of which are problematic. The first one is that it is difficult, if not impossible to see 'inside' capitalism (if it even exists in and by itself). This limitation necessitates that we look at capitalism in an indirect manner – mirroring is one way of doing that. The second consequence of capitalism's reflection is that we see ourselves when we look at it. This has a dismantling effect on the critic as she is immediately faced with the fact that she is part of the problem when questioning the legitimacy of capitalism or its related phenomena. The critic is a part of that way of life. This aggressive defense mechanism of capitalism and its advocates is well known. When Al Gore traveled the world to promote his critical documentary, *The Inconvenient Truth*, he was faced with questions about his own carbon emissions during the promotion tour. Criticizing the monstrosities of the food industry, we are likewise soon faced with our own double standards when we stand in the supermarket and decide that we cannot afford to buy the organic chicken.

According to these critics we are still as critical analysts positioned outside the system. We are therefore looking at the outer surface of capitalism, so to say. What Gore and the chicken examples show us, however, is that we as citizens, consumers, and critics are all a part of capitalism. We are 'on the inside,' so to speak. The mirroring reflections of capitalism are therefore actually not preventing us from looking in but making it (almost) impossible for us to look *outside* the world that we have created for ourselves. Herein lies the second shift in the way critical analysts have related to capitalism.

As opposed to the German-inspired critique of ideology, which peaked in the 1970s, Michel Foucault as a representative of another type of critical theory did not set out to uncover the truth of human nature behind layers of alienation and false consciousness. Neither do later critical theorists inspired by his approach, such as Judith Butler. These are currently questioning what counts as critique. In contrast to the rationalist form of emancipation, Foucault's approach to critique is that it is "an attitude and a way of conducting oneself as opposed to a type of knowledge which pretends to have a privileged access to the truth; and it is a virtue in the sense that one puts oneself at stake by resisting established truths, habits, and injustices" (Dyrberg, 2014, p. 11).

Critique does not only become ironic, cynical, and question utopian attitudes and strategies (cf. last chapter), it becomes a reflexive act when it is negotiated with and within the system that it is an inherent part of. Foucault's approach thereby marks a shift in focus: "From viewing politics outside-in to inside-out" (Dyrberg, 2014, p. 12).

The awareness that we are an inherent part of the very system that we are trying to critically analyze, that we to a certain extent are products of techniques of the self and domination, may be referred to as a *conscious inside stand*. Foucault can be seen as an example of a critical theoretician stressing how this circumstance conditions the cocksure critic. American sociologist Stephen Duncombe and critical theorist Nancy Fraser represent those who emphasize the same thing although they stress other elements of this conscious inside standpoint – the former as a cynical strategist (Duncombe, 2007), the latter as an integrating philosopher pointing towards the reflexive aspect of justice (Fraser, 2009).

Fraser has a 'transformationalist' interpretation of Foucault. She notices it as historical irony that "a new regime oriented to 'deregulation' and 'flexibilization' was about to take shape just as Foucault was conceptualizing disciplinary normalization" (Fraser, 2009, p. 117). She suggests that we need to convert Foucauldian categories to be able to explain new modes of governmentality in what she calls 'the era of neoliberal globalization.' As a critical thinker Fraser attempts to bridge the gap between the former (normative) type of critic and the latter (social constructionist) critics. She belongs to a strand of moral philosophers who examine how *critical sociology* and what Luc Boltanski and Ève Chiapello refers to as a *sociology of critique* may supplement each other. Certain readings of Fraser (e.g. Holst, 2005) stress how she has changed position with regard to these questions from her early to her later works. In my reading she has gone from a belief that social critique should not be philosophically substantiated to a position where morally based principles of justice (e.g. 'parity of participation') are defended alongside an emphasis on the importance of pragmatic forms of critique. When I asked Nancy Fraser how she viewed the link between critical sociology and critical activism, she emphasized that she "prefers to be explicit about my normative point of departure, since we all have one, whether we are aware of it or not."

The importance of acknowledging that we are part of the system that we object to (in some sense we *are* that system) is that it allows us to qualify our critique. Through reflection the hegemonic discourses of what constitutes the good life are challenged. Analysts with what is here referred to as a conscious inside standpoint have often been associated with normative relativity. Creative activists, however, working from such a position, seem to be pointing somewhere. Not because they are sure where they or we are going, but because they are confident that they have found a way to circumvent 'the postmodern hall of mirrors' that Boyd was referring to.

To a human individual whose dominant relation to society is that of subjectivity, the main problem is for the subject to 'turn its gaze upon itself' (Rabinow, 1997, p. 29). To truly understand this *art of life* as a practice of resistance we must therefore depart from the traditional notion of self-formation. This ultimately allows the playful self to utilize those power-relations one might see as exterior, dominant forces of control on to itself – and through this turn discover *a fold of freedom*. "What Deleuze here identifies in Foucault's ethical writings is the possibility of the self as the creative centre of an aesthetical practice of resistance" (Ølgaard, 2015, p. 125). Foucault "privileges localized struggle ... and ongoing resistance to the minutiae of domination over grand emancipatory projects that endorse totalizing visions of social transformation" (Tobias, 2005, p. 68). Because the self is at once the subject and the object of power-relations, it follows that it is the self that is also the site of resistant practice. This relocates the politics of resistance away from the organizing principle of representational politics and towards the individual. The aim of any strategy of resistance thus ultimately becomes to 'liberate our subjectivity, our relation to ourselves', which requires attacking the roots of the political rationalities that define power-relations and which result in modes of individualization, totalizing visions, and practices of control. The mirror is one way to turn the gaze upon ourselves while seeking to imagine and create alternative realities, the very act of which enables the subject to continuously connect its desire to these and actualize it as a practice of resistance. Central to this ethos is continuous critique, self-reflexivity, and creativity.

In the following analysis I will follow in the footsteps of some of these philosophers towards new possible components of justice and identity. Firstly, heterotopia is introduced as a theoretical concept that makes these meta-reflexive critical theorists useful for the analysis of practical resistance schemes.

Heterotopology of mirroring counter strategies

The strategies applied by creative activists may be understood as a strategic reaction to the reflexive character of capitalism, following the reasoning that the revival of critique accompanies – but always after some delay – the appearance of new kinds of protest mechanisms more attuned to the emerging forms of capitalism, in accordance with the principle that critique, in seeking to be effective, tends to become isomorphic with the objects it is applied to. (Boltanski & Chiapello, 2005, p. 518)

I agree with Boltanski and Chiapello insofar as new forms of critique are not coincidentally attuned to emerging forms of capitalism, but it seems that the mirroring counter tactics that I address, which is one of a few basic oppositional strategies, do not become isomorphic with capitalism, although it mimics the echoing force of capitalist society. On the contrary, as a reaction to capitalism these mirrors are made to cast a contrasting picture that looks nothing like what we are used to seeing and identifying with.

My spatial analysis of resistance will draw on a heterotopological approach to cultural sites and strategic, defiant positioning within a culture. In *Of Other Spaces* (1986) Foucault considers two types of spaces. They are linked with all others, but at the same time contradict all other sites. Those are utopias and what Foucault calls heterotopias. The latter is something like 'counter-sites', a kind of effectively enacted utopia in which the real sites of a culture are simultaneously represented, contested, and inverted. Heterotopias are therefore sites "that have the curious property of being in relation with all the other sites, but in such a way as to suspect, neutralize, or invert the set of relations that they happen to designate, mirror, or reflect" (Foucault, 1986, p. 24).

Between the utopia and the heterotopia, Foucault speculates that there might be a sort of mixed, joint experience – the mirror:

> The mirror is, after all, a utopia, since it is a placeless place. In the mirror, I see myself there where I am not, in an unreal, virtual space that opens up behind the surface; I am over there, there where I am not, a sort of shadow that gives my own visibility to myself, that enables me to see myself there where I am absent: such is the utopia of the mirror. But it is also a heterotopia in so far as the mirror does exist in reality, where it exerts a sort of counteraction on the position that I occupy. From the standpoint of the mirror I discover my absence from the place where I am since I see myself over there. (...) I begin again to direct my eyes toward myself and to reconstitute myself there where I am. (Foucault, 1986, p. 24)

The mirror functions as a kind of heterotopia since it is at the same time real and unreal. Since capitalism's mirroring effect partly makes it difficult to see capitalism for what it 'really' is and partly distorts our self-image, the creative activists' counter strategy is to create alternative mirrors that allow us to see ourselves and the system, not for what we and it *really* are, but for what we *also* are – and maybe also for what we *could be*. This means that two types of alternative mirrors are created. The first one is set up 'within the system' and allows for an alternative and potentially emancipatory reflection of our selves and alternative behavioral patterns. The other is set up 'outside the system' and allows for a structural critique of the system from a satellite position that is able to transcend the borders that we set up for ourselves and each other – a mirror that can only be established if we dare to cross the concrete and imaginary borders of capitalism.

Now, moving from theory to practice, what may these mirrors look like?

Critical mirrors

In the development of a tentative typology of these mirrors, two overall distinctions are made: firstly, the difference between *inside* and *outside* mirrors and, secondly, the difference between critical and proposing mirrors (cf. Brighenti's double movement of resistance and Fraser's own distinction between affirmative and transformative approaches).

The *critical inside mirror* is supposed to reflect us differently than the reflections cast by capitalist society. As Andrew Boyd puts it: "It is impossible to escape the hall of mirrors. So how do you look yourself in the eye in the midst of it? The first step is to acknowledge that that is where we are. In the field of political communication you have to become a master of the spectacle" (Boyd, interview with Harrebye). In Olafur Eliasson's words: "Mirrored political art articulates or gives form to emotions and sentiments that the individual human being has not yet found or knew existed" (interview in *Deadline*, DR, 11.04.14).

So how do Boyd and Eliasson and others like them get people to see things from a different angle? Well, if you cannot get people to move (moving from one position to another is dangerous in trench warfare), you can set up alternative mirrors that provide people with a new perspective on their own position and role in the world. To put it differently, if you cannot escape the horrifying hall of mirrors, the best thing to do as an activist may be to set up your own mirrors. Recourse to the mirror analogy metaphor in order to illuminate the nature of art has been a favorite with aesthetic theorists since Plato (see Abrams, 1953, Ch. 2). But the claim here is that they can be more than a *mere* reflector. They can also function as radiant projectors – manufactured and turned as political activists see fit.

The widespread phenomenon of beauty pageants does not represent the diversity of female beauty. Actually they celebrate the unrealistic and therefore unhealthy striving towards a narrow idea of perfect beauty attuned to support the industry behind it – the fashion industry's young, white, skinny, jewelry-covered models, who are not representative of the average woman. As media and gender researcher Karen Klitgaard Povlsen states: "The short explanation is that those who make the fashion magazines do not think that it (representing the diversity of the society that we live in) sells. (...) Here it is about being as white, as young, and as skinny as possible" (*Metroxpress*, 16.12.14). Thus many women feel inadequate when they ask 'mirror, mirror on the wall, who in the country is fairest of all?' In this aestheticized, postmodern form of action, one does not act in any autonomous sense according to one's desires, rather one fashions oneself in accordance with the dominant values of society (Kellner, 1989, pp. 99–102).

Alternative beauty contests can be seen as a critical response to this tendency (e.g. Miss Navajo Nation, Miss Land Mine). They do not try to disrupt the fashion runway shows. That would only reflect poorly on themselves. Instead they produce mirrors inside the world of capitalist female beauty contests that reflect women differently. Such alternative beauty contests may include Muslim women wearing veils or overweight women (citizens who are not commonly celebrated for their beauty in the western world owing to religious or physical minority markers). Such contests give them a chance to shine, but more importantly it disturbs the general picture of what has sex appeal, honor, and value – and what is beautiful and good.

The Truth and the Reality campaigns are large-scale direct campaign-like examples of how critical strategy increasingly chooses to apply creative tactics by holding up a different mirror than that of, in this case, the tobacco and coal industry. People were once convinced that cigarettes did not really damage your health. The Truth campaign set out to change that (thetruth.com/about). Now, smoking policies are changing, and with it the smoking culture all around the world. Just a couple of years ago most people still had doubts about whether the climate crisis was caused by man. Most people were probably not even aware that there was a crisis. The Climate Reality Project sets out to change that view (climaterealityproject.org). Today the climate is a hot topic in governments, executive boardrooms, and private homes alike. The transition is from marginalized rationales and suppressed narratives to mainstream stories about what "of course" makes sense.

The function of the critical inside mirror is to create alternative and possibly emancipatory images of who we are and who we can be – images that are not meant to sell a product or win an election, but to reflect and reflect *upon* the future potential that many people might already be pre-sensing (cf. Scharmer) but have not fully developed. Hornsleth's Village Project, the "We are all Khaled Said" Facebook page, Critical Shareholders, and The Big Donor Show are all examples of such mirrors.

*

The *critical outside mirror* is supposed to give us a critical perspective on society as a whole – one that is often lost in constantly changing news reports and suppressed by their catchy headlines. Critique (especially of a more structural nature) is difficult to maintain with a fast-moving target. Our position within society thus makes it difficult to see and evaluate the overall grand scheme of things and formulate this structural critique. Similarly it is difficult to get a sense of the world's horizontal curve when you are standing with your feet planted on the ground. The totality of things paradoxically becomes the modern man's blind spot. We cannot see the forest for the trees. We are drowned in information. We are paralyzed by the sedation of shopping. Through psychological mirroring techniques our cultural sense-receptors are numbed. The outside mirror is meant to reflect an alternative perspective on the society that we live in.

The 'Billionaires' campaign was an ironic crusade meant to draw attention to the corruption of party politics by the influence of the wealth of a few. In 2004 'Billionaires for Bush' used humor and satirical performances to sidestep traditional lobbyists when they collaborated with respected justice groups in applying viral promotion strategies, building brand and branches countrywide. Through a humorous sublimation of desire, the subject is allowed a space from which to observe and critically reflect on its actions. This 'ethical spectacle' was meant to "highlight the falsity of our supposed reality" (Duncombe, 2007, p. 47). The popular campaign was simultaneously real and unreal.

Ironic parody is a commonly used technique by the groups in question. It has an effective critical function and helps us laugh at power while imagining alternatives (Critchley, 2007). "Parody is an act of duplication where the original is placed 'beside itself' and the copy is used as a joke" (Hariman, 2008, p. 249). The ironic attitude depicted in the previous chapter seen in this light starts to resemble Foucault's heterotopologies. The mirror is also a sense of conscious displacement. In the case of the creative activist it is a joke that reveals the powerful as vulnerable, the unchangeable as contingent, and the enchanting as dangerous. Robert Hariman shows how parody is essential for a healthy political and cultural debate as it forces people to continuously look at what we take for granted from a different angle. Judith Butler (1990) uses the drag artist as an example of how gender parodies open up the traditional categories and make us question 'reality' as the parody always reveals that it is an 'imitation without an origin' (Butler, 1990, p. 175). By highlighting the tenuous nature of what we often take for granted, the ironic parody can yield a plurality of perspectives on a given matter.

By dressing up as billionaires, camping their style, the 'Billionaires' activists involved functioned as a mirror that reflected the commercial backing system supporting the political scenery that the mainstream media portrays – thereby scratching the surface and damaging the coding of capitalism's political frontrunners. By allowing the temporary suspension of normality, the parody of the pretend billionaires reinvigorated discussions that had been numbed through repetition, and by entrenched positions on either side of a stale debate (Kenny, 2009). As a heterotopological franchise the campaign spread across states and over a decade as it questioned, counterbalanced, and reversed the set of relations that it designated, mirrored, and reflected.

Workers at a company called Republic Windows and Doors adopted a more traditional mode of protest when they decided to express their discontent with Bank of America's bail-out option that followed the financial crisis of 2008. The protest was directed at their employer from whom they did not receive their salary, and right at the point of production they made an old-fashioned sit-down strike, and thus occupied their workplace. As President Barack Obama said about the protesting crowd: "What is happening to them is reflective of what is happening across this economy" (President Obama in Moore, 2009, 1:51). These workers became a symbol of justice through the alternative mirror that journalists and politicians needed to reflect a different story. The bank and the company finally agreed to meet the demands of the workers.

If an issue is 'out of sight', say the starving children in Africa or the racism in your neighborhood, it is often also 'out of mind'. With 'Da Vinci's Vitruvian Man on Arctic Sea Ice', artist John Quigley in

144 *Social Change and Creative Activism in the 21st Century*

coordination with Greenpeace (photo by Nick Cobbing), aestheticized the melting ice caps and made them 'measurable' (google the picture). The invisible is made visible and relatable.

The function of the critical outside mirrors is to create alternative and possibly emancipatory images of the society that we live in – perspectives meant to reflect and reflect upon society's status quo and the collective identity that we might otherwise have difficulties grasping. Citizenship journalism, such as OhmyNews in South Korea and bloggers like Han Han and Alexei Navalny are examples of this. The Dow Chemical prank, throwing one's shoe at the President in public, creative leafleting, setting yourself on fire to light a revolutionary regional wildfire, and the provoked televised massacre and sacrifice on the Edmund Pettus Bridge in Selma are all examples of such mirrors (Figure 6.1).

In the third generation of critical theory an idea about what constitutes the good life is the point of departure from which a structural critique of society can be formulated with the goal of inducing reflection. For the creative activist it seems to be the other way around. Through mirroring techniques they seek to provoke reflection. This process of questioning the appearance of our capitalist society and our own role in it may then result in a critical reaction or attitude. The reflexive process and the critique itself might eventually lead to the suggestion of alternatives to the status quo and autonomous ideas about what constitutes the good life.

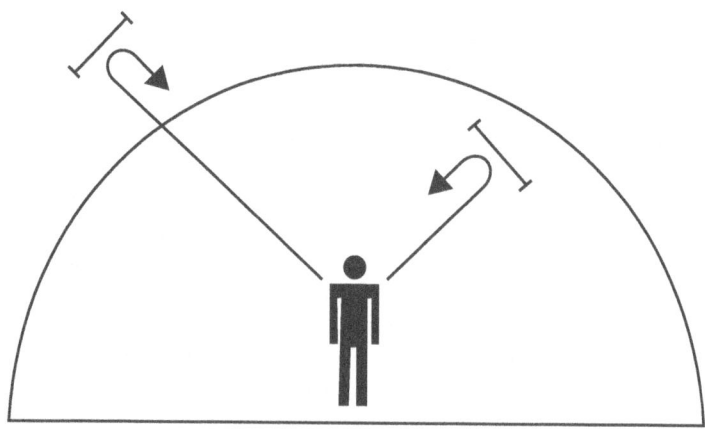

Figure 6.1 The functionality of critical alternative mirrors

Proposing mirrors

The politics of creative activists is not just one of criticism. It also tries to point forward. They do not always 'just' demonstrate *against* something or someone, they also often (try to) demonstrate *how* things might be different. To Gilles Deleuze the starting point of becoming is hence an act of creation. Elias Canetti's use of the term 'diavolution' likewise stresses the necessity of being the avant-garde of one-self when transforming what is into what could be (Brighenti, 2011). If the mirrors above are turned a little to one side, if you can imagine, the inside mirror would no longer reflect the viewer him/herself but the surrounding society and new ways for her to interact in it and with it. The outside mirror would, if turned, no longer give us a view back on our society from a transcendental position, but enable us to look beyond the world as we know it. The first turn marks a shift from the immanent critique to the creative suggestion. The second turn permits us to move from a structural critique to a utopian imaginary (Figure 6.2).

Ushahidi is an example of the *proposing inside mirror* – a civic co-creation suggesting how to solve a seemingly endless problem (ushahidi.com). Ushahidi was, in 2007, developed as an online service meant to help citizens in Kenya track and map outbreaks of ethnic violence. Neither the government nor the professional public media really covered it, and "rebuilding it from scratch, with citizen input, was easier than trying to get it (the information) from the authorities" (Shirky,

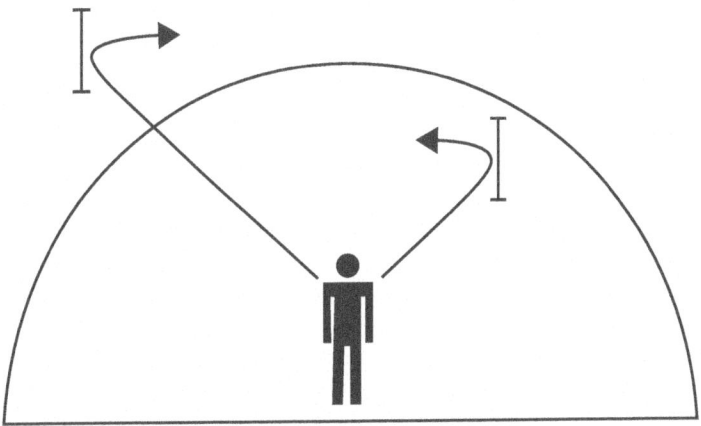

Figure 6.2 The functionality of alternative proposing mirrors

2010, p. 16). Ushahidi has since been used in many other parts of the world, such as tracking of violence in the Democratic Republic of Congo, revealing voter fraud in India and Mexico, locating the injured after the Haitian and Chilean earthquakes, etc. Social innovation is often the consequence of seeing the world through a new and different looking glass.

In Thorup Strand, Denmark, a syndicate of fishermen are buying themselves free of the capitalist market by buying up fishing quotas. They are thereby also freeing nature. In 2005 the Danish Government decided to privatize sea fishing quotas. Immediately after, half the fishing boats in the area were up for sale. The syndicate was established by some of those remaining, and within a year they bought for 25 million Danish kroner. A year later they were worth 80 million. But they didn't sell. "Our viewpoint is that we are pulling resources out of the capitalist market and using it to develop a meaningful community and a sustainable eco-system," says professor in ethnology and chairman of the syndicate Thomas Højrup (Information, 08.05.15). He is not a member of the association, though, as you have to be a full-time registered fisherman to become a member to avoid any financial speculators' takeover. The fishermen can make a decent living, but they cannot make a profit. For a number of reasons they are able to compete with big businesses. Højrup believes in fighting vulture capitalism from within and on its own terms. Just like the Danish co-operative movement their example might serve to inspire others – although in formats that fit their particular professional, cultural, financial, and biological environment.

The KONY 2012 campaign, The People's Supermarket, creating a paper air force to fight your enemies, Critical Mass bike rides, and Superflex's biogas device project can also be seen as such inside proposing mirrors and examples of how unconventional events, campaigns, and entrepreneurship can give us direction and a concrete alternative choice of action.

*

Examples of the turned *proposing outside mirror* include actual attempts to facilitate the utopian imaginary by the ecological society Damanhur in Italy (damanhur.org), the hippie experiment Christania in Denmark (christiania.org) or the spiritual ashrams in India. Temporary autonomous zones (Bey, 2011) can do the same. Carnivals and festivals can do it. In the absence of these real heterotopias, imaginary places such as those in the fairytales that we tell our children, the fake *New York Times*, or the one John Lennon asks us to imagine, may do the same thing – they allow us to dream and to move beyond the daily deadlines and headlines that make up the borders of our modern capitalist society. These activists all work with utopia not as a fixed end that we should all strive for but rather as what Martin Parker defines as "statements of alternative organizations" (Parker, 2002, p. 2).

One of the reasons why political ideologists resign from utopian projects seems to be fear of the link between the pursuit of radical utopias and totalitarianism, so closely linked with the collective memory of the horrors of the 20th century. But, as I have shown, these new activists do not have a *specific* utopia in mind. They do however utilize utopian 'techniques' to revisit our own actual world through an otherworldly reference point. As noted, they are process- rather than result-oriented. This critical detour has several functions for the creative activist, the most important one being disruption. I therefore, as Valérie Fournier (2002) does, use utopianism to emphasize movement over static visions of a better order as I focus on its critical, transgressive, and transformative functions rather than its form and content (so do Levitas, 1990; Sargisson, 1996; Harvey, 2000).

It is often stated that politics is 'the art of the possible'. However, it also seems that we are too often constrained by 'the tyranny of the possible'. One of the trademarks of creative activism is the way it insists on exposing us to the impossible, thus forcing us, at a minimum, to reflect on our axiomatic truths. As Fredric Jameson (2004, p. 43) puts it, "utopia emerges at the moment of the suspension of the political."

The options that these mirroring tactics offer are numerous. The mirrors they set up inside and outside 'the system' (large or small, intimate or public) not only enable us to view ourselves and our society in new and critical ways, but the best ones also facilitate a dialogue about how we might do things differently in the future.

In some instances activists are capable of setting up mirrors that can give both critical *and* proposing perspectives on ourselves and the society that we are part of. Gandhi's Salt March, Wooloo's New Life festivals, and the Wiki organization are good examples of this. Also, "Stewart and Colbert's (re)significations of voices, discourses, and contexts create a multiplicity of angles in which their targets and audiences are called to be reflexive about themselves and society, as fallible and mistaken, but not evil" (Waisanen, 2009). Jon Stewart and Stephen Colbert do more than conduct critiques of organizations and actors outside of the media. They also turn their critiques back on both themselves and the general strategies of news making, opinion reporting, etc. They playfully identify the substances and patterns of power and thus indirectly point to possible alternatives by combining poetic imagination with concerns for a better politics. They demonstrate that illusory boundaries need not be drawn between entertaining and rational approaches to deliberation. Fundamentally these mirrors are all meant to get us to reflect upon the ideological automatization of deliberation, which seems to prevail. Creative activists do therefore not (always) have a fixed agenda, but rather offer us a new set of spectacles – they pose a certain type of question and facilitate a different sort of listening (cf. Scharmer). This openended approach to critical participation therefore does not demand a strict ideological consistency either (cf. Kolakowski). The counter mirroring reaction to the reflective nature of capitalism should rather be seen as a claim for justice – one that calls for reflection. In accordance with this, the point of my work is not to celebrate these new social actors as bearers of better societal alternatives. It is to explore the conditions that they offer for the cultivation of such alternatives.

We began this chapter with some theoretical hypotheses, a societal diagnosis, and some conceptual clarifications, and then moved on to describe how the mirror as a metaphor can be used to describe what creative activists actually do. We will now go back and see what the theoretical implication of this metaphorical typology is.

Towards a critical theory of reflection

The following model attempts to schematize the development in critical theorizing over social struggles for justice. The model's top-down progression can be seen as a delineation of the historical inclusive development from the beginning of the 20th century to today in terms of the focus of the justice claims made by political movements (with a conscious western bias). A more strategic bottom-up reading of the model suggests the reverse logic presented earlier, when reflection and critique precede more substantial questions of justice – such as recognition and redistribution *concretely* or what the conditions for the good life should be *formally*.

The revolutionary social movements of recent years have unfolded with vigor – from Tahrir Square in Cairo over Puerta del Sol in Madrid and Zucotti Park in New York to Independence Square in Kiev, and many other places around the world. They have been a display of the traditional repertoire of contention with their mass demonstrations, sitins, and occupations calling for a fair redistribution of wealth and a better regulation of the financial sector in the wake of the financial crisis (the economic sphere), claiming the recognition of minority groups and

Table 6.1 The development in critical theorizing over social struggles for justice

Justice claims	Crises	Spheres	Analytical levels	Central agents	Historical demarcations	Overall aim	Perspective	Dimension
Redistribution	Inequality of class structures	The economic sphere	State regulation vs. market mechanisms How much vs. how little	Trade unions and political organizations	The birth of the welfare state	A decent standard of living for everyone	First order perspective	The 'what' of justice
Recognition	Discrimination of status hierarchies	The cultural sphere	Private sphere of love Juridical sphere of law Social sphere of solidarity	New social minority movements	The 1968 revolution against the authoritative traditions	Freedom understood as cultural diversity through individual particularity		
Representation	Democratic deficit	The political sphere	Ordinary political misrepresentation Misframing Meta-political misframing	Global activists and international federations	Globalization and the dismantling of the territorial state	Democracy understood as the possibility of those effected to participate	Second order reflections	The 'who' of justice (pointing towards the 'how')
Reflection	Automatization of deliberation and totality of mass-mono-cultivation	The contemplative sphere	Reflexive character of capitalism Mirroring counter tactics Triggers of reflection	Creative activists	Hegemony of the headlines/ deadline-society	A fixed agenda is deliberately not (always) in place	Blind spot awareness	The 'how' of justice (pointing towards the 'why')

a democratic opposition, free from discrimination (the cultural sphere), and demanding equal rights and to be heard (the political sphere) – cf. Fraser's three-dimensional conception of justice. On the other hand, the activists that made up the coordinating forces behind these movements were creative in their conceptualization, mobilization, communication, and organization of the movements. Furthermore, the *lack* of concrete demands by a heterogeneous crowd has for many commentators actually become a defining factor – for better and worse – in many instances for the broad and inclusive movements, where fixed agendas were deliberately not always in place. They focused more on the open reflexive process than the static designed vision. In short, creative activists played a central role in these movements (despite the movements' own and the media's romanticizing of the spontaneous self-organizing crowd) and did so as a practical organizer, a mediator between traditionally divided actors, and a facilitator of dialogue. The question of how well they played their part is a different evaluative matter.

So Fraser's conception of justice does not seem to fully be able to explain current developments within this field. I have therefore suggested *reflection* as a fourth dimension of justice. This also suggests a move from *theories of social justice* to *theories of democratic justice* as the way best suited to explain many of the current unrests. Fraser operates with two fundamental scales of justice: *the balance*, where an impartial judge weighs the relative merits of conflicting claims, and the map, where spatial relationships are framed and it is considered what, if anything, should delimit the bounds of justice. The balance represents the instrument needed when dealing with 'the what' of justice; *the map* represents the instrument needed when dealing with 'the who' of justice. I propose *the mirror* as a third kind of instrument needed to orient oneself today when questioning, analyzing, and facilitating processes that deal with 'the how' of justice.

In my discussions with Nancy Fraser she was (quite naturally so) hesitant towards including the idea of reflection as a fourth dimension of justice. Rather she sees it as one element of the meta-practices of politics that has to do with how we change the way we deliberate about what constitutes the good life. She does however explain her position as a contextualized grounded reflexivity:

> I think it would be accurate to characterize my approach as a variant of left Hegelianism. To negate oppression and to try to move beyond it is always something that emerges from within history, from within the context in which we are operating. (...) It is a grounded

reflexivity that is rooted in a specific situation. (Fraser, in interview with Harrebye)

Fraser continues by clearly distancing herself from what I earlier defined as critics with a conscious outside stand:

I am not the sort of thinker who thinks of critique as if I were somehow standing outside history and in some abstract almost platonic way saying what ought to be. I think what ought to be emerges out of a dialectical tension from what is. And I think social movements are the sorts of actors who navigate this tension. (Fraser, in interview with Harrebye)

Let me therefore list some arguments as to why a fourth dimension of justice *does* need a category of its own (even though the argument that reflection is an integrated part of redistribution, recognition, and representation has been visually incorporated in Table 6.1).

Firstly, the reflexive aspect of the possibility of democratic participation and deliberation is (as the quote above illustrates) related to Fraser's concept of 'meta-political misframing,' but the analysis above suggests that reflection needs a category of its own, since it refers to distinct features of justice that are related to the interconnectedness of capitalism, critique, and creativity (cf. Chapter 1). Critical analyses of how creativity is instrumentalized in the critical activist practices are not (always) meant to reject the legitimacy of those practices, but to understand the symptomatic, diagnostic meaning of them (e.g. Boltanski & Chiapello, 2005; Heath & Potter, 2006; Larsen, 2011; Rolnik, 2011) – just as in Immanuel Kant's critique of the various capacities of reason, creativity is not just criticized, but is also somewhat actualized in the procedure of critically differentiating between the elements that it consists of and the reflexive autonomy that it demands and sometimes creates.

Secondly, Fraser's theory of framing stops just as it reaches the unfolding of the reflexive aspects of justice that she *does* point towards when she deals with meta-political misframing. Maybe because, thirdly, there are disciplinary limits for a more institutionally oriented political theory interested in the dynamics between power, resources, and the opportunity of the multilayers of autonomous democratic participation. The critical theory of reflection based on the principles of heterotopological mirroring and creative framing that I am proposing thus builds on and methodologically complements Fraser's theory rather than undermining it. Regarding the possibility of challenging society's hegemonic discourses with alternative discourses, Fraser herself concludes that when:

> Combining features of normal and abnormal discourse, the result would be a grammar of justice that incorporates an orientation to closure, necessary for political argument, but that treats every closure as provisional – subject to question, possible suspension, and thus to reopening. (Fraser, 2009, p. 72)

Thirdly, much like Fraser, Foucault (1986, p. 26) argues that: "Heterotopias always presuppose a system of opening and closing that both isolates them and makes them penetrable." As I have tried to illustrate, it is this double movement that best characterizes the creative activists' mirroring tactics. They set up alternative mirrors that reflect citizens and society differently to those looking at them. At the same time they offer platforms for new solutions and pose open-ended questions without knowing and offering the answers to them. Like agonistic models, reflexive justice valorizes the moment of opening. The intention is to get people to reflect on their own and come up with non-dogmatic answers. "The expression 'reflexive justice' expresses that dual commitment, signaling a genre of theorizing that works at two levels at once" (Fraser, 2009, p. 73). So where Fraser sees reflection as a meta-category and maintains that critique should always be reflective, I question what that actually means today.

Fourthly, it seems that when questioning why acts of reflection constitute a separate level of analysis over and above Fraser's own current framework, the objection regarding why reflection cannot just be seen as a process or a tool that occurs at each of the three levels of analysis (and hence would be superfluous as a fourth level) only really has bite with regard to the *inside mirrors* and the immanent critique that this represents. The reflection (structural critique and utopian imaginary) brought about by *outside mirrors* transcends (if successful) the substantially conditioned questions of the 'what' of justice and the structurally limited questions of the 'who' of justice.

Interviewing John Jordan, it becomes clear that his work is a rejection of representation in favor of transformation. But what does that mean? I asked him:

> I am interested in the transformation of the political realm itself, so the material is not a representation, the material is the actual action

or the actual society or the actual way of organizing. So it's not about an image of something, it is not about a representation. Now having said that, of course I do do representations.

Fifthly, if we accept the premise for the type of reasoning behind Fraser's hesitation, one might turn the criticism around and ask if the 'second order perspective' of representation could then not also in some way just be included as one recently actualized aspect of the first order perspective of redistribution and recognition.

Finally, analyzing (these) new trends calls for a theoretical framework that somewhat mirrors the practices that it analyses. Such a theory can therefore not operate with the same normative demands and standards as Honneth does when he defines formal criteria for the good life with the aim of using them as a normative foundation for subsequent critical analyses. On the contrary, a *critical theory of reflection* must curiously explore the possibilities of the new and emerging and thus stay open to what that may be, in the analysis of how critics and creative activists seek to get people to reflect upon these issues. For, as Fraser herself puts it: "The capacity to interrogate the frame, to make it an object of critique and political action, is yet another instance of reflexivity" (Fraser, 2009, p. 154).

The depolitization of politics has to do with many of the structural trends identified in this book, and ultimately with the self-imposed governmentality that renders the political subject a docile body in the face of its rulers. The disciplinary strategy of power that characterizes modern liberal democracies, where politics is moved further and further away from citizens in a technocratic de-antagonization of politics, frames the way in which citizens (the Foucauldian self) play the *games* of truth that we are all participating in (whether we realize it or not), and why the challenge of these frames can have a transformative effect on the configuration of society.

Methodological constraints

Before drawing any conclusions I want to point out some difficulties and possibilities when it comes to the methodological aspects of developing such a critical theory of reflection. I do this by forestalling the most obvious criticisms and supplementing theory with more practical methodological considerations about the reflexive theorist's relation to empirically based analyses.

There are definitely risks involved with this mode of typological theorizing:

> In attempting to refine and (re)formulate the terms and goals of the movements, the theorist may actually end up limiting and containing the radical possibilities emergent within them. The radical possibilities of new social movements are often manifest within their innovative practices, and cannot easily be grasped using older, established theoretical concepts and frameworks. (Conway & Singh, 2009, p. 78)

The last part of the argument stresses the necessity of the development of new concepts that matches the experimenting practices in the field. However, Conway and Singh also stress how the risk of attempting to label a movement sometimes misses what is most novel and challenging about the single cadres within them – and their specific struggle. They may even serve to restrain the potential of these groups by confining them within inadequate language and categories of interpretation and evaluation: "Critical theory can therefore function to inhibit the emergent emancipatory possibilities of social struggles" (Conway & Singh, 2009, p. 79). Does this book entirely avoid this conundrum? No. To some extent that is the price we have to pay in order to develop a better, shared language that allows us to understand the times that we are living in. Furthermore it is by default impossible to foresee any unintended consequences that such theorizing might have. In defense, the open-ended nature of the reflection that these political activists are causing should be stressed in the development of the theory that this chapter is pointing towards. The analyses here also avoid pinning down their practices as dogmatic expressions of a certain ideologically contingent segment. Rather the reflexive analysis of some of today's movements or project-organized activist cadres allows them, I believe, the freedom and maneuverability that is crucial to their critical enterprise.

The scope of the theory might be limited in terms of geo-political focus, but the conceptual framework is sensitive to differences in cultural traditions and the political ambiguity of – and normative ambivalence towards – creative activists in different settings (cf. previous chapter).

So, do I unintentionally fall into what I earlier defined as the confident outside stand of the first wave critics by diagnosing capitalism from an outside position? No. The diagnosis does not pretend to define what capitalism 'really' is, but portrays a certain feature of contemporary capitalism that restricts and constrains autonomous self-representation, informed structural critique, and the possibilities of doing and imagining things in alternative ways. Methodologically this diagnosis is in a dialectic relationship with the mirroring practices because:

> Reflection means thinking about the conditions for what one is doing, investigating the way in which the theoretical, cultural and political context of individual and intellectual involvement affects interaction with whatever is being researched, often in ways that are difficult to become conscious of. (Alvesson & Sköldberg, 2009, p. 269)

A 'conscious inside stand' makes such an investigation easier. Heterotopologial analyses of mirrors (in principle) further allow for the reciprocal dynamics of conditions and responses to be revealed at different levels simultaneously. As Alvesson and Sköldberg (2009, p. 317) conclude, "reflection addressing a multitude of levels of domains, not the following of set procedures, characterizes the scientific in social sciences." Consequently, I agree with Rebughini (as also stated in the beginning) that the sociological study of critical action "does not have to choose between the observation of practices carried out as small symbolic acts, circumscribed and situated, or alternatively, as the philosophical valuation of general appeals to inevitable and transcendent values" (2010, p. 477). Social critique often calls for a unitary vision of justice through analytical knowledge distinguished from common sense. But a more pragmatic vision centered upon practices requires, in Rebughini's words (2010, p. 460), "a pluralized and re-dimensioned vision of critique that can only have a localized and temporary valence."

The proposed reconfiguration of Fraser's theory of justice is a consequence of how the grammar of arguments has changed in recent years. To use her own reasoning, far from being reducible to maldistribution, disrespect, or misframing, the automatization of deliberation caused by the totality of mass-mono-cultivation of our political contemplative capacities occurs even in the immediate absence of the latter injustices, although it is usually intertwined with them. When interviewing Nancy Fraser about the past and future of progressive politics and the correlation between the claims made and the tactics applied she concurs: "what is needed is a deeper connection between these different kinds of critique – in theory and in practice."

Likewise, the contemplative dimension is implicit in and required by this grammar of justice – thus no redistribution, recognition, or representation without critical and creative reflection. The three-dimensional concept of justice therefore also needs to be questioned.

Future program

The argument in this chapter has been as follows: we do not need a clearly formulated alternative to be critical towards the development of modern civilization. In fact it seems that creative activists do the exact opposite. They reflect critically in the co-creative pursuit of a better life – for all of us – without (always) knowing beforehand where they are going.

The tactical character of this endeavor is determined by the conditions that the reflexive surface of capitalism constitutes. As a reaction, critical and inspirational mirrors are set up inside and outside our everyday horizons to get us to reflect about our own lives, our society, and our future. That goes for the Otpor demonstrators holding up mirrors in front of the police in Serbia and the array of creative tactics deployed by movement activists all around the world in increasing numbers in recent years. It also applies to alternative beauty pageants and critical creative media campaigns of all sorts. It is true for the Christiania community in Copenhagen and the development of Ushahidi software in Kenya. There is an art to every practice. Activism is no exception. From Jesus to Gandhi, Martin Luther King to The Yes Men, artistic activism has functioned as the priming pump of our political imagination through parables and symbolic acts, by making the invisible visible and de-masking those in power – and by pushing the boundaries of what is possible and legal, balancing between critique, cooperation, and cooptation on the margins of the repertoire of contention.

Accordingly, three levels of reflection have been touched upon: the systemic reflection of capitalism, the counter strategic reflection of the alternative mirrors set up by creative critics, and the cognitive, psychological, political reflection brought about by these mirrors in the citizens affected by them. A *critical theory of reflection*, which I have pointed towards in this chapter, thus both has diagnostic potential with regard to the reflexive nature of capitalism and critical potential in terms of identifying and developing the counter reflexive strategies displayed in the mirroring tactics of, not only creative activists, but all forms of resistance and social innovation. The aim is to reflect on the dialectics between crisis, diagnosis, and critique.

The actual development of such a theory therefore demands a clear, elaborated, and operationalized conceptual framework, a deep understanding of the historical demarcations and crises underlying it, and further analyses of the interconnectedness of limiting conditions, critical strategies, and co-creative potential. This book has not only pointed towards the relevance and the possibility of such a theory. It has now also sketched the contours of it.

Following the principles of heterotopological mirroring and creative framing, the role for a new critical theory of reflection should be to:

- Accept and promote the facilitation of experimental forms of dialogue as an end in itself, not only as a means, given the open and non-dogmatic political outlook of some political actors.
- Study the symbolic role and projective functionality that mirrors play and have in different kinds of cultures and societies – in history, today, and in the future.
- Approach socially sculptured mirrors as expressions of immanent critique, creative suggestion, structural critique, and utopian imagination.
- Apply the optical mechanics of mirrors in sociological critical analysis of mechanisms of contemplative reflection.
- Investigate how groundbreaking political reflection in the individual citizen may be caused by surprising and disturbing information or enactments that challenge cultural hegemony and coherent worldviews by the introduction of new cultural memes.

"Re-opening all the closures and clutches of power is what all movements of resistance need to learn in the first place" (Brighenti, 2011, p. 75). The mirroring tactics of creative activists and transformative movements outlined here are exactly one way of doing that – by recognizing, exploiting, expanding, and exploring cracks in the system – and thereby also entertaining discussions about how and why. The principle of parity of participation also readily lends itself to this analytical approach as it has a double quality that, in Fraser's own words, "expresses the reflexive character of democratic justice" (Fraser, 2009, p. 28). Capitalism as well as the organizations, activists, and movements challenging it, are changing. We as researchers need to develop appropriate analytical tools to be able to understand how and why. A theory of reflection pinpointing and investigating *the mirror effect* is one possible instrument in that critical toolbox.

Part IV
Questioning the Impact – New Trends and Future Dilemmas

7
Professionalization and Cooptation

The interplay between civil society actors and organizations and state and market is changing. Some argue that a fourth sector is emerging (fourthsector.net; Escobar & Gutiérrez, 2011) and new partnerships are being formed. But how does this change the way that today's creative activists operate with and against shifting political agents both inside and outside the established polity?

Civil society is changing, and thus the way citizens express their concerns and are active in their community is shifting too. Today many of us think and act like cosmopolitan citizens, concerned with issues that have a global perspective, but we still engage in ways that, though they might have a global outreach, are locally anchored. Based on my long standing in the Danish activist environment participating in different ways as a spectator, member, organizer, or debater on the Nordic welfare state's civic scene, in this chapter I will draw primarily on Danish-based cases to illustrate my points.

In this chapter we will discuss current trends of professionalization of activism and related dynamics of cooptation by examining three playing fields in which these trends are advancing – one that is increasingly involving the state, one intersecting with the market, and one concerned with traditional civil society organizations. While analyzing these trends it is worth considering how the broadening of, the cooperating with, and/or the cooptation of the activist domain is influencing our democratic culture and for better and worse affects the issues at hand – whether it be alleviating poverty, saving the environment, developing an integrating urban culture, or educating the next generation of change makers.

The first section will be a critical analysis of how the players that activists have traditionally been up against, the state and the private company, today include the citizens or an employee in a co-creative decision-making processes and thereby sometimes also dislocating critique in advance by meeting demands and giving the participants a sense of ownership. The second section will focus on how activism is becoming a profitable avenue for a new type of socially concerned business. The third section looks at how global civil society organizations are step-dancing on a burning hot platform that forces them to undergo organizational restructuring, political transformations, and make radical shifts in their professional focus. A renewed focus on the training of activists has resulted in new types of partnerships. On a final and more pragmatic note I discuss how creative activism and the established political system might learn to interact in the future – but maintain that it is crucial for the integrity of creative activism that its artistic discursive autonomy is maintained in the open interplay with mainstream politics.

Top-down bottom-up inclusion

Modern governance is not just about agreeing on some laws that disposition people's actions and implementing and upholding them. It is less about telling people what to do and how to do it, and more about how to include citizens in the decision-making process in order to inform decision makers and create ownership in the citizenry – and thereby also prompting their behavior around new initiatives. Furthermore it is the underlying assumption of such inclusive processes that the co-creative process frees up imaginative potential and creative capacities:

> What is stressed in mainstream participatory models is never that lay people can make a real difference to the structuration of the political regime from inside the political system. The focus is always on how people orient themselves to government from outside in civil society, whether actively, as virtuous citizens, or passively, as obedient subjects. (Bang, 2009, p. 118)

A recent survey shows that four out of ten Danish citizens would like to be more involved in the decision-making process regarding the development of their local community (see Kudahl & Jørgensen, 2013). Only three percent wish to be less included:

> It can seem paradoxical because fewer people today become members of political parties and the voter turn out has been in a steady

decline in recent years. But people have not become less interested in politics. They are just not as enchanted about only being able to vote for an election every fourth year. The citizens have generally become more competent and less authoritarian. That is also why they demand to be involved in the decision making process. (Torfing in Kudahl & Jørgensen, 2013)

It is uplifting that people want to take responsibility. But the numbers also indicate that the majority is still too busy or too skeptical about whether it will make a difference to get involved (cf. the main argument made earlier based on the regression analysis of European Social Survey data). It is therefore extremely important that local politicians think very carefully about when and how they choose to include citizens.

When I hear words like active participation, facilitated inclusion, and citizens' involvement from state-employed actors and private consultants I reach for my rhetorical revolver. On one hand, the intentions are (apparently) good and we should take responsibility by taking part in our community. On the other, creative activists in particular need to listen carefully to the skeptical inner anarchist sounding the alarm, and for a minute keep well-meaning hippie-pedagogues and cynical management consultants at arm's length before they decide to dive into bed with them. Why? To allow for cooperation without hierarchy or state rule – in other words, what James C. Scott calls 'anarchism as praxis' – to defend a politics that entails conflict and debate, and the perpetual uncertainty and learning they entail (Scott, 2012, p. xii); to celebrate the anarchist confidence in the inventiveness and judgment of people who are free to exercise their creative and moral capacities.

Participation is a plus-word and a buzz-word on the same level as democracy and diversity. Throughout this book, I have celebrated the dynamic deliberative democracy that rises and falls with the active participation of citizens – and with Half Ross and Hal Koch in hand I salute the thriving democratic participatory tradition of my folk-high school-country both as a means and an end in itself. But as the best priests do, we must all waver in our belief from time to time and question our faith. Allow me therefore to play the devil's advocate here. For I too can be sick and tired of the demand for participation in everything from a volunteer work weekend in the kids' kindergarten to phone evaluations of the service level somewhere that only takes two minutes. Sometimes we demand too much of ourselves and each other. And to a certain degree, that is not productive. The same goes for activists. Remember?

Participation does not always make everything more democratic. First of all we *should* not participate in everything. Either because it is morally appalling (mass rape and Paradise Hotel are two examples) or because we are not meant to – a drum circle is a great example where it is amazing and fun for those in it but just as annoying for the rest of us standing outside (Lambert in Boyd, 2012, p. 156). Secondly, we *cannot* participate in everything. It is therefore necessary to carefully prioritize one's participation in order to be able to contribute in a focused and qualified manner. For some it means taking to the streets. For others, helping to build an organization. For some it means contributing to the public debate. For others, changing the way they live their lives.

But if we do participate, say in a neatly state-orchestrated democracy-enhancing event, it is important that we do so with eyes wide open. We all participate with different expectations and pre-conditions. Never on equal terms. Whether it is in school, at work, or in the union, modern facilitation is a hidden form of power. When activists, consultants, the state or any other actor use such aiding techniques they do so to stimulate the co-creative process but also always to further their own agenda. To challenge this sort of covert power one has to question the frame for that participation itself. That is what I am trying to do here.

Processes designed to involve citizens in policy development are too often skin-democratic showcases that only have symbolic value. One well-known problem is that the critique raised or the suggestions put forward may never reach the decision maker's table. And even worse, of course, when such processes are merely used to create political legitimacy.

When the Nordic Construction Company (NCC) in 2013 began the construction of a line of exclusive housing blocks along Copenhagen's inner city canal, they also built a temporary 'Dome of Vision' (domeofvisions.dk/dome-of-visions) in the middle of the construction site. The Dome itself is a piece of work that is meant to challenge the construction industry and material manufacturers. Its function is to house a variety of cultural events that challenge traditional urban planning processes and inspire new development solutions. But the history of the location hints at another reason. In 2004 a plan was presented to build a handful of high futuristic skylines unlike anything ever build in Copenhagen. The public went mad. Renowned architects criticized the plans and more than 14,000 local citizens signed a petition. The pressure led to political chaos in Copenhagen's city council. Eventually the plans were dropped. A couple of years later there was another attempt to make use – and money – off the site. In 2011 NCC held a series of workshops with local citizens to launch a new plan for the site. But how would they prevent the wider community from ruining their project? And how could they best create an atmosphere around the area that would attract solid buyers? – Through the facilitation of citizenship involvement! The question, though, is how much of a say the local citizens of Christianshavn and the wider Copenhagen area actually had when it came to deciding what, when, where, and how to build and utilize this key Copenhagen location. In reality all the lines for new buildings had already been drawn. The money had been spent. But the stakeholders needed people to feel a sense of ownership in order to be able to implement a decision already made.

One of the events that took place in the Dome of Vision was a workshop (April 20–25, 2013) ordered and paid for by NCC in agreement with the Municipality of Copenhagen. It was curated and facilitated by senior research fellows from Theatrum Mundi (such as Richard Sennett and Andrew Todd) with the assistance of local expertise (such as Gry Worre Hallberg and myself). The idea was to see what happens when architects and urban planners interact with artists and creative activists. Not a bad idea. But the activists did not show up. They were not properly rallied. Nor were concerned local citizens invited. Beautiful ideas of how to alternatively appropriate the neighboring Paper Island were presented at the final session. But they were not communicated to the politicians in charge nor taken any further elsewhere. When the local head representative of the municipal committee showed up unannounced during the final presentation it was both uncomfortable and clearly inconvenient. That did not stop him from pointing to the elephant in the room – NCC, whose head of development and communication was there to overlook the grand finale. The workshop was in many ways inventive, but the intentions were unclear at best and deceiving at worst, the selection of participants did not meet the purpose, and the follow-up and actual use of the intervention was non-existent.

From Machiavelli to Boltanski and Chiapello, it has been made clear that the trickster, the public intellectual, the annoying journalist, and the creative activist are not always someone that those in power reject and distance themselves from. On the contrary, the joker allows the prince (or those in power today) to coopt critique and make minor adjustments such that they not only deflect or redirect a potential uprising but also strengthen the immunity of a system that keeps those in power in power.

Furthermore, the organizations that facilitate citizenship meetings such as future workshops, open space, panels, summits, interview meetings, and online input pools are now curious to work with creative activists because of the facilitation tools that they have, which are also aimed at mobilizing, facilitating, and convincing a participatory culture – although in other ways than the more business-oriented consultancy toolbox (cf. the discussion in Chapter 2 about how activists are reclaiming the normative facilitating principles of deliberative democracy from the management consultants of the 1990s).

But maybe our heroic belief in democratic diversity sometimes overrates the innovative value of inclusive initiatives. The mainstream mono-cultivation of pop culture, economic theory, party politics, and management strategies reduces the diversity that is the very premise for such inclusive and cooperative processes to become synergetic. Participation can therefore be a way to reproduce existing power dynamics, contrary to what one might expect. The revolutionary idea, quite contra-intuitively, often takes place when choosing to turn down an invitation – not always when following the crowd. The active citizens and do-gooders of our society tell themselves and each other that not showing up to their event equals apathy, disinterest, or exclusion (Harrebye, 2014). But the blank vote can be an expression of protest, trusting that better-qualified people will make good or better decisions, or consciously choosing to participate elsewhere on one's own terms. When analyzing how activists use and relate to media outlets one can (inspired by Rucht, 2004), as explained earlier, differentiate between four approaches: the first is adaptive: Greenpeace, for example, cooperates with existing medias and operates on their premises; but the other three, cf. the point made above, are critical in the sense that they either distance themselves from the mainstream media, attack them, or create their own alternatives to them.

Accordingly, when the turnout for a vote is low it is not necessarily because people do not care about politics. It is to a large degree because they want more than just an opportunity to vote and/or people do not feel that the politicians are in touch with public concerns – in Denmark the trust in politicians, which is relatively high compared to other countries, has plummeted in the last couple of years (survey done by A&B Analyse in 2014).

Now, it might sound as if I am undermining the very arguments that I have built up in the book so far. But what I am doing is just flagging the difference between meaningful and effective participation and futile and deceitful forms of facilitation. The focus on active citizenship as learning processes (cf. Delanty, 2010) makes sense. But if citizens experience that their input is not put to good use, then we risk that they might never come back.

So the democratic value of active participation is a central argument for many civil society romantics who believe in deliberative democracy and want to see more volunteers and engaged citizens. But one has to be aware that this also allows for a possibility to cut universal welfare state services, for example. The point here is therefore simply that citizens in general and creative activists in particular need to be aware of which overall agenda their efforts are used to serve and promote as it can be difficult to detect.

When the Foreign Ministry called the Wooloo management in for a meeting as they were preparing for their New Life festival, because they preferred that Wooloo did not match official delegates with private citizens thereby keeping it a parallel festival, the Wooloo boys stood strong and insisted on working across those boundaries. Superflex had to strike the same balance when developing their biogas device in cooperating with partnering NGOs and art foundations confused about the project's intentions due to problems of categorizations.

So how do we prevent important democratic participation from becoming false solidarity, political correctness, renunciation of responsibility, or from being used as a poorly hidden management tool? Building on the principles of what makes an ethical spectacle (cf. Duncombe, 2007), openness, transparency, and consequence are necessary – from intention, selection, format, process, follow-up, and evaluation. Yes, we have heard that before. But we rarely see it in practice. Maybe because the best process-consultants are busy teaching leaders, who can afford it, how they can most efficiently implement cutdowns and mergers instead of real bottom-up change processes where there is an actual social need for them.

There are of course numerous examples of where, when, and how these techniques make sense – from co-creative municipal development and negotiation to democratic housing schemes in Chile (see TED talk with Alejandro Aravena), from community meetings about how to privately house asylum seekers in small-town Jutland to online tools for collaborative decision making such as democracyos.org in Argentina and loomio.org in New Zealand (or gear like appgree.com, polleverywhere.com and assemblyvoting.dk), and from participatory budgeting to World Wide Views (wwviews.org).

The new political party in Denmark, The Alternative (alternativet.dk), is another example of how such inclusive processes do make sense. The Alternative publicly announced that it was going to run for parliament in November 2013. Uffe Elbæk, founder of the world-famous Chaos Pilot education and the former Minister of Culture (openly inspired by former controversial mayor of Bogotá, Antanas Mockus), took center stage. The broader vision was clear: a new political culture was needed, a political program where sustainability (financial, social, and environmental) was the fundamental principle, and where social entrepreneurship and an ingenious civil society was the means to find new solutions to the challenges we already face in society. It was also a way to position themselves in between the leftist green agenda and the liberalists' growth program. But apart from the overall vision and some guiding principles such as curiosity, humility, and humor the party was expecting the public to join in before an actual political program was drafted. How? By enabling ordinary citizens, experts in their field, and rebels without a cause to pitch ideas, raise critique, and join the conversation through a continuous series of 'political laboratories' around Denmark in the form of communal workshops, partnership meetings, interviews, and an open online platform. The preface to the party's political program states it very clearly:

> The political document that you are about to read is the result of a special political and democratic experiment. Driven by a belief that more people know more (...) we gave each other the political and organizational challenge of formulating a principal and party political program through what one might describe as a political open-source-process. That means that we invited everyone with the time and energy to become co-authors. The only condition was that you could agree with the party's six fundamental values and its overall direction and ambition: A serious sustainable transformation of Denmark. The six values are: Courage, generosity, transparency, humility, humor, and empathy. The transition process is characterized by the courage to imagine a radically different future – for Denmark and the rest of the World. More than 700 people have taken us up on our invitation and have contributed with concrete suggestions, critical questions, and curious wonder. They have done so through their participation in the many political laboratories and workshops that were held all around the country in the autumn of 2014.

The ambition was (and still is) to create a space where a new kind of political dialogue can take place and on that basis develop new political ideas and policies (see Husted, 2015 for an organizational typological analysis of the democratic implications of management in radical politics). Incoming suggestions were then gathered by the political secretariat, roughly edited, grouped thematically, and then presented for the Transitional Council (an independent advisory board of experts in different relevant fields – I happened to be one of them) whose job it was to prioritize, question, qualify, and recommend the more or less concrete proposals received. We had five such meetings (one on new political culture, one on education, one on art and culture, one on entrepreneurship, and one on sustainability). For each meeting there were 30–60 new ideas on how to do things differently. The edited list then went back to the political secretariat where political decisions were then made.

What was remarkable about this process was the amount of surprising ingenuity of many of the incoming designs and schemes (see political program online). Most important, however, was the degree to which this process actually concretely contributed and politically determined the final political program, which was presented at the People's Meeting (Folkemødet) on Bornholm. When The Alternative launched this part of their development process (which also functioned as part of the campaign, as this was of course *also* about creating legitimacy and a sense of ownership) they never could have imagined and did not anticipate such an original and also rather radical program that it left them with. Because they really had no clue what the answers were to the questions they posed – and that is an optimal starting point for an open, transparent, and effective politically bottom-up co-creative process:

> A wise man once said that if he had one day to fix one problem and his life depended on it, he would spend 90% of the time formulating a good question, because the right answers would then come easier to him. (...) We are therefore asking for your help. (Ringblom et al., Facebook call for specific political lab on peace and defense policy)

As it turned out it was also an extremely effective process. On June 18, 2015 The Alternative defied all the political commentators that had ridiculed the party prior to the election and stormed into the Danish Parliament with nine members of parliament (4.8% of the vote) in a landslide election. I believe that one of the reasons is that The Alternative very consciously deals with 'the what' of justice through 'the who' and 'the how' of justice. As an elected member of the new board, I find that our biggest challenge is to ensure the development of an actual social movement, one that entails a fruitful collaboration between the political party, the widespread activism of members and volunteers, and thirdly, developing democratic and social-economic initiatives in line with core values – thereby through pre-figurative politics demonstrating how what might seem utopian, actually can work (Reiermann, 2015).

Governance through the formation of networks composed of public and private actors might help solve pressing problems and enhance democratic participation in public policy making, but it may also create conflicts and make public governance less transparent and accountable: "In order to ensure that governance networks contribute to an effective and democratic governing of society, careful meta-governance by politicians, public managers and other relevant actors is necessary" (Sørensen & Torfing, 2009, p. 234). It is therefore also a central part of the research in this field to discuss how to assess the effective performance and democratic quality of governance networks, and why it is so crucial to develop the strategic and collaborative competences of local politicians.

Participatory processes of different kinds, when they work well, can be inclusive, creative, and dynamic. But they can also be empty buzzwords, strategic smokescreen, romantic utopia, or sweet and sour pickle pots. Facilitated participation can therefore easily become a convenient way for parents, politicians, and the unemployment worker to redirect, scrutinize, and control critics. The creative activists' finest role, should they choose to collaborate with more established political actors on such proceedings, might be to hold stakeholders accountable, ensure a representative balance of divergent interests and enable continuous critical reflection of the frame within which we are invited to participate – to set up critical mirrors that allow the propositions to be of value. So when we are asked to participate in a Facebook debate or be chosen for a subcommittee that is meant to put the issue on hold, we need to think hard about whether it is most productive to partake or obstruct, observe or do something else. As Marcus Miessen underlines in his book *Nightmare of Participation* (2011), democracy should sometimes be avoided at all costs. As Rune Lykkeberg has argued (2012), it does not work while in bed having sex, on a ship in a storm, or as an ever-presiding principle when raising our kids.

Democratic participation is desirable. But when it is facilitated by state-led actors with the support of private consultants partly based on creative activist techniques, one needs to be wary of the interests at play. If people feel cheated there is a risk they might never come back – and that would be disastrous for our democracy.

When the cause makes a profit

But it is not only state and private actors who have systematized new ways to accommodate or reallocate activist energy in ways that channel critical energy into (sometimes) constructive dialogue. A new social actor has emerged in-between the traditional civil society organization and the businesses that operate based on pure market logic. The *social business* is another example of how a new professionalization of what activism stands for has been coopted by businesses or reconfigured to fit the market by activists suiting up for it. We will look at examples of both kinds. Let us start with the former.

Spark is a little but ambitious consultancy shop. It was founded just a few years back by two headstrong women who had both quit their well-paid jobs at one of Denmark's most respectable consultancy firms to start up a new, more value-based and agile company. Today they have rapidly increased their number of employees and have won the Gazelle prize for their rapid growth and job creation. Spark specializes in what they call 'sustainable change'. More specifically they help organizations within both the private and the public sector to design and implement change that will last and that is geared to the social, environmental, and economic standards identified.

But none of them are activists in any traditional sense of the word. So how do the high heels fit the pirate? Well, Spark wants to challenge existing models of development and encourage clients to pursue value-based change processes and business models – in all sectors, locally as well as abroad. They offer their services in three arenas of change: (1) sustainable business models and value creation, (2) democratic development and participatory models, and (3) learning and capacity building (sparkcph.dk). Furthermore, they have an explicit philosophy that also informs their external advisory profile: making money and doing good are not necessarily counter-productive values – on the contrary even. 'Less mandate, more pirate' their new strategy spells. In fact, according to agents like Spark, a lot more could be done by creative activists, social entrepreneurs, NGOs, cultural institutions, critical artists, etc. if they only knew how to make a business plan. That is also why one of Spark's many initiatives is to try to teach such agents and organizations how to make money as this will, that is the belief, give them the drive and the independence necessary to make them serious, self-sustainable change makers. The question of course is whether they do not risk just playing another man's game.

With my knowledge of Spark[1] they are tightrope walking between long-established political institutions, politically oriented civic organizations, and cynical profit-seeking companies. On one hand, the work that they do is important and noble (given that they do not help companies with a less noble cause). On the other hand, they do not sell their services cheap and the owners get the profit. In their mind they give the critical and creative communities a helping hand in redefining capitalism, and putting food on the table at the same time. In a more skeptical perspective they are smoothing out the edges that, according to theorists such as Chantall Moufe (2007), are necessary to maintain and communicate an agonistic struggle against the exploiting system through and under which we live and work. And by redefining capitalism, Boltanski and Chiapello (2005) would argue, they are making its continuous survival possible and thus undermining feasible alternatives. Some activists will even go so far as to say that companies like these are doing so by piggy-backing on the 'real' activists out there by applying their tools to build a business. Finally, one might also question their use and understanding of the sustainability concept. If we apply the tripartite definition and question Spark's own environmental, social, and economic sustainability I am not sure they would do very well – primarily due to the growth and profit margins their employees need to hit. But the business is innovative according to the 'connective theory' perspective and provides an option for activists (those who want to) to get out of the streets and into the middle of the battlefield where they might change things from within instead of shouting in from the outside.

Innovation, we are told, is important if we are to come up with better solutions, grow our economy, and sustain our welfare. But critical bottom-up participation is also needed in these processes to challenge and complement the market-driven agenda.

To challenge and develop the concept of creative activism we therefore need to compare it to related concepts developed within less critical and more business- and production-oriented approaches to social innovation, broadly understood as "new ideas that work in meeting unmet social needs" (Mulgan, 2007).

Innovation can simply be defined as 'new ideas that work,' and can thereby sometimes be differentiated from improvement, implying incremental change, and creativity, which may sometimes lack a market-driven implementation and diffusion. A narrower definition depicts it as "innovative activities and services that are motivated by the goal of meeting a social need and that are predominantly developed and diffused through organisations whose primary purposes are social" (Mulgan, 2007). It is thus not driven by profit maximization the same way as business innovation is.

Muhammed Yunus, who is the founder of Grameen Bank and the originator of micro-credit loans, defines social business as "a non-loss and a non-profit company with a social purpose" (interview in Hulgaar & Holm-Pedersen, 2009). This does not mean that one cannot make a profit. It just means that the profit generated should not go to owners or investors but be reinvested in the business of doing good – whether that means employing the disadvantaged or helping to create environmental solutions to everyday problems – so that people can pursue and further develop their business in a healthy and progressive manner.

Yunus insists on the difference between a social business and a social entrepreneur. If you establish and manage a social business, he argues, you are also a social entrepreneur. But you do not necessarily run a social business because you are a social entrepreneur. The Night Ravens (Natteravnene) is one example that fits the description, as they are basically parents who go out in groups on patrol on Friday and Saturday nights to make the city life safe for kids that are not yet familiar with their own drinking limits. From when the society was founded in 1998 it has now grown to include well over 200 local unions. The Night Ravens has an explicit social purpose but they are not (and have no known intentions to become) a social business.

Social innovation overlaps with related concepts such as social entrepreneurship (Defourny & Nyssen, 2010), collaborative entrepreneurship (Miles, Miles, & Snow, 2005), collaborative innovation (Sørensen & Torfing, 2011), and participatory innovation (Buur & Matthews, 2008; Kristensen, 2011). Social innovation is not a new phenomenon, but the need for conceptual clarity and comparisons of principles of facilitated acceleration has never been bigger (www.tepsie.eu; www.emes.net/what-we-do; Hulgaard, 2007; Howaldt & Schwarz, 2010; Kristensen & Voxted, 2011b; Moulaert et al., 2013; Defourny, Hulgaard & Pestoff, 2014; Tanggaard, 2014). Community-based and more grassroot-oriented kinds of social innovation (cf. the Belgian School, Moulaert, 2010) are relevant to look at when discussing social businesses here because of the way they link up to the more radical, artistically inspired, critical, and activist aspects of the innovation process. Throughout history social movements have caused their own organizational, political, and social innovations.

Examples of what can (also) be defined as social innovation include self-help health groups, Wikipedia, neighborhood nurseries, consumer cooperatives, Ushahidi, restorative justice and community courts, zero carbon housing schemes, The Open University, Linux software, participatory budgeting models, Grameen microcredit bank, etc.

Climate change, the financial crisis, rising health care issues, increasing intercultural challenges, and the democratic deficit all require new ways of thinking about how we reorganize our companies, the city, our political system, etc. Economic growth, new technologies, and political top-down decisions will not themselves be enough. Social innovation that helps change behavior is also required. The questions here then becomes how the political balance between social movements and social businesses influences the type and application of social innovation we will see in the future.

Shared value creation (Porter & Kramer, 2011), which is closely related to measurements of social return of investment (Scholten, 2006) and ABC value (Lund & Meyer, 2011), are concepts and approaches that attempt to capture the social impact of civic entrepreneurship through a combination of traditional value-chain theory and critical stakeholder theory. Inspired by sociological organization-evaluation methods and value-network analyses, impact metrics are typically developed to compare benefits (e.g. Weinstein, 2009 and www.robinhood.org/metrics). Inspired by these advances, but aware of their limitations as well, we will in the final chapter include the synergic implications of other dimensions that are harder to measure but equally important for critical participants, the experimental organizational process, and the entrepreneurial spirit. In alternative evaluative frameworks, mistakes for example can be said to have a value of their own. But how do we reconcile 'success' and 'failure' in a continuous, open-ended approach? This becomes necessary when we are not evaluating corporate social responsibility (CSR) initiatives in private profit-maximizing companies but a particular type of civic engagement that strives towards social change and facilitates the active participation of the everyday maker – a kind of activism that is key to understanding today's broader patterns of participation, volunteering, and social entrepreneurship.

In this context Porter and Kramer's framework is interesting because it insists that there is no conflict of interest between making money and doing good. In fact companies, it is argued, must take the lead in bringing business and society back together. According to this paradigm, shared value creation (SVC) is not just old wines in new bottles (CSR), where societal issues in the social responsibility mindset are at the periphery, it is here at the center. Furthermore CSR has historically been a reaction to external pressure where the perspective that Porter and Kramer propose is integral to competing: "The solution lies in the principle of shared value, which involves creating economic value in a way that also creates value for society by addressing its needs and challenges" (Porter & Kramer, 2011). Underlying this argument lies the idea that the competitiveness of a company and the health of the community that surrounds it are closely intertwined. Global companies, however, do not today have the same sense of 'home,' and with outsourcing and offshoring that premise is further challenged.

In neoclassic thinking, social improvement, say hiring disabled workers or reducing energy consumption, equaled a constraint on the corporation, say a rise in costs or a reduction in profits. These new perspectives rather see such initiatives as a possibility to save money, innovate, and create new markets.

One difference from the more justice-oriented activist approach becomes clear when comparing the Fair Trade movement, which is essentially about redistribution, to this methodology, which in similar kinds of cases has been more interested in improving growing techniques, leading (ideally) to a bigger pie of revenue that benefits both the farmers and the companies who buy their products.

As examples Porter and Kramer refer among others to WaterHealth International, which is a fast-growing for-profit organization that uses innovative water purification techniques to distribute clean water at minimal costs to more than one million people in rural India, Ghana, and the Philippines. Its investors include not only the socially focused Acumen Fund and the International Finance Corporation of the World Bank, but also Dow Chemical's venture fund (remember The Yes Men's prank on Dow Chemical in relation to the catastrophe that they never took responsibility for).

Another example, this one showing how health conditions can be innovatively improved while earning a substantial growth margin, is Waste Concern, which is seeded with capital from the Lions Club and the United Nations Development Program. Waste Concern is a hybrid profit/non-profit enterprise started in Bangladesh in 1996, which has built the capacity to convert 700 tons of trash, collected daily from neighborhood slums, into organic fertilizer, thereby increasing crop yields and reducing CO_2 emissions.

When taking point of departures in these successful cases, this sort of business is making a huge difference to better the circumstances of people in need. From an activist standpoint, the question still remains, however, whether they have altered the *structure* of the economy and the state or the inner *composition* of the hegemonic apparatus as such.

Where Spark entered the grey zone in-between business and social entrepreneurship from the business end of things, the social business Baisikeli (Baisikeli.dk) has entered that space from the other end. They wanted to make the world a better place and combined a social need with untapped resources and a business opportunity.

Baisikeli (which means bike in Swahili) is a private company dedicated to improving the life quality of those who suffer by making transport easier and cheaper for the poorest people in the world. Specifically they are working towards developing a thriving bike culture in Africa. Concretely they fix bikes up and ship them south in containers. They primarily get these used or stolen bikes from the police or insurance companies who have no use for them. It is a win–win situation. To ensure a sustainable bike industry they also educate bike mechanics both at home and abroad in collaboration with local expertise. They sent off their first container shipment in 2007. Today they have workshops in Denmark, Sierra Leone, and Mozambique. To make money they fix, rent, and sell used bikes in Denmark – to the everyday peddler and through special leasing agreements with companies such as Ikea and Novo Nordisk. Baisikeli does not receive any financial donations because they believe that the best way to develop Africa is through sustainable growth. Baisikeli create the possibilities to utilize unused resources. "Goods that have little or no value in one place can make a tremendous difference somewhere else." By moving, changing, or adding resources Baisikeli therefore activates assets that would otherwise be wasted but now makes a difference in people's lives.

The work they do builds on the following principles (Baisikeli.dk): (1) we utilize otherwise wasted resources, (2) we invest the money we make in Denmark in bike-shops in Africa, (3) we are a financially (self) sustainable project, and (4) we do a proper job.

Walking into the bike-shop on Ingerslevsgade, Vesterbro, Copenhagen you immediately see how technical pride has not suffered from altruistic values. The bikes are beautifully made. A trademark model is now about to hit the streets. The former chaos pilot who co-founded Baisikeli is obviously proud of the work that he does: "Bikes are often rebuilt when they land in Africa – for hospital-bikes, water-purifying-bikes, different types of transportation, etc. The creativity there is great because it needs to be" (founder Henrik Mortensen).

In *Unboss* (2012) Bøtter and Kolind portray how some of today's cutting-edge companies act like movements to make themselves useful and change the world. The editors, together with a hundred collaborators from around the world who contributed to make the book, obviously also think that it is the right thing to do:

> You are no longer employed by an employer, you are a partner in a team. Your manager does not have all the answers, but she can ask the right questions. You don't work to earn money for some owners

Professionalization and Cooptation 177

you don't even know, you work for a cause. And you get a fair share of the profit you generate. You do not go to work from 9 to 5, you work where you are and when it suits you. Your company does not sell products to customers, it creates value with customers. And, if you work in the public sector, it is not the budget that counts, it is the value you create for citizens. (unboss.com)

Social businesses are typically characterized by not letting the ambition to make money and the aspiration to work for the greater good stand in the way of one another. These businesses promote a noble cause – either by working *for* say a certain target group (generating knowledge or money to support it) or by working directly *with* that group (e.g. by employing fragile groups in society, taking care of the elderly, or caring for the environment through more sustainable production). They usually make money through sales of innovative products or services. Profits are transparently reinvested in the development of the business or given in support of the greater cause. Finally, they are organizationally and politically independent from the public sector.

They differ from the activism we have analyzed here in a number of fundamental ways, but they pose important questions about the activists' politically correct and sometimes restricting ideas about how we fight the good fight most effectively and ethically responsibly.

Historically, social business dates back to the end of the 19th century when political parties, trade unions, charities, and religious and public movements really emerged. The seeds for the socially conscious way of doing business were not least laid with the co-operative movement, the co-operatives, and self-owned institutions. The development of social businesses is in that way closely tied to the development of a strong civil society where ordinary citizens get involved and work together in the solution of shared societal challenges. In the last couple of decades the New Public Management wave has led to an increased focus on outsourcing and/or the involvement of alternative actors in the solving of welfare services such as cleaning, integration, elder care, etc. which further opens up the avenue for such companies. The environmental and financial crisis has further created demands by citizens and consumers for socially responsible, environmentally viable, and economically sustainable and accountable solutions and options.

For Spark it is about making money in a responsible way while helping people create real value. For Baisikeli it is about helping people in need while being able to maintain a decent living standard. They each occupy their end of the social business scale – which is kind of unclear as it is since it covers the activists who need a budget to do what they want, to the capitalists who have grown a conscience and who operate with the logic that making money is not (only) an end in itself but a means that gives you the independence and the possibility to create more social value – a shift (possibly) in the fundamental logic of capitalism as we know it.

Dugnad (www.koeb-socialt.dk/cafe-dugnad) is an example of how social businesses can function as a kit that binds the state, the market, and civil society together in new ways. The Dugnad initiative helps drug addicts in inner Copenhagen. A café is opened as a safe-haven for the addicts. Relevant products have been developed for the users (such as a specially designed box for used needles, in collaboration with local businesses), and a connected 'health-room' has been established in cooperation with the Municipality. Money is made by selling food at various events. The entire concept has been born and grown over a long period of time and in close collaboration with 300 local citizens who have actively contributed to how the addicts (who are a serious problem on the streets of Vesterbro) and the rest of the community can actively work together to improve the situation for everyone (Pedersen, 2009).

Such projects challenge what creative activism is and can be. Social change by business development therefore also points towards a possible addition to the six types of activism summarized in Table 4.2. The seventh type (developed in talks with Richard Georg Engström) would be characterized by the proactive characteristics suggested in Table 7.1.

Table 7.1 Activism Inc.

TYPES OF ACTIVISM	ACTIVISM INC.
FUNDAMENTAL LOGIC	DO IT WITH OTHERS TO BE ABLE TO COMPETE
TYPICAL ACTIVITIES	CREATING SHARED VALUE THROUGH NEW SOCIAL BUSINESS MODELS
INTENDED GOALS	SUSTAINABLE DEVELOPMENT
SAYINGS	"We are what we repeatedly do. Let's do better. For everyone's sake." (job advert)
DOMINATING PERCEPTION OF FRAMING AGENTS (police, politicians, and media)	DOERS (not seen as an activist agent)

Social business is more than just corporate social responsibility, bottom of the pyramid, and triple bottom line. It is in the shared value perspective, a way to add a solidary and altruistic dimension to the capitalist system, which today builds on the accumulation of capital and maximization of one's own self-interests – a system that may lead to an overall growth in wealth, but also an increase in material inequality, human alienation, and environmental decay.

Activists must figure out whether or when to get involved with such endeavors. When deciding to do so, it is key to consider the dialectics between resistance, critique, and social change (Brighenti, 2011; Rehmann, 2013). Where the former often by association in this context implies drama, performance, and spectacle, the latter implies a clear vision and a pragmatic plan. But since this is (sometimes) a false dichotomy and as it is possible to mediate (analytically and practically) between incremental reforms and revolutionary breaks, short-term gains and long-term progress, and parliamentary, market-based, and extra-parliamentary forms of participation without compromising with one's core values, then it is worth pursuing possible synergies between activist creative critique and profitable social innovation.

The fundamental question, however, remains whether and how the social business entails a fundamental clash with – or a substantial supplement to – the economic model that is dominating the global scene today.

To promote progressive pre-figurative corporate politics we need new forms of social stock exchanges, funding schemes, crowd equity mechanisms, and partnership collaboration across sectors. With world-wide networks such as Grameen, Ashoka, BancaEtica, Young Foundation, Skoll World Forum, Social Stock Exchange, and Schwab Foundation as some of the central actors, supported by national alliances, coalitions, and social movements, this new trend is worth recognizing – not only because it is challenging (or aiding, depending on your viewpoint) capitalism, but also because it is doing the same to traditional forms of activism and its necessity and/or possibilities to form new partnerships and maybe cut their ties to old allies as a consequence of such new ways of working and funding activities. As governments and NGOs likewise begin to think more explicitly in concrete and alternative value terms their interest and possibility to collaborate with businesses and activists alike will also grow – as will consequently new kinds of hybrid enterprises. On this note let us look at how the international NGO searching for new partnerships can be seen as an example of this political conundrum.

New partnerships wanted

In the new millennium civil society is the burning platform on which international NGOs stand. Such organizations are now redefining their internal structure, their external communication, and the theory of change itself. In the future they will have to operate more as social enterprises and collaborate in new ways with social movements. But how? Luckily, some argue (e.g. Gnärig, 2015), disruptive innovation springs from necessity: "In order to survive and thrive, civil society organizations need to reinvent themselves." Education and capacity building seem to be one way in which these different actors are able to work together.

A new trend within this field is (therefore) the systematic professionalization of training of creative activists. Where they used to be artists gone political or activists with a flair for the aesthetics that would experiment with new versions of the old repertoire (without really knowing what they were doing and why), we now see courses offered around the world where tactics, strategies, and philosophies are taught to cultivate a certain strand of community building, campaigning, and protest. This is a more systematic way of working with our imaginative, inventive, and creative individual capacities and socio-political possibilities. Where we used to have master and apprentices, guerilla community-theater (e.g. Theater of the Oppressed), or lone avant-garde explorers we now (for better and for worse) have certified *ritual masters* helping us take those first daring baby steps into the world of fun and frightening activism.

Yes, Martin Luther King, Rosa Parks, and Pete Seeger all went to Highlander Institute, a school that Myles Horton built in 1932 based on in-depth studies of Grundtvig and the Danish folk-high-school tradition combining the broadening of civil right claims with the training and education of civil campaigners. But there is a rise in both temporary activist camps that move around and prepare people to make efficient needle-stick operations[2] and internationally oriented, professionalized activist training centers that either support campaign developers in practice or teach NGO managers, social entrepreneurs, and active citizens how to become better organizers.

Here I will briefly outline how some of the leading actors in the field work to educate the new generation of change makers. The underlying question of this discussion is whether revolutionary potential and ingenious energy are lost when the distance between lobbyists and die-hard activists is narrowed down to a course curriculum, and what the moral and political implications might be of this new role of the traditional state-funded service provider NGO and the once-isolated anarchists.

When it comes to activist education centers we can distinguish between two overall kinds. The first includes minor specialized training hubs set up by seasoned activists who do courses and advise larger organizations about campaigns and media stunts. The second and more formalized NGO type offers a wider array of courses. The grey zones are flourishing. Examples include Yes Lab, The Leading Change Network, Alliance of Community Trainers, CANVAS, Escola de activismo, Ashoka, Center for Artistic Activism, the Beautiful Trouble Team, Center for Story Based Strategy, etc. They differ in curriculum, financial set-up, in the assignments they take on, and style – some of them deliver fixed modules for contextualized inspiration whereas others believe in teaching fundamental facilitation of creative processes that will lead to the participants' own culturally adjusted solutions. Action Aid International is yet another example: a civil organization that works with 25 million people in over 40 different countries to eradicate poverty and injustice. We will look at Action Aid Denmark (a national division of the international umbrella organization) as a prime example of how NGOs have dealt with some of the challenges outlined and examine the new partnership between Action Aid and Beautiful Trouble as part of that transformation.

Action Aid Denmark was founded in 1944 and joined the Action Aid umbrella in 2010. It has over 8,000 individual and around 65 organizational members. Action Aid Denmark works with local organizations to support impoverished people around the world to know and demand their rights so that they can help build democratic and sustainable societies. Action Aid Denmark currently has ten Global Platforms (in Denmark, El Salvador, Ghana, Jordan, Myanmar, Mt Kenya, Nairobi Kenya, Nepal, Tanzania, and the United States). More are opening up. These constitute a worldwide network of education centers where courses and workshops in human rights, global citizenship, campaigning, social media, social entrepreneurship, and creative activism are offered. Courses in the latter often include a historical and political introduction to the field, a theoretical ABC, analyses of illustrative best and worst cases, a concrete tactical toolbox, tests of planning models and evaluation tools, future workshops, mapping the political field, and a variety of exercises.

The theory of change that is underlying this part of Action Aid's work is that capacity building is crucial to support people's own ability to take action and fight for themselves and their rights. The impact logic behind has however not yet been sufficiently backed by independent evaluations (Garbutt & Haddock, 2012). The Operations Management planning, monitoring, and evaluation (PME) template suggests that steps are taken to focus and quantify day-to-day practices and ensure alignment to overall strategic objectives.

A new partnership was established in 2014 between Action Aid Denmark and Beautiful Trouble with the support of the Danish national development agency Danida, who had a call out for new 'innovative partnerships.' The new initiative, called Beautiful Rising, is meant to provide a dynamic web platform where creative activist principles, tactics, ideas, and stories for inspiration can be exchanged. A collection of key examples from the Beautiful Trouble project along with Action Aid Global Platform training tools form the basis of the operation. One of the key challenges is to 'translate' mainly European and US examples of inspirational interventions and campaigns into and place within an African, Asian, or South American context. Intercultural communication therefore becomes a key competence in converting knowledge but also when facilitating the mutual exchange of untapped local knowledge that might have never been hatched or shared between ingenious but often isolated local heroes who have come up with an effective way to combat harassment of women on the street or unions that have made an original campaign that allowed for a new type of dialogue with otherwise divided social actors. Concrete examples of what is to come include: *Divestment* – a tactic call for investors to withdraw their money from targeted companies, corporations, and investment funds involved in structural or social injustices to either pressure power holders to shift position or isolate a harmful industry. Keromela Anek's story about terrible loss, myth, courage, and *disrobing* in Uganda (Wilmot, 2015), chasing off officials and preventing land grabbing, is an example of how some tactics that work well there would never work on the other continents.

In early June 2015, members of the Beautiful Rising team assembled in Harare, Zimbabwe's capital, to work with a group of 20 experienced human rights activists, feminists, and writers over four days of knowledge exchange, discussion, collaboration, and writing (similar workshops have been held in Myanmar, Tunisia, Palestine, Jordan, Egypt, Amman, Bangladesh, Tanzania, Mexico). Natasha Msonza is a local human rights activist who participated in the workshop. This is part of her account in a letter about the event:

> The timing could not have been better: Activists in Zimbabwe are struggling with a wide range of issues, from growing civil society and

donor fatigue, to increasingly shrinking democratic spaces, yet are able to draw on an incredible legacy of struggle in terms of thinking through approaches for building a better future. Expectations of participants ranged from the desire to 'Africanise' Beautiful Rising, to wanting to learn new tactics and finding ways of 'rejuvenating' social movements or addressing the burnout many activists are feeling.

Many of the participants were excited to be in the same space with other activists, and wanted to explore ways of building collaborative networks that would enable the strengthening of each other's work; or, in the words of one of the facilitators, Francis Rwodzi, to "find ways of using the right tactics, at the right time, for the right reasons." The participants also spent time discussing ways of building meaningful relationships while reflecting on the commonalities and differences among their various political struggles.

The main endeavor of the workshop was to document some of the successful and inspiring local action stories, tactics and principles of nonviolent collective activism and organizing, with the ultimate goal of contributing to the global Beautiful Rising creative activism toolbox. Participants felt that by creating a contextualized toolbox of stories and tactics for Zimbabwe, this would go a long way in strengthening the ability to organize by articulating effective approaches through documenting old and new tactics. Such a toolbox would also seek to strengthen the capacity of frontline activists to facilitate effective change.

In this context it is not only interesting as a new way of facilitating diffusion and brokerage across the North and South divides, it is also noteworthy because of the organizational and political implications of such new types of partnerships.

According to *Time Magazine*, the person of the year 2011 was The Protester. Towards 2030 Africa's population will grow to over one billion. That makes Africa our youngest continent – a huge challenge, and maybe a huge potential. In 2013 an ambitious policy-oriented Civil Society Rally was held in Copenhagen. Joanna Keer (Director, Greenpeace Canada) gave the opening keynote speech and kicked off proceedings by proclaiming that, "When people say that the young generation are the leaders of *tomorrow* they couldn't be more wrong!" I was dreading where this was going as I was sitting in the panel discussion coming up, but "No," she said, "the young generation are the leaders of *today*." This set the tone for the rest of the rally and marks a shift in politicians' view of the political relevance and creative potential of our youth.

As a former member of the Board in Action Aid Denmark (2013–15) I can affirm that a substantial amount of time within the development field is devoted to discussing the changing role of civil society organizations and what our strategy should be during this process of transformation. An open letter that was sent out to 'fellow activists around the globe' signed by a long list of some of the world's biggest international NGOs representatives has reinvigorated that debate:

> Sadly, those of us who work in civil society organisations nationally and globally have come to be identified as part of the problem. We are the poor cousins of the global jet set. We exist to challenge the status quo, but we trade in incremental change. Our actions are clearly not sufficient to address the mounting anger and demand for systemic political and economic transformation that we see in cities and communities around the world every day. A new and increasingly connected generation of women and men activists across the globe question how much of our energy is trapped in the internal bureaucracy and the comfort of our brands and organisations. They move quickly, often without the kinds of structures that slow us down. In doing so, they challenge how much time we – you and I – spend in elite conferences and tracking policy cycles that have little or no outcomes for the poor. They criticise how much we look up to those in power rather than see the world through the eyes of our own people. Many of them, sometimes rightfully, feel we have become just another layer of the system and development industry that perpetuates injustice. We cannot ignore these questions any longer. (Sriskandarajah et al., 2014)

The letter goes on to stress how international NGOs must to a greater degree ensure that the principal account is not to donors but to recipients and collaborators, rebalancing power from rigid organizations to informal networks in recognition of the importance of 'the wisdom of the street', supporting people's movements, and facilitating self-organization. The warning is sent out not because the work already done is not important. The boots on the ground need lobbyists, just like everyday makers sometimes benefit from an established organizational platform – and vice versa. The critique should rather be read as an expression of how traditional civil society agents feel that they have been coopted by complex systemic (political and administrative) processes to a degree that has threatened the bottom-up power that they rely on. One of the ways in which international civil society organizations are now trying to regain some of the energy, legitimacy, involvement, and outreach that they so badly need if they are to meet their own expectations is by forming new partnerships. The Beautiful Rising collaboration is an illustrative example of how attempts are being made to do so. With regard to such new partnerships the four following inherent dilemmas of working with unaffiliated activist cadres and social movements were highlighted in a discussion paper drafted by an internal working group presented to the board:

- We need to recognize that many social movements have both radical and long-term goals that cannot be fitted neatly into project cycles, and that 'empowerment' through social movements entails a certain degree of politicization and risk.
- We need to recognize that we (as Action Aid Denmark and Action Aid International) are bound by certain donor requirements that to a certain extent hinders an organizational flexibility, but also that these requirements actually come or are bound by a very specific political agenda.
- While social movements to some extent can be characterized as rhizomatic in 'structure', NGOs tend to be arborescent and hierarchical. This leaves challenges to how we approach and formalize 'partnerships', but also how we define accountability.
- There is also the challenge specifically with AADK in working with social movements that it entails an open discussion with our (potential) supporter base that tend to see development in its traditional sense. (Warburg et al., 2014)

From service delivery to new kinds of partnerships – such a change thus presents a number of these challenges and opportunities to the traditional state donor-financed NGOs in terms of their political status and independence, alternative fund-raising efforts, and organizational flexibility.

Once a year the board goes on a weekend retreat in an isolated location in order to look in depth at a pressing issue. In 2013 we spent a weekend preparing the organization for the hypothetical but not unrealistic scenario that the Danish state would completely shut down its funding to the organization in the not so distant future. These talks are not only instigated due to decreasing funds but also for the way it is given: in my interview with Helle Munk Ravnborg (chairman) on the changing development aid landscape, she says:

> Today, government-to-government development cooperation tends to be shaped through a policy dialogue rather than through a more

context-specific and technical dialogue based on the concrete experiences of poor and marginalized people which previously tended to be more important.

In 2014 Danida (Denmark's development corporation operating under the Ministry of Foreign Affairs) funds covered 59% of Action Aid Denmark's annual account. Income-generating activities covered 22%. Only ten years earlier state funds covered 89% and income-generating activities only 10%. This shows that this organization, like so many others of its type, has begun to look and operate more and more like a social business. The training happening on the Global Platforms, to which Beautiful Rising should be seen as a complement, is a central part of that process – and Action Aid Global Platforms continue to grow fast in terms of numbers:

> When we start to make our own money, yes we become less dependent on state funding, but that also means that we become more dependent on making money. (...) One of the dangers is that the weight will slowly shift from ultimately justifying our work and our approaches with who and how we best help those in need, to how much we earn doing it – a shift from a developmental rationality to an economic one. (Vibeke Vinther, National Director, Action Aid Denmark)

So Action Aid Denmark (AADK) has taken steps towards being more economically self-sufficient. In interviews with board members as well as the leadership team I asked them explicitly about what the implications of such a shift from a traditional state-funded service provider NGO to something that is partly starting to resemble a social business within the international NGO would look like. It is immediately clear that opinions are divided. But they all agree that if things change *too* fast the organization and its members lose sight of who they are and where they are going:

> I see great potential in NGOs influencing companies like food processing companies, medical companies, pension companies, and energy companies in order for them to improve their human rights and environmental behavior. New partnerships may emerge where NGOs and companies test out alternative approaches. It is essential that such partnerships do not compromise the NGOs' independence and right to critical external communication. To do it right we need

to consult the critical consumers, the volunteers, and the frontline workers before doing so. Prior attempts gone bad have taught us so. (Frans Mikael Jansen, Secretary General)

Steen Folke (Board Member and member in Action Aid International) urges caution: "It should never distort our mission. Of course we are more aware of our spending costs today, but we risk simplifying complex matters to make ends meet." Dines Justesen (Vice Chairman) agrees: "There is a risk that we lose the coherence and related synergy between the activities that we do in the organization. (...) Worst case we will lose the people's interest if/when money starts running the show. I fear it might be a slippery slope."

Most of them see the potential, but they are also acutely aware of the risks that it implies. Jakob Kirkemann Boesen (International Director) is likewise open for change but alert to the unknown territory that they are stepping into: "We should explore new collaborations. We have to. But we need to maintain a critical distance when doing so."

One of the driving forces behind growing the entrepreneurial spirit in Action Aid, Peter Christiansen (Regional Director and former International Training Director), has plenty of hope, but reminds us to set the bar high when building on lessons learned:

There are plenty of small-scale examples of how we can make social enterprises work, but we still need to figure out how to upscale them in a way that can really make a difference. We need to be more ambitious and more daring if we are to live up to the full potential of what I am certain a social business within our field can be.

Critique, cooperation, and cooptation

Today it seems obvious that private companies alone cannot meet the challenges that the world faces – and neither can the public institutions nor the civic sector. That is the reason why so many are beginning to collaborate across the three classical sectors and develop a fourth characterized by companies, institutions, organization, and looser networks combining the best from the former – economic efficiency and customer service from the private sector, a focus on the common good from the public sector, and purpose-driven diversity in the organizational culture from the voluntary sector.

Significantly on the relationship between critique, cooperation, and cooptation with regard to the challenges of a new kind of professionalization of training, creative activism is at risk of becoming a one size fits all merchandise and of being coopted by systemic, corporate, or organizational interests, thereby losing its critical edge. On the other hand, this tendency might be the greatest political opportunity in the history of progressive politics to test new ideas and stimulate social innovation. The world is in too dire straits not to take a leap of faith. Whether it is the local municipality's facilitated inclusion of active citizens, social enterprises, or traditional civil society organizations seeking new partnerships, creative activists are in high demand because they have the credibility, the social capital, and the creative toolbox necessary to open up new territory, build new alliances, and constructively challenge and improve experimental approaches tested by more established agents flirting with the public movement of everyday makers. In so doing it is crucial for the integrity of creative activism that its artistic discursive autonomy is maintained in the open interplay with mainstream politics.

8
The Gordian Knot – Measuring Effect and Revisiting Theories of Change

Most critical journalists and skeptical politicians – and probably the majority of citizens too – ask the same question when it comes to social movements, and especially the creative actions that play a particular role for these and that are dealt with here: do they actually make a difference? And many activists ask themselves the same thing: how do we know when what we are doing is successful?

Oddly, there is a lack of work on how artistic activists think about the social and/or political efficacy of their work. Implicitly the question has been dealt with throughout the book, but in this final chapter we will address it more directly, along with the overall question that scholars within this field are always faced with, but never really dare to tackle: how do we come to grips with the democratic value of activist interventions?

In this chapter we will discuss why we need to develop new and better ways to measure the impact and value of alternative civic engagement, why this exercise is so difficult, and how we might begin to do so despite these difficulties. Finally, this chapter points to the necessity of rethinking and reorganizing existing theories of change.

So the aim with this last chapter is to discuss why it is so difficult to measure the impact of creative activism and especially temporary spectacular happenings with no tangible goal, but also try and demonstrate how we can begin to quantify these matters and thus qualify the democratic value of the agents and practices in question.

When exploring patterns of participation, the breadth of democratic movements, the openness of the political system, the perceived efficacy of participation, and the possibility of political change are all factors to be considered (Stoker et al., 2011).

But to make sense of the work that creative activists do, they have to operate with a more or less conscious theory of change that will justify their means and help them strengthen their strategic apparatus. To see the value of the role that these change agents play in our society, we as spectators and participants can also benefit from having an idea of how what they do make sense and make a difference. The problem is that we don't really. Hopefully this book has up until now partly functioned as a way to clarify this issue by explaining the activists' facilitating role, seeing them as disruptors, tricksters posing inconvenient questions, and triggers of actions and reflection through the metaphorical mirrors they set up around us. It is a practice intimately linked with the epistemic regime it seeks to challenge. Behind all these different images and explanations lies a cloudy theory of change that valorizes agonistic models of deliberation, open-ended questions, and the revolutionary moment where the necessary or commonsensical is challenged. Here I will try to be more quantifiable by identifying evaluative parameters and possible methodologies that can measure the impact that the activism in question does or does not have.

The evaluating culture

Today we live in a world where there is a steady increase in demands to monitor, document, and evaluate oneself and each other. For better and worse the school teacher has to fill out forms that she didn't forty years ago, the social worker is forced to follow an Excel sheet when she visits the elderly instead of weighing the individual needs in a given situation, and performance management systems have become standard operating tools for private and public consultants alike – the development organizations, as we have just learned, have them too. Some sociologists (e.g. Sennett, 2000; Østergaard & Willig, 2005) have pointed out how this development can be seen as part of the explanation for the boom in social pathologies such as stress, anxiety, and depression. The exercise of weighing out what is lost at the price of what is gained is not for me to make here, but a reasonable question is whether and why we need to turn up the demands for volunteers and activists to document the value of their work.

The main argument is that since we are doing so anyway, why not do it better? Today civic activist organizations primarily measure number of members, flyers handed out or money raised for a given course. These are output (not outcome) indicators. While those variables are certainly important, they do not, I claim, capture all of what is at stake for the actors and audiences, contractors and donors. We need a more appropriate approach – because one's aim is better when you know what you are shooting for. State institutions, private foundations, philanthropists, and private donors increasingly demand that organizations produce proof of their relevance and the impact they have on society at large. When it comes to projects in civil society that in one way or another are political, we need to measure a set of parameters and indicators that capture *all* of the things that such activities are about, since value cannot *only* be measured in currency and econometrics.

As I will list further below, there are many good reasons why one would refrain from measuring the causal mechanisms that link one action to a certain change of heart down the road. But there are demands that we need to comply with, measurement practices that we need to challenge and improve, and creative design and implementation habits that can be sharpened earlier in and throughout the planning and implementation process by thinking systematically about why we are doing what we are doing, to what end, and by which means. We also need to consider by which standards and indicators we wish to be evaluated. Instead of being busy pushing evaluation protocols away, we should take control of them and make them fit our own needs and practices. That is the progressive response to conformity.

There is no doubt that SWAT teams better their operations by debriefings, consultants sharpen their customer-suited service through feedback, and organizations become more efficient when monitoring their efforts and impact. So why shouldn't activists do the same by testing techniques and interventions in a more systematic manner? What is important to keep in mind here is that it needs to be done in a way that doesn't undermine the autonomy and professional integrity of the employee or social entrepreneur in question. Trust and self-initiative is key when striking a reasonable, productive, and sustainable balance between efficiency, creative and strategic development (often based on a trial and error approach), and the ideological integrity that is the cornerstone of every activist's endeavor.

But why is this exercise so difficult? The answers to this question are many and have been dealt with at length in many other places, as they are the reasons people need not to embark on the journey of actually proving that they make a difference. I will therefore keep it brief and boil them down to aspects to be aware of when trying to do so anyway.

When Scottish independence activist Robin McAlpine was asked why he and his movement didn't win the referendum in 2014, he replied:

Depends on how you define victory and when you choose to measure it. We lost the election, yes, but three years ago the idea that we introduced was laughed upon; today we have half the population with us. (...) For twenty years I myself have ridiculed the effect a movement of butterflies might have on an Empire. Today I see that I was wrong – and I feel good not even knowing whether I am even right standing here today.

With that Robin smiled out to the rest of us in the room, grabbed a flower from the audience, stuck it behind his ear and sat down, the crowd cheerfully thundering his humble engagement.

If one is active during a presidential election, one might measure one's success based on whether one is elected or not. Such success criteria make sense – but it is still difficult to measure what role your specific campaign events played. When we talk about long-term effects of social movements the success criteria are rarely as simple and not always clear (e.g. Occupy Wall Street, OWS). Sometimes they have too many (e.g. the alter-globalization movements), and often they change over time (e.g. the feminist movement). Even when politicians deem them successful they may not think that they are. All of which makes success difficult to measure.

As with all matters of measurement, it is paramount what we measure, how we measure, and when we choose to measure. It is one thing to measure success based on certain criteria set up by the activists themselves or others. It is another is to measure the relative effectiveness of particular strategies. The latter demands comparative analyses and is a complicated matter given the vast variations in political environment, set of actors, culture, types of resistance, etc. It is also a well-known problem in sociological measuring of any kind that cause and effect can be hard to separate. Movements often spring from historical developments that also point towards the solution of the problem that a movement has mobilized to solve. The period that led to the American Civil Rights Movement, for example, also in some ways led to the eventual improvement in the lives of millions of black and brown people in America through improved social awareness, legislative reforms, etc. – a development that cannot (entirely) be attributed to the movement. As explained earlier, their success largely depended on recognizing, exploiting, expanding, and exploring the cracks in the system as a result of structural trends. So one might ask: would the black community have gained equal civil rights without the movement? Maybe it would 'just' have taken longer.

A central challenge here is thus to prove the causality between a given action, campaign, or movement and a certain change in behavior. To be able to talk about causality (in a more simplistic positivist sense) we need to meet four basic criteria (Andersen, Hansen, & Klemmesen, 2012, p. 104).

Firstly, there needs to be a connected variation between X and Y variables, here meaning a given protest and its effects. In the case of the Danish Mohammed cartoon crisis, Lindekilde, Mouritsen, and Zapata-Barrero (2009, p. 163) were for example able to prove such connected variation between the way Muslim actors communicated the drawings and the coverage and impact this had in the media.

Secondly, causality demands a plausible timeline, meaning that the cause must come before the effect. When kidney donations suddenly exploded throughout Europe in the summer of 2007 it did so exactly after (not before) The Big (fake activist stunt) Donor Show had aired.

Thirdly, causality in this context also requires that we check for third variables. In other words, we need to be able to rule out (or minimize the importance of) other factors than the ones we are concerned about that might produce or influence the observed outcome. Comparative studies are one way of doing this. Experimental design methods including control groups are another. Control for third variables is about ruling out competing explanations in effect studies so that one avoids so-called spurious correlations. Entirely ruling out other factors than the narrow ones that one's analysis might be focusing on, however, runs the risk of simplifying matters to a degree where the complex dynamics of multiple causality of real-life change are lost. So this becomes a question about how high and narrow are the standards for knowledge we require of others and ourselves. Contextual epistemology (Hendricks, 2008) allows us to explicitly and deliberate adjust the criteria for and modify our ambitions about when something can said to be proven and certain or agreeable knowledge.

Fourth and finally, causality demands a plausible theoretical explanation of the patterns we may identify. Say studies show that provocative actions made at the beginning of the month seem to create more activity in the social media than actions made later in the monthly cycle. If we could not explain this pattern in any meaningful way we probably need to reject the claim of causality or come up with a new theory to support such claims.

These challenges all demand certain things of our research designs when we study activism, social movements, and civic engagement in more general terms, including data collection, case selection, and theoretically informed analytical strategy. The new evaluative culture also demands that activists themselves are more conscious about what they do, why they do it, and how others experience it.

Key variables

Social movements come in all shapes and sizes. Some explicitly try to influence policy. These are often labeled political movements. Cultural movements are more occupied with changing the way we think, communicate, and live our lives. The former often have a more direct and measurable objective, whereas the latter have a more indirect long-term impact on our society – and are in that sense of course also political. As explained in earlier chapters, most movements are neither one nor the other. They are both.

I have been investigating the effect that activists are seeking, directly and indirectly, instantly and in the long run. But primarily, creative activists have the ability to create an interest and get people thinking – what I have coined as *the mirror effect* – and therefore have a closer affinity to the cultural than the directly political elements of a social movement.

Art works when it 'moves' us – aesthetically, emotionally, and sometimes even physically. Artists express themselves to generate *affect*. Political activism also moves us. Activists take action that is meant to have an *effect*. Creative artistic activism can be said to be a combination of the two, which is why the *affective effect* or the *effective affect* (Duncombe & Lambert, 2016) is of special interest when making sense of this practice and its *raison d'être*. In a study of the ritualized politics of transformation in the Kiev uprisings Georgsen and Thomassen (2015) display how their informants emphasize that they themselves feel forever changed as they were *marked* by the drama of the events, and conclude that

> effective change *is* affective change. The ritual and mythical activities that unfold in the liminal are even beyond the subject–object divide. It is reality itself, which is in play; subjects, objects and their interrelationship. Thus the analysis of political transformation must engage the level of ontology.

The question then becomes how this should influence the way we ascribe meaning, value, and measure this kind of civic engagement. In kindred worlds we have fairly good metrics: commercial and institutional success for mainstream art, sales for marketing, and the voting population and elected candidates in electoral politics. Some of these can be quantified, some allow for control groups. We need to develop an independent metrics for success appropriate to the practice of creative activism. I will suggest a couple of ways to do so, which leads me to develop key evaluative categories.

As I previously pointed out, there is obviously a difference between measuring whether you are successful in saving a community garden or creating a democratic laboratory, and evaluating more profound and far less apprehensible indicators like shifts in language and consciousness, but we need to find the linkages between short-term and long-term, effect and affect, and material and ideological change.

Furthermore, maybe the most devastating argument against trying to come up with new and better measurement tools for questioning and/ or justifying the impact and relevance of creative activism in particular is that creative activists do not often even themselves (deliberately) know what they want or where exactly they are going. Which of course makes it very difficult to test whether they have achieved their goals – as they have none (officially anyway). This is why dimensions of process and intention are so important to include.

Key variables to consider[1] when categorizing, measuring, and analyzing the efficacy of new types of civic engagement are important to establish and include a temporal and an instrumental dimension (Table 8.1).

Whether the listed outcomes and impacts are educating activists, raising funds, winning an election, or raising public awareness, they have to do with the next couple of parameters that I will discuss. But, for now, let's try and see how the use of these variables condition the evaluation of Greenpeace's action on the Queen's red carpet during the COP15 climate summit in Copenhagen and start to think about how such an intervention might move the social.

Table 8.1 Key variables of time and intention

Evaluating variables	Short-term	Long-term
Intended	*Outcomes*	*Impact*
Unintended	*Consequences*	*Influence*

Copenhagen is bubbling with life. The streets are full of citizens, both with hope and in despair. Heads of states from around the world, NGO representatives, and business lobbyists have gathered to discuss climate change and what we as a global community can and will do about the challenges ahead. Journalists from all the major networks are circling for a festive feeding frenzy.

It is December 17, 2009, and the official COP15 climate summit meeting negotiations are now on hold as everyone high on the social ladder is going to have dinner with the Queen of Denmark. The politicians have not made much progress, and the Danish Prime Minister Lars Løkke Rasmussen has been "banging" on tiresomely as chairman. Just before Hillary Clinton is about to arrive on the red carpet, an unknown aristocratic-looking husband and wife enter the castle. They have passed two police security screenings to get here with their Bentley chauffeur. As they step through that ten seconds window and onto the red carpet where you have the attention of the whole world, they both take off their scarf and unfold it into a one-meter yellow banner with the words "Politicians talk – Leaders act." Each of them holds the statement up in front of them as they continue to march into the castle with cameras rolling.

It only takes seconds, of course, for security to grab them and drag them away. But they still managed to intervene in, disturb, and redefine an agenda mostly preoccupied with starters and dinner gowns. The world was disturbed. Viewers were watching a well-orchestrated gala event receiving random information about what the menu was and what people were wearing. Suddenly an abruption reminded them that outside the palace an alternative summit, consisting of all the people not invited to the official one (thousands of them sleeping in private Danish homes thanks to the Wooloo organizers), was questioning the very premise for the celebration – that politicians were showing leadership.

Now let's take a moment to remind ourselves what kind of action this can be classified as. Using the typology of activism developed earlier, this action qualifies as a confrontational intervention. Bearing witness in the way that these agents of civil disobedience are doing leads to an accentuation of the emotional intensity of participation – which is closely linked to the confrontational activists' emphasis on individual sacrifice as a civic duty. Operating with a *logic of disclosure* can be said to be the strategic reasoning behind this protest, as their most important purpose might have been to reveal the summit's true democratic colors by sacrificing themselves to what they see as its abuse. What they want is more open procedures. The action is creative in the sense that it tricks the system, takes the spectator by surprise, and reframes an issue by hijacking an event.

It is also important to stress, yet again, that one type of activism is not necessarily better than another. We need lobbyists to groom the decision makers, and we need boots on the ground to channel the people's raw commitment. Some are critical, some cooperate with the formal institutions, and some fully opt into the official circus. All principled approaches however need a creative tactical spin to break through the noise. An 'everyday maker' can for example apply a tricky lobbyist approach, and a demonstration aimed at mobilizing as many people as possible can apply creative tactics etc.

On May 16, 2012, thousands of bicycling activists ended their campaign "Tour de Future" in front of the Danish Parliament Christiansborg in Copenhagen. Some had cycled from the far end of the country to get there. The locals had joined the tour on the final route through the city. I was one of them. In the square bands were playing, everywhere people dressed as Robin Hood were advocating lower taxes, campaigners were handing out flyers, and rallying speeches of course were thundering from center stage. When the Danish Minister of Development Christian Friis Bach spoke to the crowd he referred to a conversation he had just had with one of the former chief ambassadors of the renowned 1992 Earth Summit in Rio twenty years earlier. Preparing for the upcoming climate summit in Rio the minister had asked the ambassador what he thought was the most important thing to do to ensure that real decisions were also made at this summit. The answer was clear: an active civil society full of active citizens who lead by example and who can put pressure on the politicians to take things seriously. That was what the four red carpet activists (as they have become known) tried to do three and a half years before. But how can they be said to have had an effect?

The activists' short-term goal was to get a lot of attention and raise awareness of the widespread democratic frustration and climate-related anxiety in the global public. This intention was met immediately. To measure it you need only to register how many media outlets ran the story, in how many countries, and for how long. A comprehensive investigation would also include activity on social media. To qualify the quantitative record one would have to look into how the event was framed and how it was received. This is when it becomes tricky. The short-term goal was not to raise awareness because the four activists were exhibitionists. The immediate awareness-raising also had a long-term perspective in terms of changing people's viewpoint on the democratic nature and political value of such summits – and subsequently their daily habits and political support patterns. Maybe even causing a few to take action themselves. In that sense the red carpet activists were not holding up yellow scarf banners, they were holding up mirrors.

Internally the action was a way for Greenpeace to test new campaign tactics that push the boundaries for what is possible and in that way develop their own and other's critical repertoire of contention. To quote Art Tinnitus from the Beautiful Trouble team, "Instead of an all-out assault on the castle, the prankster slips through the gate wearing a fool's outfit." Creative activists often reveal those in power without taking on the armored guards head on. As discussed in the previous chapter, the education of future activists is an essential part of the theory of change of many organizations' internal long-term strategy.

One of the unintended consequences of this particular action, my communication with investigating journalists has shown, was an immediate decline in membership as some of the existing elder members of Greenpeace thought the action was going too far in sabotaging a royal event and opted out. New members have later joined, so the action in that sense altered the member profile – and therefore also Greenpeace, one could argue. The four red carpet Greenpeace activists – Nora, Juanxto, Christian, and Joris – were arrested on the red carpet and detained for twenty days before their release. And the summit failed to deliver an ambitious and binding deal with the Copenhagen Accord.

Regarding the long-term impact of such happenings and protests, then, who is to say *when* something can be deemed a success or a failure? What we proclaim as either a success or a failure often depends on the time span that we operate with. COP15 was not seen as a success. But in 2015 a very ambitious sustainable development agreement was made between the 193 UN members to fight hunger, extreme poverty, and climate problems. The global plan now commits *all* countries, and the United States is (finally) taking the (necessary) strategic lead. This shift in commitment is about shifting the spectrum of allies. Rarely is a political fight won by overpowering the active opposition, but by shifting the support out from under them. This has taken visionary politicians, an aligned field of global climate researchers, an increasingly proactive business community, *and* a critical activist environment challenging and collaborating with all of these.

In one of the interviews that I conducted with Nancy Fraser she reflects on why we need a long-term perspective on social struggles before we deem them meaningless or useless:

> Walter Benjamin and Hannah Arendt had this sort of idea of crystals that get deposited in history. Sometimes these are the ideas of the loser, but they can be very powerful ideas, and fifty years later someone else might come along and the crystals get dug up and reactivated. The

idea of racial equality has been a losing idea for much of our history, but it's been planted there by slave revolts, which failed in terms of normal criteria of success. But these revolts have somehow left something for future generations. These are ideas that sometimes come, you might say, too early to succeed. Nevertheless they can inspire people later on who do something new with the idea in a new context. So 'good activism' is not just the obvious successes. It is also the patient changing of attitudes over time. (Fraser, in interview with Harrebye)

In line with my previous definition of critique, based on its relevance for the object of my analysis, the success of the activities analyzed in this book depends to a large extent on their ability to gain attention, communicate conflicts and/or solutions when and where no one else can or will, and provoke a change in daily practices and ways of thinking. In short, to formulate a critique that is heard and sinks in – sooner or later. An action that may at first seem fruitless may turn out to be a crystal for later generations' political art collectors and campaign inspirers. Artistic activist Steve Lambert, speaking at a workshop on the efficacy of creative activism in New York, calls for double standards:

You should aim for the stars. But you are always gonna fall short. So when we fail we can tell ourselves, well I didn't turn the world into Utopia, but we did do this and we laid the groundwork for the things that come next – because its a long ongoing process.

Other key variables to consider when categorizing, measuring, and analyzing the efficacy of such interventions include an organizational dimension (as I have already touched upon), and one that has to do with what counts as effect and affect and whether and when it makes sense to focus on particular politically set goals or the process that is meant to get you there (Table 8.2).

Table 8.2 Key variables of space and politics

Evaluating variables	Internal	External
Material (political)	e.g. funds or members	e.g. reforms or election
Ideological (cultural)	e.g. educating activists and developing repertoire; or the unintended, e.g. fragmentation and radicalization	e.g. changing discourse and breaking down prejudices; or the unintended, e.g. repression and counter movement

If we consider the external outcomes and impact of the material political dimension then one might (as Gamson, 1975) differ between gaining a new-won accept in the form of recognition and status, and new gained advantages such as concrete admissions or institutional change. A movement can receive full response, a preventive reaction, or be coopted, as is the case with women movements in a number of Muslim countries where the authorities have accepted the work for women's rights but where no real admittances have been given (Mohmood, 2005). Many one-time actions never get noticed and several more or less known movements collapse.

The ideological dimension, which covers what one might also call the cultural consequences (Giugni, 2008) of an intervention, campaign, or movement, includes new lifestyles, symbols, norms, frames, and counterculture. Consider the hippie movement, for example. Hippies are not least known for their experiments with new collective ways of living together, fashion, music, and attitudes – all of which link up to more or less conscious values and strategies that ultimately promoted a free and experimental lifestyle that for better (and sometimes for worse) has shaped society today. I therefore differentiate between immediate effects in opinion shifts or concrete policy or election results and more long-term impacts on our way of life through a change in habits and ways of navigating in the world – in that way the mirror counter-strategies in late modern capitalism are one way of redistributing the sensible.

If we therefore think back to the mirroring metaphor applied earlier and then consider the development in the justice claim of many movement activists, from redistribution to recognition and representation to reflection, it becomes clear that in many instances it is now more appropriate to measure activists' ability to impact culture and conduct rather than law and letters. When evaluating the success of the Civil Rights Movement we evaluate whether their demands were met. They were. Today all Americans regardless of their color have the same legal rights. But the uprisings before and after the shooting in Ferguson, Missouri in November 2014 were concerned not with the rights of Michael Brown but with the racism that still seems to infest the American police corps and juridical system. The push from below along with reports verifying racism in the police forced the Chief of Police to resign and the politicians to intervene. To measure the impact of the new generation of activists involved in and around the shootings that currently plague the country one would have to look not so much on whether new rights are given, but more on how these are protected and implemented in a culture where race is so neatly interwoven into the very fabric of culture. As pointed out at the beginning, quoting an anonymous creative activist, "you cannot legislate away child abuse or sexism. You have to change the hearts and minds of people." Creative activism is one way of bringing about such change.

With regard to the internal investment, many activities have a more or less explicit parallel purpose where it is not only about, say, passing a sexual harassment act that is up for review or changing the way we talk to our affected family, friends, or colleagues about such incidents; but also about fundraising and member recruitment, and training new activists, keeping momentum, and developing the organization. If there is no focus on the internal development of an organization, big or small, formal or informal, activists will burn out and the movement cannot be sustained. In some (e.g. New Age) movements the biographical development is actually not the secondary focus and instrumental necessity but the main purpose of their activities (e.g. Heelas, 1996). Recognizing that time is not ripe for change, some sharpen their tools for later or future generations. As Brazilian popular educator Paulo Freire asked, "What can we do today, so that tomorrow we can do what we are unable to do today?"

Many of the theories of social movements that we have touched upon previously relate to the question of what determines outcomes and consequences of political protest internally and externally. Resource mobilization theory focuses on the importance of internal resources; theories of political opportunity structures stress the significance of the external context; framing theory looks at how communication strategy enables understanding and mobilization; and theories of values and norms approach and explain the effect of movements as something that is shaped by a movement's ability to relate to central societal values, develop identities, and in different ways appeal to emotions in the political struggle. These factors need to be weighed differently from case to case, but most often internal factors such as resources, organization, and framing are mediated by external factors such as political opportunity structures, media coverage, and public opinion. The causal dynamics are complex.

Neighborhood Moms (Bydelsmødre) is a network of 350 groups of women in Denmark who together speak a total of more than 50 languages and who are dedicated to helping 'sisters in need get back on their feet.' In November 2014 they won the Livia award for their courageous work. When they won, fifteen beautiful women of all colors and ethnicities came on stage, many of them wearing Muslim scarfs. A young woman, Madam President of the union, stepped up to receive the honor and to thank the committee. When she was to explain to the crowd in front of her what kind of work they did and how it mattered, she did so with an anecdote. "I don't know how else to explain how what we do matters," she said. She told the story of a woman who was alarmed by the continuous noise and trouble she heard in the neighboring apartment. She didn't dare take action herself and didn't know what else to do, so she called Neighborhood Moms. Her call was answered and one of the union's mothers went to knock on the door. When she did the door opened, and a little frightened woman with three crying kids in the background looked out from a condemned apartment. The first thing she said was, "can you help me?" A husband traumatized by war had left the family a couple of days earlier. The woman got help. With the assistance of the stranger knocking on the door she got in contact with the authorities, the children started in school, the mother got a job, they all acquired friends and a network, she eventually learned Danish and now she is getting an education.

As the young woman on stage was telling the story, an older one far to her left on stage had tears rolling down her cheeks. I am guessing she was one of the women in that story. Which one I don't know. When I approached the young woman who received the award after the official ceremony, I asked why she felt the need to excuse the anecdote as a way to convey the impact these women have on other women's lives. She said she knew how much quantifiable measurements means for sponsors and donors, which was also why the international consultancy firm Deloitte was now about to help them make a systematic evaluation of the impact of the work that they did. I still don't know whether I think this is good or bad news. It is not surprising. A dilemma for new social actors is how to deal with the call for boldness and inventive innovation on one hand and the demand to predict the outcome of their activities and document their effect on the other – two types of practices that seemingly undermine each other. Or do they?

Let us take a closer look at another example and briefly attempt to apply relevant variables when we deem those actions successful or not. Much has been written about the political legitimacy of Occupy Wall Street (OWS) and its contested impact on all of us. David Graeber and Barbara Epstein both more or less implicitly operate with the dichotomy between verticalists and horizontalists – although with reverse political intentions. Critics argue that OWS is a fundamentally 'anarchistic' movement without any realistic perspective on social change. The movement's "insistence upon egalitarianism, its suspicion of the state and aversion to mainstream institutions and culture, and its emphasis on the creation of alternative communities, intended to be, as far as possible, beyond the reach of the state and mainstream society" (Epstein, 2013, p. 66). As Jan Rehmann (2013) convincingly argues, this view is based on an undialectical opposition between 'resistance' and 'social change,' according to which the former "calls for drama, performance, spectacle," whereas the latter "calls for thinking about how to get from where we are to the society that we want" (Epstein, 2013, p. 81). But this dichotomy misses the strategic importance of a revolutionary Realpolitik (cf. Rosa Luxemburg) designed to mediate the contradictions between short-term and long-term goals, reform and revolution, parliamentary and extra-parliamentary practices. A Gramscian analysis of OWS is not obvious since the movement is said to have been leaderless and did not channel its energy into an actual political party or network that was able to consolidate temporary achievements. But understanding how the movement created a counter-hegemony through symbolic acts of reappropriation of the commons, the creation of new forms of democratic participation, and slogans that captured the people's imagination is needed to grasp its relevance. Up until mid-September 2011 the Tea Party movement was the only vibrant and expanding social movement in the US. One month later the hegemonic landscape had changed considerably after interventions into the symbolic order. According to a poll of late October 2011, 43% of US citizens agreed with the views of the OWS movement, compared to an approval rate of 9% for Congress at the time (Rehmann, 2013, p. 10). The question remains whether the sympathies had changed or just found representation. Politics should not be reduced to electoral politics, but neither should activism be afraid to consider how their efforts might play into a coherent organizational strategy. If OWS wasn't afraid it was hesitant.

Where The Battle in Seattle was aggressive, OWS was peaceful. Despite the motto that "Another world is possible," the activists in Seattle did very little to showcase the wonders of this new world. They demonstrated against the summit, but failed to demonstrate what a different world might look like. The OWS motto was "This is what democracy looks like." Trying to honor their motto community-based initiatives were taken – the general assembly, the people's microphone, the barber, the open education, the community kitchen, and the library. These things did not serve any real purpose (the general assembly was an ineffective nightmare and people stole the books in the library), but they did have an important symbolic one – as pre-figurative politics, acting out and experimenting with ideals of democratic public life, small town meetings, etc. – and in that way functioned as proposing mirrors for the public imagination to reflect itself in.

Hence when looking back at what we have been through, the typology of activism that we have developed might help us remember to consider and clarify the different types of activists' goals when we are to evaluate their relevance and effectiveness. Both because they should be measured according to the goals that they set for themselves, but also because each contributes to our society with voices that are valuable and/or precarious in so very different ways. Because even though activists' relation to such analytical typologies is like birds' relation to ornithologists, meaning that neither cares much about the human need to label and categorize, birds do move freely despite whereas activists today cannot help hearing about how the world perceives them and are increasingly utilizing or actively challenging such preconceptions in their practice and goal setting.

The OWS-related network is vast. A systematic mapping of how central coordinating activists continue their work now behind closed doors and in open arenas is missing, but there is no doubt that the internal education of active citizens is considered a success within their own ranks. Think of spin-offs such as Occupy the Hood, The 99% Spring, Occupy Sandy, etc. (movementnetlab.org).

Now OWS may have altered the public discourse but not the structure of the economy or the state – nor the inner composition of the hegemonic apparatus. Some argue that this needs the courage of taking on the responsibility to translate the protest into tangible development projects and convincing policy platforms. But today, some argue, there seems to be a general distrust in some activist environments when it comes to anything that starts to resemble the power needed to make change happen and sustain it on a larger scale:

> This is an obvious but unspoken cultural difference between modern youth protest movements and those of the past. (...) Anybody who sounds like a career politician, anybody who attempts to use rhetoric, or espouses an ideology, is greeted with visceral distaste. (Mason, 2012, p. 45)

This is part of the reason why pessimists like Ivan Krastev (2014) see protests as an insurrection against the very institutions of representative democracy, but without offering any alternatives within the democratic system or openness to non-democratic alternatives. Google's Eric Schmidt predicts that "the future will be full of revolutionary moments" but short of "revolutionary outcomes" (Schmidt & Cohen, 2013).

Experimental design

Now let us take a brief look at what one might consider when designing a new kind of impact study. We will look at examples of how one can construct them in ways that take into consideration new types of civic engagement using mass internet data, quasi-experimental designs, and getting self-identified creative activists themselves to, in their own words, clarify what they want and expect (e.g. raising awareness, fostering dialogue, exposing power, creating and reinforcing communities, reimagining the possible, creating a new language, etc.).[2] The aim here is not to present a final design, but rather some possible routes of inquiry and in a preliminary way flesh out some ways of exploring them.

New forms of civic engagement have been criticized for political ineffectiveness compared with more conventional forms. Not least the online part of it. In a broader popular context Gladwell (2010) points out that activism through social media does not produce the structure that is needed to mobilize effectively. The argument is that social networks like Twitter and Facebook involve weak ties rather than strong ties (Granovetter, 1973), and that the weak ties do not lead to high-risk activism and/or participation that is also able to play constructively into the more established polity. The KONY 2012 campaign has been used as a case in point. In line with this type of argument, Van Deth (e.g. 2013) argues that newer forms of online engagement do not provide sufficient links between citizens and the political system. Other scholars disagree with the assumption that new forms of engagement are ineffective (Shirky, 2008; Bennett & Segerberg 2013; Gerbaudo, 2012; González-Bailón, S., Borge-Holthoefer, J. & Moreno, 2013). They claim, as I also did earlier, that the horizontal nature of online community-building strengthens necessary networks over time in a way that supplements other and more 'grounded' types of participation.

Much critique of these studies of new forms of political activism has focused on the dominant use of case studies, which cannot be generalized. To develop new and more meaningful approaches, future projects aimed at measuring the effect of new types of civic engagement in general and creative types of activism in particular should: (1) explore activists' own perceptions of success and the means used to achieve them, (2) map citizens' attitudes and opinion towards different kinds of civic engagement, and (3) test over time the affective effect of different forms of activism – both in terms of generated virtual and real-life activity of a certain sort – and change understood according to the four key variables identified.

The *methodological* aim of such undertakings should be to develop new evaluation criteria for organizations in the field and new research methods for scholars that work with the social and political impact of new forms of civic engagement. The *theoretical* aim should be to develop new models for understanding the impact of these, which combine classical theory on social movements and contentious politics with political theory of efficiency and new theory about social media, social networks, and aesthetics. The *practical* aim should be to develop new tools, strategies, and tactics for creative activists and their collaborators.

Step one of such an undertaking should primarily have an explorative and qualitative character, and consists of three layers and approaches.

Firstly, an analysis that can map out organizations' existing theories of change and planning, monitoring, and evaluation (PME) mechanisms must be conducted in order to determine how groups and organizations in the field, as institutions themselves, perceive and measure change.

Secondly, interviewing key staff and participants would be valuable – by asking questions such as "what does success look like to you?" and "why do you do what you do?" in order to develop new categories and concepts for the collection and analysis of data. This includes an analysis of how they themselves perceive and measure change. Interviewing Ève Chiapello about the difference between social and artistic forms of critique she is, not surprisingly so, critical and requests such an inquiry: "You have a lot of movements who are using art to question capitalism, but what are they asking for? We should interview them to know what they are looking for." Deva Woodly is one of those who has done so (although primarily talking to more traditional union activists and campaigners), and her data also supports a more and a more focused inquiry into this part of the activists' work: "When talking to actual activists in the different movements they had rather different perspectives on how these things ought to be done – and what counted as a win." Interviewing an activist about designing, implementing, and promoting new (unauthorized) bike lanes in Katmandu, Nepal, and asking her about the result, she highlighted the attention the campaign had gotten in the media. Make sense if you want to inspire public debate and influence policy makers. But when drilling her about it, I was surprised to find that they never bothered to measure whether their efforts had any effect on the daily number of cyclists, their end goal being exactly that.

Thirdly, ethnographic participatory observations – taking part in actions, training, and campaign meetings – would make it possible to compare organizational set-ups, individual perceptions, and actual practice. These three qualitative approaches can be used with different weight and adjusted according to the cultural and political context and cases that they are applied to.

Step two, focus on the population's attitudes and opinions towards different kinds of activists, might use factorial surveys (e.g. horizontal vignette), which allow the researchers to manipulate different stimuli that are supposed to have an impact on the attitudes and perceived effectiveness of different activist interventions. In this quasi-experimental design it is possible to study the formations of attitudes experimentally using clearly defined respondents and control groups. To analyze how different kinds of creative activism influence peoples' beliefs and habits controlled experiments where two groups of people are presented with a story or a video about activists that try to achieve the same political goal but with different political means, or better yet unaware exposed to and involved in an intervention, are needed to subsequently get their immediate reactions and follow their habits and behavior down the line. The controlled experiments could also include staged happenings on the street, covert organizational interventions, and popular but particularly targeted campaigns.

Step three focuses on the impact of concrete forms of interventions in terms of information exchange, opinion shifts, and concrete political change measured by different data sources. The categories deducted from step one and the patterns emerging from step two should influence the final design of step three, but in order to measure activity on the social media data, from Twitter, Google, and Facebook should be examined more systematically and independently than is the case today (e.g. medialab. sciences-po.fr and smapp.nyu.edu[3]). With the development of computer technology and digital data, "every day new public and private archives are swallowed by computers' memories, economic transactions migrate online, social networks root in the Web and the more this happens, the more traces become available on the collective dynamics that used to be hidden by the quali-quantitative divide" (Latour et al., 2012). One of the advantages of internet data is that it gives access to time-series datasets with a huge number of individuals. Internet data gives the opportunity to observe the dynamic effects and causal mechanism that shape political participation. By connecting existing internet data with own surveys one will be able to analyze the relationship between online activism and offline civic engagement. This will also enable clearer analyses of whether and how the increasing use of social media enhances active participation or if 'clicktivism' becomes 'slacktivism' and creates apathy.

These are just a few ideas about what a new civic assessment initiative might include. The aim here is not to present a final model, but to introduce elements of what such a model would need to take into consideration: the activists' perspective, the activities a given intervention creates, and the affective effect this has on the individual participant or spectator – from awareness and contemplation to recall and action, to consolidation of new beliefs and habits. The long-term political–material impacts need historical comparative studies, as we know them. But there is plenty of room for inventive methodological approaches here. In fact the main purpose of new leads in this area should be to allow for such experiments.

Rethinking existing theories of change

The last part of this chapter, and this book, points to the necessity of rethinking and reorganizing existing theories of change – these considerations follow naturally from the arguments made above.

In the 19th century change was explained through elaborate theories focused on the impact of evolution, the advance of reason, the corrosion of character, technology, and class struggle – along with simplistic tendencies to ascribe change to either visionary individuals, crowd psychology, or national will.

All efforts to define an overarching grand unifying theory of change trying to synthesize the insights of particular fields fail because of a common misconception: although all aspects of social life are connected, no single theory can explain the change-driven dynamics of phenomena as diverse as family life, urban development, employer and employee relations, identity shift, pragmatic politics, and principled ideology – unless it is very broad and saying very little.

Accordingly, many different theories can be read as explanations of how change takes place, but few theories deal with change processes directly as such – not, say, how spouses deal with losing their loved ones, but how that loss changes them; not how mergers impact on an organization, but how the change itself affects the employees and the plausibility of a successful merger; not what conditions allow for revolutions to take place, but how these are expressions of change.

However, there are a few things that we can do when it comes to understanding the inner dynamics of fundamental change processes – where and when they take place. One of them is to point to some shared features of major societal transformations as, say, the liminal character of revolutions, the acceleration of mediatization, the paradoxically local stimulus of globalization, etc.

Another is to point to some common themes when designing, testing, and analyzing change, e.g. the role of barriers in galvanizing change, turning personal resentment into social forces, the role of knowledge and ideas, the enabling role of resources, structural conditions, and political opportunities. In an implementation process these things factor in, from the generation of ideas, through prototyping and piloting, to scaling up, learning, and adjustment. The body of social movement literature can be viewed as an example of how this has been done within the context of creating social and political change from below.

Finally, which has not yet really been done, it would be fruitful to compare theories of change on the individual, the organizational, and the overall political level. I have done this with my students through a couple of courses over some years now, identifying differences and similarities between theories as diverse as Inglehart and Welzel's data-heavy Human Development Sequence, organizational complexity theory, and Gladwell's popular Tipping Point.

Overall we can differentiate (at least in theory) between two kinds of theories of change: the ones that analyze change that has taken or is taking place, and the ones that can help us make such change happen. The first is diagnostic. The second type is instrumental. In practice, however, as with most other kinds of theories, the use of most theories can be both analytical and instructive.

But even though creative activists are often savvy tacticians they do not always have a clear idea about *how* what they do makes a difference. When Skype interviewed seasoned activist Andrew Boyd in class about this question his response was, "I don't know. In the end I guess I just cling on to the hope that what we do makes a difference."

Change can come as a revelation or happen as part of a learning process. It can be incremental or revolutionary, and it can mean a break with the status quo or an adaptation. It can be understood as a critique or a solution, a defeat or a victory, disruption or innovation, but rarely conservative as it is always pointing forward.

According to Buddhist philosophy change is constant. The only thing that we know for sure is that nothing stays the same. But it seems that change today happens quicker than ever before. Hartmut Rosa, a fourth generation critical Frankfurt School theorist, has developed a theory of what he calls the 'acceleration society' (2014) based on the three types of social acceleration that he identifies. The first one is technical acceleration, and includes faster transportation, production, and new communication technologies such as the mobile phone and the internet. The second is the acceleration of social change, which means that the fundamental institutions of our society such as family and work have become less stable. In early modern society you would become a carpenter if your father was a carpenter, and you would marry whom your position in society allowed you to marry. In classical modern times (say 1850–1970) you would to a larger degree choose your own profession and marry who you fell in love with. In this postmodern era that we live in, many people change profession and family several times over the course of a lifetime. We have therefore moved from an inter-generational to an intra-generational pace. The third type of acceleration is then the acceleration of the pace of life. Today micro behavioral sociology shows that our tendency to do more things at once is increasing. We talk on the phone while cooking and helping our children do their homework. We also do things faster. The time spent to eat dinner with our family, for example, has been reduced considerably. This tendency partly has to do with the paradox of having the conditions that allow for us (in the privileged western world) to do this. One might think that the time saved by being able to send an email instead of waiting a week for a response by snail mail would free up time. No. Instead we have just ended up with a hundred more messages and spam in our inbox. So we wind up feeling we have less time to do what we feel we must. According to Rosa, we are caught in what he calls a 'frantic standstill'.

The consequences of these accelerations are individual alienation, social pathologies, and democratic crises (2005). According to Rosa, the acceleration society is a totalitarian one because it pressurizes individual citizens to keep up and no one can really escape the acceleration regime. But are we not also witnessing some counter-movements, such as so-called deceleration trends, e.g. natural speed limits, different oases of deceleration, dysfunctional consequences of acceleration, intentional deceleration, and structural and cultural inertia? There does, however, seem to be an asymmetry in the weight of these trends (acceleration influences our lives more than the minor counter-movements of deceleration), Rosa defends his theory, and secondly most of the examples of deceleration that we are witnessing are instrumentally used as ways to accelerate further when leaving these zones of deceleration. Our routine visits to the psychiatrist or the yoga class are obvious examples of this.

So maybe a radical reaction to this constant need to change and keep up with colleagues, news streams, and gossip in the social media is to stop and think. Take a pause. When consultants, social entrepreneurs, or politicians are to design and implement a change they typically follow the same plan. For theorists like the much-used John Kotter (kotterinternational.com), (organizational) change is a transformation that should be approached and led as a planned, sequential process. Although change is usually messy and complex, the key to success is actually to follow eight rigorously defined steps. First you set the stage by (1) creating a sense of urgency and (2) pulling together the guiding team. Then you decide what to do by (3) developing a change vision and a strategy. Then you make it happen. Here you should (4) communicate the plan to the masses to make them understand, accept, and buy-in, (5) empower others to act, (6) produce short-term wins, (7) consolidate results, and continue ahead. After the implementation phase you make it stick and help create a new culture.

This approach builds on a rather linear understanding of change processes as something that takes place in rather traditional organizations that operate much like a machine where a handyman can make change happen if he is familiar with the nuts and bolts of the organization. Creative activists intervene in a political field that operates more like a complex organism and where there is a relatively high degree of disagreement and uncertainty. Both of which are factors that make change more a matter of responsive processes constantly balancing how to sustain continuity and some degree of stability while generating instability and change. Such change processes should, according to theorists such as Ronald A. Heifetz and Ralph Stacey, be led by facilitation, not control. In an episodic perspective the professional organization, or in this case the individual citizen or the political field, is seen as a static entity that needs to be melted in order to be able to regroup or introduce new things before freezing the organization back into the new state that is envisioned. In a perspective where change is something that is constantly taking place between human beings, the logic is reversed (Høpner et al., 2010).

In today's organizations where this is often the case or in a postmodern era where everything is fluent and up for negotiation (within a given framework), the opposite is needed. When nothing ever seems to stand still, meaningful change comes about when we freeze for a minute to consider where we are going before letting go – a sort of 'anchor management' where leadership suddenly becomes about helping the rest of us stop and breathe, reconnect with what matters, and test our moral compass. In mono-cultivated acceleration societies the creative activists' finest task is to make us stop, take a look in the mirror, and think.

One might also question to what extent it is possible at all to plan for change. When you do, it most often becomes a process that is driven from top-down. If you want to facilitate a change that is driven from below you quickly run into the control paradox touched upon earlier. On one hand, you need direction and management. On the other, you need legitimacy, engagement, creativity, and ownership from the involved parties to create valuable and sustainable change.

In an anthropological context, the concept of liminality has been used to describe how different cultures around the world use similar rituals to mark the transition from one stage in your life to another – say boyhood to manhood. Arnold van Gennep (1909) was the first to study the significance of rituals accompanying the transitional stages in a person's life – 'rites de passage' – birth, puberty, marriage, and death. Three stages reappear – that of separation, margin, and reaggregation. In the Aboriginal culture the boy is separated from his known world. In practice he is cast from the village and into the bush where he has to survive on his own for several days. This is the liminal state where normal rules do not apply. He is forced to see the world in a new light. He is in danger and becomes uncertain about who he is and what he can handle. If he survives he comes home and is reintegrated in the community – but with a new status. He is now a man.

Several scholars (e.g. Thomassen, 2012; Armbrust, 2013; Horvath, Thomassen, & Wydra, 2015) have pointed to the possibility of applying this concept in a more sociological context, and have used it to analyze how revolutionary chaos can be understood as a liminal phase that needs its own ritual masters and follow a similar pattern. Following that line of thought, one might think of liminal stages as something that can include more than one person (the single individual, a group of people, and society as such) and be stretched over time for each of these loose categories (a particular moment, a certain period, and whole epochs). If we do so we come up with a map where the creative activist in a political sense often acts as both the trickster trigger and the ritual master, designating a character and a narrative found in various forms across all modern cultures and in antiquity. What distinguishes the creative activist of today is that she often has a clear direction, political will, and strategic discipline.

To link up with the theoretical relevance of the ambiguous but nevertheless analytically useful concepts of utopia, cynicism, and irony discussed in Chapter 5, let me quote Paul Radin's classic study of the Trickster:

> Laughter, humor and irony permeate everything Trickster does. The reaction of the audience in aboriginal societies to both him and his

exploits is prevailing one of laughter tempered by awe. (...) Yet it is difficult to say whether the audience is laughing at him, at the tricks he plays on others, or at the implications his behavior and activities have for them. (Radin, 1956, p. x)

Closing the circle, the liminal phase can also in this context be understood as the space in-between (cf. also Turner, 1964), that I started out arguing that the creative activist is occupying. In Victor W. Turner's own words, liminality may be described as "a stage of reflection" (1964, p. 53), as those ideas and sentiments that have hitherto been accepted as natural hard facts around which we build our lives suddenly dissolve and resolve into new configurations as everything is questioned when all known hierarchies are suspended in *sacred poverty* – "For a while, anything goes: taboos are lifted, fantasies are enacted, indicative mood behavior is reversed, the low are exalted and the mighty abased" (Turner, 1988). This is also why these *neophytes* are so dangerous for the normal, stable community and why the young men are cast away in their passing to become men. European upper-class young men of means have for centuries taken the 'grand tour' around Europe. Uprisings – large-scale revolutions or trembling of the individual's core belief system – involve all the essential features of liminality: suspension of ordinary rules, fundamental questioning of power structures and political legitimacy, and a situation marked by volatility, ambivalence, and potentiality. "The potential of liminality, both creative and destructive, is at the heart of the trickster, who is exquisitely ambivalent: potentially powerful, ridiculous, and dangerous" (Armbrust, 2013, p. 846).

The phenomenon of ambivalence is in many ways what drives the process of social communication. The sociology of ambivalence claims that disturbances, paradoxes, misunderstandings, and exceptions are not critical risks to social order (as traditional sociologists tend to argue), but rather indispensable elements of this order. Social action too often presupposes a cultural order that is generated by applying distinctions and classifications:

> The two sides of a distinction refer to contrasting or oppositional meanings that, by this opposition, constitute each other: (...) But although this reconstruction of the excluded other of an opposition is widely accepted, mainstream cultural sociology has only marginally theorized a third possibility – the space in between the opposites, the third possibility, the transition between inside and outside, the "neither ... nor", or the "as well as ...", the space of hybridity. (Giesen in Horvath, Thomassen, & Wydra, 2015, p. 61)

What the creative activists are doing is to bring the bush into the village. They explore the cracks in our seemingly coherent ideologies. By setting up mirrors, creating a space in-between, a social interstice, a space of potentiality, playing an act on the stage of political theater, and transcending the given, they ask questions that make us think differently about what we usually take for granted. Thereby they represent the possibility to position oneself *outside inside* and thus reflect an alternative worldview.

One way to get an alternative perspective from the outside is to create a physical distance from your everyday life. Many people still travel around the world to get it. I travel with our kids because of the humility that a change in perspective gives us. Whether it is having child beggars surround us in Mumbai, dancing in the streets of Santiago de Cuba, fishing in Greenland, studying in Africa, or doing nothing on a beach in wherever, our thinking about the life that you live back home changes. You see how petty your career concerns are, you realize how fortunate you are, or you dare to revisit some of your fundamental beliefs. Sometimes it is not simply a matter of understanding one's own existential predicaments. It is more a matter of how you do so. Perception and understanding are not flat experiences and concepts. There is a depth to them, with layers ranging from the mere 'mechanical' understanding of hearing what you are saying and making formal sense of the combination of words you are putting together and the depth of understanding that comes from experience, taking a moral stand, and living with the consequences, which gives you a different and deeper understanding – whether we talk about raising children, going to war, or understanding the subtle dynamics of local communities.

In the meditative book *Zen and the Art of Motorcycle Maintenance* Robert Pirsig (1974) opens by describing how he with his son on the backseat of the motorcycle sails through the American countryside. When he spots a blackbird he turns to the son, points, and yells "blackbird"! The son is not impressed. "I have seen plenty of those dad," he yells back at him. As an eleven-year-old it is difficult to see why this stupid little bird has particular value. But for the father, for Pirsig, the sight takes him back to how he as a boy ran across the burned cornfields when the hunting season set in. His history gives the apparent trivial experience a depth that the boy cannot fathom.

The movement between these different layers of understanding sometimes happens over longer periods of time without us maybe even noticing. Sometimes it happens in leaps of faith or due to an occurrence that tips your belief system and opens up a whole new world of opportunities. The penny drops. Thomas Rochon, when describing how culture moves through dialectics between critical communities and social movements (1998), differs between value conversion, creation, and connection. The revolutionary idea, the redeeming laugh, the divine revelation, the tears in your eyes – they are all expressions of that deep moment of understanding and reconciliation.

Our prejudice can be inhibiting for our understanding and thus our moral judgment. In the documentary *Promises* we follow a handful of children – some Israeli, some Palestinian – who all live in Jerusalem. They each have their own more or less indoctrinated understanding of blame and right in this mother of all conflicts. But when these kids meet each other it becomes equally clear for them that the enemy's children are just kids – just like themselves. As one of the Israeli boys says after having spent a day with his new Palestinian friends, "Before I just thought that you were all terrorists. Now I understand the graffiti on the wall. I would probably feel the same way if I was you." He can suddenly put himself in their position. A Palestinian boy continues, "I am torn. Part of me wants to get to know you. Part of me is struggling." He starts to cry. I too was moved just watching it. The worldview that he had and the people that he now knows do not match up, which creates a cognitive dissonance between his different layers of understanding as an alternative mirror has been put up in front of them.

It is said that astronauts who get to see planet Earth from outer space as a little thing floating in free space have an emancipatory and life-changing experience. Sometimes you can get that perspective with both feet on the ground. The curiosity that has driven me to write this book (and probably you to read it) often functions as a driver and precondition for people's creation and experience of this sense of clarity, transcendence, and challenge in their own lives – not on an extended vacation or a trip around the moon, but in their own homes, walking down the street, or fighting for what they believe – not through unrelenting arguing or extremist religious belief, but just for a moment. Sometimes just the smallest push in just the right place at just the right time can cause you to change direction since a sudden splash in one's (seemingly) coherent belief system can cause the ripple effect of existential political insight and send gentle rocking motions through generations.

Hartmut Rosa's analysis can help us understand why people in general, and why creative activists in particular, feel that it is necessary to be resourceful when communicating their message, challenging those in power, and demonstrating how things might be different:

Ordinary people tend, today, to be more "intelligent", "rebellious" and "creative" than in the past insofar as they are constantly called upon to make value judgments and life choices where previously there was only conformity to a pre-established destiny. (Oliveira, 2008, Ch. 6)

Accepting Rosa's diagnosis has several direct implications for creative activism. One of them is that politicians, financial markets, and the media are setting new agendas in a tempo that makes it difficult for many people to follow them. Formulating a critique, mobilizing people, organizing hearings, etc. takes time. This leaves us in a democratic crisis. The target for our critique is, as opposed to earlier times, constantly moving, and now faster than ever. This makes it difficult for activists to aim, shoot, and hit. It also means that a lot of the work that they are doing becomes single issue-oriented and temporary comments that are non-binding – what Bauman has called 'camping critique' (Bauman, 2001). People come and go without much interest in challenging or renegotiating the managerial philosophy of the site. Visitors pay rent, make demands, and might even occasionally complain but generally stick to themselves. When they break up to follow each of their individual itineraries they leave the place untouched for the next guests to arrive. The problem arises if no structural critique accompanies the more fragmented one, if no realistic coherent alternative follows the utopian pre-figurative politics, if the revolutionary energy is not channeled into an institutional structure, if no hope underlies the cynical and ironic attitude. The creative activist argues that the latter enables the former, and not the other way around.

Creative activists operate on the margins of the repertoire of contention because change often begins where the limits for what is possible can be pushed. As poets and philosophers challenge and experiment with the limits of language, creative activists test and expand the boundaries of critique and political reasoning. In practice change happens from smaller to larger circles of influence – from those that one cooperates with about a certain event to those who end up (willingly or unwillingly) taking part in it, to those in the activist environment who get encouraged by the work one is doing, to the friends and family of those who accidentally ended up reading about one's idea. The media's attention, the politicians' responsiveness, slowly changing a culture – it ripples on from those you can touch.

"While they may help to unleash a reform process, protest waves are not sufficient to produce significant reforms – they also require the presence and entrepreneurship of well-placed reformists who can turn the impetus for change into concrete proposals and pilot them through the political process" (Tarrow, 2012, p. 158). Elites are unlikely to be persuaded by challengers outside the system. New feminist organizers might have dressed up as witches demonstrating, but they were *also* simultaneously pushing the policy agenda from within party ranks to make sure the ends met.

One of the big questions that my work keeps circling around is *how* social change takes place. Considering the totality of cases studied, of which only a few have been referenced and analyzed here, the power of intelligent action seems clear to me. A few minor actions by the right people at the right time in the right place can make a big difference. How? Well, in a number of ways. But first and foremost I have come to believe, and creative activists, as I have shown, surely believe so as well (otherwise they would not be doing what they do), that people *can* radically transform their behavior or beliefs in the face of the right impetus. Little causes can have big effects, and sometimes social and political change is triggered by seemingly small events. When Mohamed Bouazizi set himself on fire, nor he nor the Tunisian government could foresee how his death a couple of weeks later would spark a regional wildfire. Surely the Arab Spring was caused by a multitude of interrelated factors, but his self-emulation marks a tipping point. Again the structural opportunities are only worth something if there are change agents who understand how to widen and explore cracks in the established system. When Andrew Boyd coordinated a group of fake supporters when Steve Forbes in 1999 announced his candidacy for president, and reframed the event entirely, he could not have known that it would expand into a decade-long do-it-yourself grassroots media campaign. But using humorous parody and cynical irony to expose politicians who, in their view, support corporate interests at the expense of everyday Americans, the organization has grown to around hundred chapters across the US.

Creative activism seeks to start a trend, change the game, bend the rules, and can when at its best act as an epidemic where questions, ideas, or actions spread just like viruses do. Surely the answer to the questions of how social change take place depends on whether we are talking about an immediate change in someone's view on a given matter or the long-term change of an entire civilization. But the latter begins with the former. When evaluating creative activism's political influence it is crucial where one chooses to focus.

Walking the streets of Copenhagen with an academic mentor, an activist veteran and a good friend, Stephen Duncombe, we ended up under a random bridge by the central lakes of the city. Here a party was quickly growing, rumor running fast, started by the youth chapter of the Danish Bicycle Union, it turned out. Keep in mind that Denmark is famous around the world for its proud bicycle culture. From a monster of a rebuild Christiania bike with subwoofer stereo, beautiful music was echoing between the graffiti-ridden walls of the tunnel. The youth chapter is making sure that riding bikes stays relevant for the new generation of commuters. The men and woman here are busy getting cyclists riding by to grab their flyers, and each time it happened it activated an excited roar from the crowd, who were joint-smoking, well-educated, good-looking, fast-speaking, trendy hipsters. The rare but effective combination of the three archetypes that Malcolm Gladwell's Law of the Few principle tells us that we need to create a cultural epidemic: the salesman, the connector, and the maven. They are creating a commuting culture by making it cool to ride a bike and thereby having a real but not easily measurable impact on total carbon emissions.

Sometimes activism is about changing and passing laws. Sometimes it is about changing the hearts and minds (and the daily habits) of people. Politics itself therefore needs to be thought of in broader terms than electoral tactics and legislative reforms. It is (also) about when, how and why people think, believe and act as they do – and how we can strengthen the nuts and bolts of the democratic mechanisms that trigger and steer these processes. In many wealthy liberal democracies the social movements that have momentum are the so-called lifestyle movements, such as the slow food movement endorsing ecology (and as such part of the greater climate movement). One way of measuring the success of activists, campaigners, lobbyists, and NGOs in this area is to review price and demand on organic groceries and products. In Denmark, for example, the trend is significantly clear: prices are coming down and sales are booming in recent years (dst.dk).

Extra-parliamentary participation *can* make a difference. But distributing leaflets in a creative way captures people's imagination and increases the possibility that you reach an audience. When signing a petition it matters how the signatures are delivered. Boycotting products, you are more likely to have people do the same if you communicate why (google 'target boycott flash mob').

If you close your eyes for a moment and think about the best and the worst actions that you have helped plan, participated in or just read about, then I am sure a few stand out. Go on – it will only take a minute.

Learning from our successes and failures, we need to identify what works, how and why, and what was missing when things didn't go as planned. Doing so, we need to at least think about goal setting, contexts, openings and pressure points, target and audience, capacity and resources, strategy and tactics, story and action logic.

So called 'band-aid solutions,' often by critics related to the single-issue politics of creative activists, do not have a good reputation. But thinking of David, who, like the creative activists, had to be resourceful in using what he had to his advantage so that he could slay Goliath, such solutions are inexpensive, convenient, and remarkably versatile temporary answers to an array of problems. The band-aid keeps you walking until you reach where you want to go to or going while you come up with a more sustainable solution. In the days after The Big Donorshow, remember, the hoax TV program featuring patients desperately competing to be chosen to receive a kidney from a terminally ill woman, was aired on Dutch television, thousands of citizens across Europe, an unprecedented number, registered as donors.

The dialectic dynamics between systemic culture and change-agent, capitalism and creative activism, are complex. That is why social change is so unpredictable and somewhat inexplicable. Influence goes both ways, but my *structurally pragmatic but agent optimistic standpoint* is upheld since creative activism has proven that it is able to overcome structural limitations and challenge hegemony head on.

When the student movement Otpor overthrew Milošević in Serbia, they used graffiti, public pranks, and cool campaigns to do so. By proving to the public that the regime could be made fun of, they induced hope. Today CANVAS teaches their non-violent philosophy and tactics around the world. Since its creation in a squatted military compound in Copenhagen in 1971, Christiania has experimented with alternative ways of living together, and to this day force politicians to justify themselves when they try to privatize it. When the KONY 2012 viral media campaign spread like a virus it was a testament to how weak-ties activism can be used creatively and effectively to advocate one's cause. But it was also a reminder that creative online activism cannot and should not stand alone. High-risk activism, Doug McAdam has pointed out, is a 'strong-tie' phenomenon. When four college students sat down at the lunch counter at the Woolworth's in downtown Greensboro, North Carolina on February 1, 1960 and asked for a cup of coffee, they were good friends. At first they were told that Negroes could not be served. In the days to come their college friends joined them, and after a week the sit-ins had spread to the neighboring town. This was the beginning of the civil rights strife that erupted in the Southern states in the US during the 1960s. Such change could never have come from low-risk weak-tied networks alone. As Malcolm Gladwell notes when arguing why social media cannot provide what social change has always required, "It makes it easier for activists to express themselves, and harder for that expression to have any impact." However, the young girl struggling to breathe under a cloud of teargas outside a Danish asylum center, portrayed at the beginning of the book, the one who chose to take a picture of herself lying there instead of just fleeing the scene, might in hindsight be seen as an example of how the new generation does not see a problem with undertaking both high-risk activism where they put themselves on the line and low-risk weak-tie activism online where posting your picture certainly serves to polish your profile, but also to make your 'friends' aware of the injustice you experience during a peaceful demonstration. There is thus, as Hannah Arendt describes it, an element of creative performativity at the very heart of politics (Arendt, 1993, pp. 143–171).

What I have done in this book, then, is to examine *how* creative activism functions as a driver of the imagination, the resourcefulness, and the inspiration that is so badly needed in the political environment today. We have looked at *why* it is important to also consider the political environment with which it has to interact in order to have a possibility of a tangible impact. To conclude, creative activism should be understood as a kind of meta-activism that tries to facilitate critical and creative dialogue in-between traditional divides and actors, and as such functions as a priming pump for the political imagination if and when it manages to push the boundaries of the known repertoire of contention in its attempt to get the individual citizen to reflect on her responsibility in moving humanity forward.

Creative activists critique and sometimes point to solutions, but whether they make invisible theater, do a hoax, infiltrate, go naked, turn the tables, block, reclaim or make prefigurative interventions – their finest task is to pose questions that open up the political. As Henrik Kaare Nielsen concludes his work on the democratic potential of artistic interventions:

> The establishment of a well functioning democratic public sphere requires not only constructive, dialogical forms of practice and appreciation of diversity but also a universalist political culture and an associated reason-based political judgement that is capable of reflecting conflicts and process them in the view of the common good. Artistic interventions, in other words, cannot replace more classical forms of political practice and experience, but they may open their established formations of meaning and prompt them to rethinking practices and making new experiences. (Nielsen, 2015)

Let me therefore say it again: the point of this book is not to celebrate these new social actors as bearers of better societal alternatives. It is to explore the conditions that they offer for the cultivation of such alternatives. Through their acts of resistance the creative activist and the grassroots movements that they are part of "expose the 'irresistible forces of capitalism' as being the product of decisions and choices; and as such, as being possibly resistible and reversible" (Fournier, 2002, p. 200). The point is that decisions, by definition, can be otherwise. As James Baldwin (Beasley & Hager, 2014) put it: "The world changes according to the way people see it, and if you can alter, even by a millimeter, the way people look at reality, then you can change the world." That is the wonder of the mirror effect.

That being said, precautionary measures have been taken all along and should be explicated and repeated before closing: a creative activist is not something you can apply to become as no standards apply. It is actually against the philosophy of most of the creative activists that I have interviewed, studied, and worked with to try and fit them into one specific category. In fact they spend most of their time escaping fixed frames. I have done so well aware that they all stick out their own way and believe that a better understanding of what they do and who they are serves to develop an important research field – both scientifically and politically.

As I have shown, throughout history but remarkably today, the active citizen may through playful forms of action appropriate practices of domination and control as a valuable tactic of resistance, critically reflect on its own relation to society by subverting hierarchies and creating autonomous space for performance and mimicry, and constitute new realities through the prefigurative acting out of its fantasies and desires, interrupting the status quo by showing rather than telling the change they want to see. But the question is left open: does the playful action of creative activists finally break down the barrier between art and protest, and deliver on its promise of releasing the creative potential of the desiring subject into the arena of politics?

As I have shown, playful forms of political action are constantly challenging the established order of things, engaging people's resourcefulness, and facilitating new political opportunities for change. We must renounce the wish for an administrative politics of 'truth' and 'necessity', and foster forms of action that dare to celebrate the vacuum it leaves and the possibilities that follow in relation to how we conduct ourselves as political subjects – in praise of an elusive but valuable revolutionary ethics of political imagination.

Notes

1 Occupying the Space In-Between

1. Cf. the definition of ambivalence by Henrik Kaare Nielsen in Larsen and Pedersen, 2011, pp. 26–27, emphasizing its sociological aspects in late modernity.
2. See Henrik Kaare Nielsen in Larsen and Pedersen, 2011, pp. 157–158 for a concise sociological definition of imagination and its relation to aesthetic practices.
3. In May 2011 I participated in this education held in New York by the School for Creative Activism at the Center for Artistic Activism. Participants remain anonymous.
4. Nicolas Bourriaud (2002, p. 16) explains Marx's term as follows: "The interstice is a space in human relations which fits more or less harmoniously and openly into the overall system, but suggests other trading possibilities that those in effect within this system."

2 Creative Activism Today

1. This line of argument builds on an article that I published in 2015 in *Culture and Organization*, Vol. 21, Issue 2 (see Harrebye, 2015).
2. This line of argument builds on an article accepted for publication in 2016 in *Open Social Science Journal* (see Harrebye, 2016).

3 First Movers and Circular Cycles of Contention

1. For an overview discussion of how these characteristics of the new social movement have been dealt with within political and cultural strands of new social movement theories, see Johnston, Larana, & Gusfield, 1994, and Buechler, 1995.
2. I am especially interested in the 'cultural' versus the 'political' versions of new social movement theory, cf. Buechler's distinction (1995, p. 457).

4 Paradoxes of Participation

1. The figure is a condensed version of the multi-level regression analysis we made in the article printed in *Comparative European Politics* (see Harrebye and Ejrnæs, 2015). The data we used in this article comes from the European Social Survey (ESS) round 4, conducted in 2008. The sample includes 37,377 respondents from 20 EU countries.

   Dependent variable: In order to measure the level of extra-parliamentary activity an index based on the following questions have been constructed: There are different ways of trying to improve things in [country] or help prevent

things from going wrong. During the last 12 months, have you done any of the following?
- Worn or displayed campaign badge/sticker? (yes/no)
- Signed petition? (yes/no)
- Taken part in lawful public demonstration? (yes/no)
- Boycotted certain products? (yes/no)

The range of the scales goes from 0 (have not been involved in any of the four actions) to 4 (have been involved in all four actions). In the multi-level regression model it has been analyzed how different individual and macro-level variables influence the mean value of extra-parliamentary activities.

Independent variable: At the individual level the central independent variable is here dissatisfaction with the government, and is scaled on the following question: Now thinking about the [country] government, how satisfied are you with the way it is doing its job?

The scale goes from 0 (extremely dissatisfied) to 10 (extremely satisfied). To ease the interpretation of the coefficient we rescaled the variable so it now goes from 0 (extremely dissatisfied) to 1 (extremely satisfied). The micro multi-level regression analysis also included such variables as age, education, employment status, gender, satisfaction with the government, and feeling of being a member of a discriminated group.

2. (1) *The radical activists* were represented by groups such as NTAC (nevertrustacop.org) and Black Block (autonominfoservice.net).
(2) Examples of groups practicing *confrontational civil disobedience* include Climate Justice Action group (climate-justice-action.org) and major events such as Reclaim Power and Shut It Down (shutitdown.dk).
(3) The hunger strike and the numerous artistic installations around Copenhagen city are examples of *creative activism*. The Green Men, The Red Climate Agents, and the Blue Wave were similar kinds of colorful happenings, which added a creative element to other events during the COP15.
(4) *The professional activists* were represented by the organized civil society – e.g. the NGOs at DGI Byen and, those who were allowed inside, at Bella Centre.
(5) *The occasional activist* participated in the larger demonstrations or at the sponsored Hopenhagen at Rådhuspladsen (hopenhagen.org).
(6) *The everyday maker* can be motivated to engage directly in helping to reduce pollution or other environmental hazards by making a difference in their everyday lives.

3. In social sciences, a typology is usually based on a combination of key underlying factors (e.g. in cross tables), whose various possible interaction may result in a series of other types. Furthermore they are often thought of as comprehensive and/or exhaustive. The referenced typological analysis develops conceptual representations of concrete summit activities in order better to be able to label different types of activism. Empirical examples are used as illustrations of the 'ideal-typical sensitizing construct' (Buechler, 1995, p. 457), which cannot capture all the complexities of the field and will inevitably oversimplify some of its dimensions, but nevertheless allows for

an organization of diverse dimensions and debates into somewhat coherent positions with a fair degree of internal consistency across various issues.
4. Approximately 30,000 global citizens came from all over the world to Copenhagen to negotiate and demonstrate. One of the greatest challenges for a broad democratic conference is to secure accommodation for the many thousand visitors arriving. The hotels in Copenhagen were booked by the most powerful nations and organizations long in advance. Some lesser-funded visitors stayed on the floors of schools and sports halls, but more than 5,000 activists and campaigners had no place to stay approaching the summit. New Life Copenhagen matched over 3,000 of these visitors with Danish citizens who volunteered to open their homes and host the many guests.
5. To mention some of the most relevant, there were a Climate Justice Fast, the Home Away Resort project, Healing Ritual Host performances, the Guestbook dialogue, the Copenhagen intervention in collaboration with India Research Center and The Yes Men, and the Ecological Burial designed in cooperation with Superflex and a biologist.
6. When the Foreign Ministry called the Wooloo management in for meeting because they preferred that the festival did not match official delegates with private citizens, thereby keeping it a parallel festival, Wooloo stood strong and insisted on working across those boundaries.

5 The Ambivalence of Cynicism, Irony, and Utopia

1. This chapter partly builds on the article that I published in 2015 in *Culture and Organization*, Vol. 21, Issue 2 (see Harrebye, 2015).

6 Mirroring Counter Strategies

1. The cases included in the book are meant to illustrate how the creation of such 'pockets' are facilitated. My understanding of the *raison d'être* of these groups were further qualified in my interviews with renowned creative activists influential at a global scale through their own avant-garde practices and teachings.
2. I would like to thank Nancy Fraser whom I studied under as a visiting scholar at The New School for Social Research in New York in 2011 and who has functioned as my co-advisor in the following last phase of my PhD – and thus has been given the dubious privilege of aiding me in questioning her own work.
3. To supplement her conceptual framework for understanding struggles of social justice, Fraser has developed her normative principle of 'participatory parity'. According to Fraser, public opinion is legitimate if and only if it results from a communicative process in which all potentially affected can participate as peers, regardless of political citizenship.
4. The original German term *ungleichseitigkeit* has also been translated into nonsynchronism (Bloch, 2000), noncontemporaneity (Bloch, 2009), and nonsimultaneity (Durst, 2002).
5. Mirroring neurons (subneurons to the motor-command neurons of the premotor cortex, discovered by neurophysiologist Giacomo Rizzolati in 1992)

adopt other persons' point of view and are able to perform a virtual reality simulation of the other person's action due to their imitation and emulation qualities. When we watch someone else being touched we are therefore able to understand it and feel it. But we do not feel it the same way as when we are touched ourselves. Why? Because our sense receptors tell us that we have not actually been touched. People who have an amputee arm do feel as if they have been touched on their phantom hand when they see someone else's hand being brushed. Their mirroring neurons tell them so, and their sense receptors cannot argue with them (neuroscientist Vllayanur Ramachandran on blog.ted.com). If our 'cultural sense receptors' are numbed, we may find it difficult to distinguish between what we are bombarded with every day (commercial narratives, images, symbols, product associations, and hidden morals) and our own life stories, motivation, and ethics. In this case the human being's neurological disposition for empathy becomes an enabling factor for a cannibalistic culture of silenced greed.

6. Mirroring is the behavior in which one person subconsciously imitates the gesture, speech pattern, or attitude of another. It is a way for individuals to build rapport with others. For infants mimicking and mirroring, acknowledgement allows the infant to establish a sense of empathy and thus helps them build a positive sense of self, self-worth, and self-expression (Meltzoff, 1990, and Rasborg, 2014). As adults it is important, however, that we are presented with a multitude of mirroring possibilities. Seemingly we are. But if we look around us dominating pop politics permeate most of them – and since we know (e.g. Mintz, 1985) that individuals are likely to mirror the person or trends of higher status or power, alternative mirrors create potentially emancipating temporary autonomous zones where the self can be explored or re-evaluated. "When we respond to narcissistic behavior by changing our own behavior, the mirror effect is at work. (and) can in turn evolve into fixed personality traits (...) reflecting the behavior back to the public at large" (Pinsky, 2009, p. 137). The psychological technique called mirroring allows a person to gain control over someone else's actions, even without them being consciously aware of it by mirroring their behavior until it is hard to tell who is copying whom. When they are in sync the person who was initially copying the other, can start to reverse the process so that the unaware is now mirroring the mirroring agent's actions. I point to how similar cultural mechanisms are in place and working at a societal level. The alternative mirrors set up by activists are meant to counter-balance these classical confirming, duplicating, and reproducing psychological and cultural mirroring mechanisms.

7 Professionalization and Cooptation

1. I have done training with them and have visited with my students to drill them about their theory of change. Go to sparkcph.dk for a list of the type of projects that they work on.
2. See, for example, Rosendahl's (2015) account of a thousand plus Climate Camp set up in vicinity of Europe's largest coal mine to train experienced as well as first-time activists to take civil disobedience action.

8 The Gordian Knot – Measuring Effect and Revisiting Theories of Change

1. The variables suggested in Tables 8.1 and 8.2 are inspired by Rucht, 1999; Snow and Soule, 2010; and Olesen and Lindekilde, 2015.
2. Ideas for new impact study designs have been developed in close collaboration with colleague Anders Ejrnæs and the rest of the New CAP (New Civic Assessment Project) team.
3. Smapp is an example of a research center whose goal it is to "forge interdisciplinary collaboration that examines the impact of social media on political behavior by iterating through stages of model development, testing, refinement, and validation. First, from social psychology and political science we derive fundamental hypotheses about how, why, and when social media affects citizens' cognitions and motivations with respect to political participation. Second, we express these questions as empirically testable hypotheses derived from behavioral models (e.g., with quantitative response and predictor variables). And third, drawing from biology and computer science we adapt sophisticated computational methods of approximate inference and machine learning (adapting methods developed for the analysis of Systems Biology data) to evaluate our behavioral models using extremely large social media and social network datasets" (smapp.nyu.edu).

Bibliography

Abrams, M. H. (1953) *The Mirror and the Lamp: Romantic Theory and the Critical Tradition.* Oxford University Press.
Adler, P. and Adler, P. (1987) *Membership Roles in Field Research.* Sage.
Albrow, M., Anheier, H., Glasius, M., Price, M. E. and Kaldor, M. (Eds.) (2008) *Global Civil Society 2007/08 – Communicative Power and Democracy.* London: Sage, pp. 198–223.
Alexander, J. C. (2006) *The Civil Sphere.* Oxford University Press, p. 4.
Alvesson, M. (1993) The Play of Methaphors. In J. Hassard and M. Parker (Eds), *Postmodernism and Organization.* London: Sage, pp. 114–132.
Alvesson, M. and Sköldberg, K. (2009) *Reflexive Methodology: New Vistas for Qualitative Research.* Sage.
Amoore, L. and Hall, A. (2013) The Clown at the Gates of the Camp: Sovereignty, Resistance, and the Figure of the Fool. *Security Dialogue,* Vol. 44, Issue 2, pp. 93–110.
Anderson, B. (1991) *Imagined Communities.* Verso.
Andersen, B. S. (2008) Ironiens kultur og kulturens ironi: En undersøgelse af senmoderne sensibiliteter [The Culture of Irony and Culture's Irony: An Investigation of Late Modern Sensibilities – Own Translation]. *Dansk Sociologi,* Vol. 19, Issue 1, pp. 9–30.
Andersen, L. B., Hansen, K. M. and Klemmesen, R. (2012) *Metoder i Statskundskab.* Hans Reitzels Forlag.
Andersen, S. S. (1997) *Case-studier og generalisering.* Oslo: Fakbokforlaget.
Annan, K. A. (2004) *We the peoples: Civil society, the United Nations, and global governance.* Report of the Panel of Eminent Persons on United Nations – Civil Society Relations (online). Available at: http://www.un-ngls.org/orf/Final%20report%20-%20HLP.doc (accessed 5 Mar. 2010).
Arendt, H. (1993) *Between Past and Future. Eight Exercises in Political Thought.* Penguin Books.
Armbrust, W. (2013) The Trickster in Egypt's January 25th Revolution. *Comparative Studies in Society and History,* Vol. 55, Issue 4, pp. 834–864.
Aronoff, K. (2015) *The Beauty of COP21 Is in the Street.* Wagingnonviolence.org.
Asimov, I. (1970). *Asimov's Guide to Shakespeare.* Gramercy Books.
Aune, J. A. (1994) *Rethoric and Marxism.* Boulder, CO: Westview Press.
Bäck, H., Teorell, J. and Westholm, A. (2011) Explaining Modes of Participation: A Dynamic Test of Alternative Rational Choice Models. *Scandinavian Political Studies,* Vol. 34, Issue 1, pp. 74–97.
Bakhtin, M. (1984) *Rabelais and His World.* Trans. He´le`ne Iswolsky. Bloomington: Indiana UP.
Bang, H. (2009) Yes We Can: Identity Politics and Project Politics for a Late Modern World. *Urban Research and Practice,* Vol. 2, Issue 2, pp. 117–137.
Barber, B. (1984) *Strong Democracy – Participatory Politics for a New Age.* Berkeley, CA: University of California Press.
Bauman, Z. (1999) *In Search of Politics.* Stanford University Press.

Bauman, Z. (2001) *The Individualized Society*. Cambridge: Polity Press.
Bauman, Z. (2006) Kritikken – privatiseret og afvæbnet. In Jacobsen, M. H. (Eds), *Baumans mosaic. Essays af Zygmunt Bauman om etik, kritik og utopi 1990–2005*, pp. 249–257. Sydansk Universitetsforlag.
Beasley, M. M. and Hager, P. M. (2014) Intervention, Instigation, Interruption: Art, Activism, and Social Policy. *Journal of Poverty*, Vol. 18, Issue 1, pp. 1–4.
Beck, U. 2006. *The Cosmopolitan Vision*. Cambridge: Polity Press.
Beck, U. 1997. *Risikosamfundet – på vej mod en ny modernitet*. Hans Reitzels Forlag.
Beck, U. and Beck-Gernsheim, E. (2002) Authors preface: Instutionalized individualism, in *Individualization*. London: Sage, pp. xx–1.
Benhabib, S. (1992) *Situating the Self. Gender Community, and Postmodernism in Contemporary Ethics*. Polity Press.
Bennett, L. W. and Segerberg, A. (2013) *The Logic of Connective Action: Digital Media and the Personalization of Contentious Politics*. Cambridge University Press.
Bens, I. (2000) *Facilitating with Ease* (Jossey-Bass).
Bey, H. 2011. *T.A.Z. Temporary Autonomous Zones*. Seattle: Pacific Publishing Studio.
Bhaskar, R. (1998) *Critical Realism: Essential Readings*. Routledge.
Bloch, E. (2000) *The Spirit of Utopia*. Stanford University Press.
Bloch, E. (2009) *The Heritage of Our Times*. John Wiley and Sons.
Bloch, N. (2015) *Protest Ban Will Not Stop Creative Actions at COP21*. Wagingnonviolence.org.
Blumer, H. (1939) Collective Behaviour. In R. E. Park (Eds), *An Outline of the Principles of Sociology*, pp. 220–280. New York: Barnes and Noble.
Bobel, C. (2007) 'I'm Not an Activist, Though I've Done a Lot of It': Doing Activism, Being Activist and the 'Perfect Standard' in a Contemporary Movement. *Social Movement Studies*, Vol. 6, Issue 2, pp. 147–159.
Boese, D. (2010) *Activism, Conceptual, Project Organizing* (April Issue). Artforum.
Bohman, J. and Rehg, W. (1997) *Deliberative Democracy*. MIT Press.
Boje, T. (2010) *Active Citizenship, Participation, and Governance*. (Baden-Baden: German University Press).
Boje, T. and Potucek, M. Eds. (2011) *Social Rights, Active Citizenship, and Governance in the European Union*. Nomos, Baden-Baden.
Bolt, M. (2005) *City Rumble – kunst, intervention og kritisk offentlighed*. Forlaget Politisk Revy.
Boltanski, L. and Chiapello, E. (2005) *The New Spirit of Capitalism*. Verso.
Boltanski, L. and Thévenot, L. (2006) *On Justification: Economies of Worth*. Princeton University Press.
Borch, C. (2012) *The Politics of Crowds – An Alternative History of Sociology*. Cambridge University Press.
Boren, Z. D. (2015) Spain's Hologram Protest: Thousands Join Virtual March in Madrid Against New Gag Law. *The Independent*.
Bourdieu, P. and Wacquant, L. J. D. (1992) *An Invitation to Reflexive Sociology*. The University of Chicago Press.
Bourraud, N. (2002) *Relational Aesthetics*. Les Presses du Réel.
Boyd, A. Ed. (2012) *Beautiful Trouble – A Toolbox for Revolution*. O/R Books.
Brand, K.-W. (1990) Cyclical Aspects of New Social Movements: Waves of Cultural Criticism and Mobilization Cycles of New Middle-Class Radicalism. In R. J. Dalton and M. Kuechler (Eds), *Challenging the Political Order*, pp. 24–42. Oxford University Press.

Brannen, J. Ed. (1992) *Mixing Methods: Qualitative and Quantitative Research.* Aldershot: Avebury.
Brighenti, A. M. (2011) Power, Subtraction and Social Transformation: Canetti and Foucault on the Notion of Resistance. *Distinktion: Scandinavian Journal of Social Theory*, Vol. 12, Issue 1, pp. 57–78.
Bruner, L. (2005) Carnivalesque Protest and the Humorless State. *Text and Performance Quarterly*, Vol. 25, Issue 2, pp. 136–155.
Buechler, S. M. (1995) New Social Movement Theories. *The Sociological Quarterly*, Vol. 36, Issue 3, pp. 441–464.
Bühlmann, M. and Müller, W. (2011) *The Democracy Barometer: A New Instrument to Measure the Quality of Democracy and Its Potential for Comparative Research.* European Political Science Symposium.
Butler, J. (1990) *Gender Trouble: Feminism and the Subversion of Identity.* Routledge.
Buur, J. and Matthews, B. (2008) Participatory Innovation. *International Journal of Innovation Management*, Vol. 12, Issue 3, pp. 255–273. Imperial College Press.
Bøtter, J. and Kolind, L. (2012) *Unboss.* Jyllands Postens Forlag.
Calhoun, C. (2009) *Social Science for Public Knowledge.* Social Science Research Council. See: publicsphere.ssrc.org/calhoun-social-science-for-public-knowledge.
Castells, M. 2004. *The Power of Identity, the Information Age: Economy, Society and Culture.* Vol. II. 2nd ed. Cambridge, MA: Oxford, UK: Blackwell.
Castells, M. (2012) *Networks of Outrage – Social Movements in the Internet Age.* Polity.
Carstens, A. L. and Jensen, K. (2011) *Version 0.8.* Roskilde University (Unpublished Thesis).
Chenoweth, E. and Stephan, M. J. (2011) *Why Civil Resistance Works: The Strategic Logic of Nonviolent Struggle.* Columbia University Press.
Cohen, J. L. (1985) Strategy or Identity? New Theoretical Paradigms and Contemporary Social Movements. *Social Research*, Vol. 52, pp. 663–716.
Conway, J. and Singh, J. (2008) Is the World Social Forum a Transnational Public Sphere? Nancy Fraser, Critical Theory, and the Containment of Radical Possibility. *Theory, Culture & Society*, Vol. 26 Issue 5, pp. 61–84.
Critchley, S. (2007) Humour as Practically Enacted Theory, or Why Critics Should Tell More Jokes. In Westwood, R. and Rhodes, C. (Eds), *Humour, Work, and Organization*, pp. 17–33. Routledge.
Cuninghame, P. (2007) "A Laughter that Will Bury You All": Irony as Protest and Language as Struggle in the Italian 1977 Movement. *International Review of Social History*, Vol. 52, Issue S15, pp. 153–168.
Dalton, K. and Burklin (1990) The Challenge of the New Movements. In Dalton and Kuechler (Eds), *Challenging the Political Order*, (pp. 3–20). Cambridge.
Dalton, R. J. and Kuechler, M. (1990) *Challenging the Political Order: New Social and Political Movements in the Western Democracies.* Oxford University Press.
Danermark, B. et al. (1997) *Att förklara Samhället.* Studentlitteratur.
Danermark, B. et al. (2002) *Explaining Society: Critical Realism in the Social Sciences.* Routledge.
Danielsen, E. et al. (2012) *Roskilde Festival: A City.* Roskilde Festival.
de Waal, M. and Morais, R. J. (2010) Creativity, Brands, and the Ritual Process: Confrontation and Resolution in Advertising Agencies. *Culture and Organization*, Vol. 16, Issue 4, pp. 333–347.
Debord, G. (2004) *Society of the Spectacle.* Rebel Press.

Defourny, J. and Nyssen, M. (2010) Conceptions of Social Enterprise and Social Entrepreneurship in Europe and the United States: Convergences and Divergences. *Journal of Social Entrepreneurship*, Vol. 1, Issue 1, pp. 32–53.
Defourny, J., Hulgaard, L. and Pestoff, V. (2014) *Social Enterprise and the Third Sector*. Routledge.
Delanty, G. (2000) *Citizenship in a Global Age – Society, Culture, and Politics*. Buckingham: Open University Press.
Delanty, G. (2005) *Social Science*. Open University Press.
Delanty, G. (2010) Citizenship as a Learning Process: Disciplinary Citizenship Versus Cultural Citizenship. *International Journal of Lifelong Education*, Vol. 22, Issue 6, pp. 597–605.
Delhey, J. and Newton, K. (2003) Who Trusts? The Origins of Social Trust in Seven Societies. *European Societies*, Vol. 5, Issue 2, pp. 93–137.
Della, P. and Diani, M. (1999) *Social Movements: An Introduction*. Blackwell Publishers.
Della, P. and Diani, M. (2006) *Social Movements – An Introduction*, 2nd ed. Oxford: Blackwell.
Della Porta, D. (2011) Eventful Protest, Global Conflicts – Social Mechanisms in the Reproduction of Protest. In J. M. Jasper and J. Goodwin (Eds), *Contention in Context: Political Opportunities and the Emergence of Protest*. Standford University Press, pp. 256–275.
Della Porta, D. and Mattoni, A. (Eds.). (2014) *Spreading Protest: Social Movements in Times of Crisis*. ECPR Press.
Diani, M. (2011) The Concept of Social Movement. *The Sociological Review*, Vol. 40, Issue 1, pp. 1–25.
Docker, J. (1994) *Postmodernism and Popular Culture: A Cultural History*. Cambridge University Press.
Dryzek, J. (2000) *Deliberative Democracy and Beyond: Liberals, Critics, Contestations*. (New York: Oxford University Press).
Du Plessis, E. M. (2014). *Drinking Coffee with Zizek*. (Paper presented at 9th Organization Studies Workshop, Corfu, Greece. (Or as suggested: Unpublished)).
Duncombe, S. (2007) *Dream – Re-Imagining Progressive Politics in an Age of Fantasy*. The New Press.
Duncombe, S. (2012) *Open Utopia*. Wivenhoe/New York/Port Watson: Minor Compositions/Autonomedia.
Duncombe, S. and Lambert, S. (2016) *How to Win*. Forthcoming.
Durst, D. C. (2002) Ernst Bloch's Theory of Nonsimultaneity. *The German Review: Literature, Culture, Theory*, Vol. 77, Issue 3, pp. 171–194. Routledge.
Dutton, M. (1998) *Streetlife China*. Cambridge: Cambridge University Press.
Dyrberg, T. B. 2014. *Foucault on Power, Critique and Parresia*. Palgrave.
Edwards, B. and McCarthy, J. D. (2004) Resources and Social Movement Mobilization. In S. Snow and K. Kriesi (Eds), *The Blackwell Companion to Social Movements*, pp. 116–152. Oxford: Blackwell.
Edwards, M. (2004) *Civil Society*, 2nd ed. Polity Press.
Eisinger, P. (1973) The Conditions of Protest Behavior in American Cities. *American Political Science Review*, Vol. 81, pp. 11–28.
Enrique, L., Johnston, H. and Gusfield, J. R. (1994) *New Social Movements*. Philadelphia: Temple University Press.
Epstein, B. (2013) Occupy Oakland – The Question of Violence. Socialist Register 2013: The Question of Strategy, pp. 63–83.

Escobar, J. J. and Gutiérrez, A. C. M. (2011) *Social Economy and the Fourth Sector, Base and Protagonist of Social Innovation*. CIRIEC.
Esping-Andersen, G. (1990) *The Three Worlds of Welfare Capitalism*. Oxford: Polity Press.
Etzioni, A. (1995) *The Spirit of Community*. London: Fontana Books.
Fischer, F. (2000) *Citizens, Experts, and the Environment: The Politics of Local Knowledge*. Durham: Duke University Press.
Flacks, R. (1967) The Liberated Generation: An Exploration of the Roots of Student Protest. *Journal of Social Issues*, Vol. 23, Issue 3, pp. 52–75.
Flacks, R. (2003) Review of Dynamics of Contention. *Social Movement Studies: Journal of Social, Cultural and Political Protest*, Vol. 2, Issue 1, pp. 99–102.
Flyvbjerg, B. (2010) Fem misforståelser om casestudiet. In Brinkmann and Tanggaard (Eds), *Kvalitative metoder – en grundbog*, pp. 463–487. Copenhagen: Hans Reitzels Forlag.
Fominaya, Christina Flescher. 2014. *Social Movements and Globalization*. Palgrave.
Foucault, M. (1972) *Power/Knowledge: Selected Interviews and Other Writing 1972–1977* (C. Gordon, Eds). Pantheon Books.
Foucault, M. (1986) Of Other Spaces. *Diacritics*, Vol. 16, Issue 1, pp. 22–27.
Foucault, M. (1995) *Discipline & Punish – The Birth of the Prison*. Random House, Inc.
Foucault, M. (2001) *Fearless Speech* (J. Pearson, Eds). Semiotext(e).
Foucault, M. (2007) *The Politics of Truth*. Semiotext(e).
Fournier, V. (2002) Utopianism and the Cultivation of Possibilities: Grassroots Movements of Hope. In Parker (Ed.), *Utopia and Organization*, pp. 189–216.
Fraser, N. (2009) *Scales of Justice: Reimagining Political Space in a Globalizing World*. Columbia University Press.
Fraser, N. and Habermas, J. (2003) *Redistribution or Recognition? A Political Philosophical Exchange*. Verso.
Freud, S. (1938) *Wit and Its Relation to the Unconscious*. The Modern Library.
Fukuyama, F. (1992) *The End of History and the Last Man*. The Free Press.
Fukuyama, F. (2000). *Social Capital and Civil Society*. Washington, DC: IMF working paper No. 00/74.
Gamson, W. (1975) *The Strategy of Social Protest*. Dorsey Press.
Gamson, W. and Meyer, G. (1996) Framing Political Opportunity. In McAdam, McCarthy, and Zald (Eds), *Comparative Perspectives on Social Movements*. Cambridge University Press.
Gansky, L. (2010) *The Mesh – Why the Future of Business Is Sharing*. Portfolio Penguin.
Ganz, M. (2010) Leading Change. In Nohria and Khurana (Ed.), *Handbook of Leadership in Theory and Practice*. Harvard Business Press.
Ganz, M. (2010) *Why David Sometimes Wins: Leadership, Organization, and Strategy in the California Farm Worker Movement*. Oxford University Press.
Garbutt, A. and Haddock, P. (2012) *Evaluation of Action Aid Denmark's Training4Change*. INTRAC.
Gennep,V. (1909) *The Rites of Passage*. University of Chicago Press.
Georgsen, M. and Thomassen, B. (2015) *Affectivity and Liminality in Ritualized Protest: Politics of Transformations in the Kiev Uprising*. Unpublished.
Geraint, P., Moyser, G. and Day, N. (1992) *Political Participation and Democracy in Britain*. New York: Cambridge University Press.
Gerbaudo, P. (2012) *Tweets and the Streets – Social Media and Contemporary Activism*. Pluto Press.
Gibson-Graham. 2006. *A Postcapitalist Politics*. University of Minnesota Press.

Giddens, A. (1979) *Central Problems in Social Theory: Action, Structure, and Contradiction in Social Analysis*. University of California Press.
Giddens, A. (1994) Risk, Trust, Reflexivity. In U. Beck, A. Giddens and S. Lash (Eds), *Reflexive Modernization. Politics, Tradition and Aesthetics in the Modern Social Order*, pp. 184–197. Cambridge: Polity Press.
Giddens, A. (1996) *Modernitet og selvidentitet. Selvet og samfundet under sen-moderniteten*. Hans Reitzels Forlag.
Ginsberg, E. (2011) *The 'Enlightainment' Project – An Analysis of the Satire of Jon Stewart and Stephen Colbert*. Unpublished Master Thesis.
Giugni, M. (2008) Political, Biographical, and Cultural Consequences of Social Movements. *Sociology Compass*, Vol. 2, Issue 5, pp. 1582–1600.
Gladwell, M. (2000) *The Tipping Point – How Little Things Can Make a Big Difference*. Little, Brown and Company.
Gladwell, M. (2010) *Small Change: Why the Revolution will not be Tweeted*. The New Yorker.
Gnärig, B. (2015) *The Hedgehog and the Beetle. Disruption and Innovation in the Civil Society Sector*. Vorschau.
Goffman, E. (1974) *Frame Analysis: An Essay on the Organization of Experience*. Harper & Row.
Gold, R. (1958) Roles in Sociological Field Observation. *Social Forces*, Vol. 36, Issue 3, pp. 217–223. Oxford University Press.
González-Bailón, S., Borge-Holthoefer, J. and Moreno, A. (2013) *The Dynamics of Protest Recruitment through an Online Network*. Scientific Reports, Nature Publishing Group.
Goodwin, J. and Polletta, F. (2000) The Return of the Repressed: The Fall and Rise of Emotions in Social Movement Theory. *Mobilization*, Vol. 5, Issue 1, pp. 65–84.
Goodwin, J. and Polletta, F. (2001) Why Emotions Matter. In J Goodwin, J. M Jasper and F. Polletta (Eds), *Passionate Politics*, pp. 1–24. Chicago: University of Chicago Press.
Gorz, A. (2010) *The Immaterial*. Seagull Books.
Gramsci, A. (1992) *Prison Notebooks*. Columbia University Press.
Granovetter, M. (1973) *The strength of weak ties. American Journal of Sociology*, vol. 78, Issue 6, pp. 1360–80.
Gundelach, P. and Siune, K. Eds. (1992) *From Voters to Participants*. Politica.
Gurr, T. (1970) *Why Men Rebel*. Princeton, NJ: Princeton University Press.
Gusfield, J. A. (1994) The Reflexivity of Social Movements: Collective Behavior and Mass Society Theory Revisited. In Larana, Johnston, and Gusfield (Eds), *New Social Movements*, pp. 58–78. Temple University Press.
Habermas, J. (1984–1987) *The Theory of Communicative Action*. Beacon Press.
Habermas, J. (1989) *The Structural Transformation of the Public Sphere*. Polity Press.
Habermas, J. (1990). *Moral Consciousness and Communicative Action*. Polity Press.
Haddad, M. A. (2006) Civic Responsibilities and Patterns of Voluntary Participation Around the World. *Comparative Political Studies*, Vol. 39, Issue 10, pp. 1220–1242.
Hanson, N. R. (1958) *Patterns of Discovery: An Inquiry into the Conceptual Foundations of Science*. Cambridge University Press.
Hariman, R. (2008) Political Parody and Public Culture. *Quarterly Journal of Speech*, Vol. 94, Issue 3, pp. 247–272.

Harrebye, S. (2011) Global Civil Society and International Summits: New Labels for Different Types of Activism. *Journal of Civil Society*, Vol. 7, Issue 4, pp. 407–426. Routledge.

Harrebye, S. (2014) *Jeg er træt af kravet om aktiv deltagelse*. Information.

Harrebye, S. (2015) The Ambivalence of Creative Activism as a Reorganization of Critique. *Culture and Organization*, Vol. 21, Issue 2. pp. 126–146. Taylor & Francis.

Harrebye, S. (2016) Facilitating Active Citizenship – Creative Activism in-between Critique and Suggestion at the COP15 Climate Summits in Copenhagen. Special Issue. *Open Social Science Journal*. Forthcoming.

Harrebye, S. and Ejrnæs, A. (2015) European Patterns of Participation – How Dissatisfaction Motivates Extra-Parliamentary Types of Participation Given the Right Institutional Conditions. *Comparative European Politics*, Vol. 13, Issue 2, pp. 151–174. Palgrave Macmillan.

Harvey, D. (2000) *Spaces of Hope*. Berkeley, CA: University of California Press.

Heath, J. and Potter, A. (2006) *The Rebel Sell – How the Counterculture Became Consumer Culture*. Capstone.

Heelas, P. (1996) *The New Age Movement*. Blackwell Publishers.

Hendricks, V. (2008) *Mainstream and Formal Epistemology*. Cambridge University Press.

Herriott, R. E. and Firestone, W. A. (1983) Multisite Qualitative Policy Research: Optimizing Description and Generalizability. *Educational Researcher*, Vol. 12, Issue 2, pp. 4–12.

Hess and Martin (2006) Repression, Backfire, and the Theory of Transformative Events. *Mobilization*, Vol. 11, Issue 1, pp. 249–267.

Hill and Rothschild (1992) The Impact of Regime on the Diffusion of Political Conflict. In Midlarsky (Ed.), *The Internationalization of Communal Strife*, pp. 189–206. Routledge.

Himmelstrup, J. (1964) *Terminologisk ordbog til Søren Kierkegaards samlede værker*. Gyldendals Forlag.

Hirschman, A. (1970) *Exit, Voice, and Loyalty: Responses to Decline in Firms, Organizations, and States*. Harvard University Press.

Hochschild, A. R. (1983) *The Managed Heart. Commercialization of Human Feeling*. University of California Press.

Hogan, K. (2002) *Understanding Facilitation*. (Kogan Page Publishers).

Holmes, M. (2004) The Importance of Being Angry: Anger in Political Life. *European Journal of Social Theory*, Vol. 7, Issue 2, pp. 123–132.

Holst, C. (2005) Nancy Fraser I kritikkens Landskab. *Kvinder, Køn og Forskning*, No. 4.

Honneth, A. (2000) *Suffering From Indeterminacy: An Attempt at a Reactualization of Hegel's Philosophy of Right – Two Lectures*. Uitgeverrij Van Gorcum.

Honneth, A. (2003) *Behovet for anerkendelse*. Hans Reitzels Forlag.

Honneth, A. (2006) *Kamp om anerkendelse*. Hans Reitzels Forlag.

Høpner, J., Sørensen, H. B., Jørgensen, T. B. and Andersen, T. (2010) *Modstillinger I organisations- og ledelsesteori*. Hans Reitzels Forlag.

Horkheimer, M. and Adorno, T. W. 2007. *Dialectics of Enlightenment*. Stanford University Press.

Horvath, A., Thomassen, B. and Wydra, H. (2015) *Breaking Boundaries – Varieties of Liminality*. Berghahn Books.

234 Bibliography

Hoskins, B. and Mascherini, M. (2009) Measuring Active Citizenship through the Development of Composite Indicators. *Social Indicators Research*, Vol. 90, pp. 459–488.
Howaldt, J. and Schwarz, M. (2010) *Social Innovation: Concepts, Research Fields and International Trends*. Sozialforschungstelle, Dortmund.
Hulgaard, L. (2007) *Sociale entreprenører – en kritisk indføring*. Hans Reitzel.
Hulgaard, L. and Holm-Pedersen, P. (2009) *Den sociale virksomhed*. Turbulens.
Hunt, B., and Snow (1994) Identity Fields: Framing Processes and the Social Construction of Movement Identities. In Larana, Johnston, and Gusfield (Eds), *New Social Movements*, pp. 185–208. Temple University Press.
Husted, E. (2015) Organiseringen af Alternativ Politisk Deltagelse: Udkast til en Typologi. *Politik*, Vol. 18, Issue 2, pp. 13–23.
Hutcheson, D. S. and Korosteleva, E. A. (2006) Patterns of Participation in Post-Soviet Politics. *Comparative European Politics*, Vol. 4, Issue 1, pp. 23–46.
Inglehart, R. (1990) Values, Ideology, and Cognitive Mobilization in New Social Movements. In Dalton and Kuechler (Eds), *Challenging the Political Order*, pp. 43–66. Oxford University Press.
Inglehart, R. and Welzel, C. (2005) *Modernization, Cultural Change, and Democracy. The Human Development Sequence*. Cambridge University Press.
Innes, J. and Booher, D. (2004) Reframing Public Participation: Strategies for the 21st Century. *Planning Theory and Practice*, Vol. 5, Issue 4, pp. 419–436.
Jacoby, R. (1999) *The End of Utopia*. New York: Basic Books.
Jameson, F. (2004) The Politics of Utopia. *New Left Review*, Vol. 25, pp. 35–54. http://newleftreview.org/II/25/fredric-jameson-the-politics-of-utopia
Janik, V. K. (1998) *Fools and Jesters in Litterature, Art, and History: A Bio-Bibliographical Sourcebook*. Greenwood.
Janoski, T. (1998) *Citizenship and Civil Society: A Framework of Rights & Obligations in Liberal, Traditional, and Social Democratic Regimes*. Cambridge: Cambridge University Press.
Jasper, J. M. (2006) Emotions and the Microfoundations of Politics: Rethinking Ends and Means. In S. Clarke, P. Hoggett, and S. Thompson (Eds), *Emotion, Politics, and Society*, pp. 14–30. New York: Palgrave Macmillan.
Jenkins, J. C. (1983) Resource Mobilization Theory and the Study of Social Movements. *Annual Review of Sociology*, Vol. 9, pp. 527–553.
Jensen, A. F. (2009) *Projektmennesket* [The Project Human Being-own translation]. Aarhus: Aarhus Universitetsforlag.
Johnston, H. and Klandermans, B. (1995) *Social Movements and Culture*. Minneapolis, MN: University of Minnesota Press.
Johnston, H., Larana, E. and Gusfield, G. R. (1994) *New Social Movements. From Ideology to Identity*. Temple University Press.
Junker, B. (1960) *Field Work*. University of Chicago Press.
Kaldor, M. (2008) Democracy and Globalization. In Albrow, M., Kaldor, M., Glasius, M., Anheier, H. and Price, M. E. (Eds), *Global Civil Society 2007/08 – Communicative Power and Democracy*. Sage.
Kant, I. (2007) *Critique of Pure Reason*. Penguin Books.
Kaner, S. (2007) *Facilitator's Guide to Participatory Decision-Making*. (Jossey-Bass).
Kellner, D. (1989) *Baudrillard – From Marxism to Postmodernism and Beyond*. Stanford University Press.

Keniston, K. (1967). The Sources of Student Dissent. *Journal of Social Issues*, Vol. 23, Issue 3, pp. 108–137.
Kenny, K. (2009) 'The Performative Surprise': Parody, Documentary and Critique. *Culture and Organization* Vol. 15, Issue 2, pp. 221–235.
Kessler, G. (2014) *One in Five Women in College Sexually Assaulted: An Update on the Statistics*. The Washington Post.
Kierkegaard, S. (1920–1936) *Samlede Værker* (1–15) (Collected Works). Copenhagen: Drachmann, Heiberg, and Lange.
Klandermans, B. (1992) The Social Construction of Protest and Multiorganizational Fields. In Morris and Mueller (Eds), *Frontiers of Social Movement Theory*, pp. 77–103. Yale University Press.
Kliman, A. (2012) *The Make-Believe World of David Graeber: Reflections on the Ideology of Underlying the Failed Occupation of Zuccotti Park*. Marxist Humanist Initiative. http://www.marxisthumanistinitiative.org/alternatives-to-capital/the-make-believe-world-of-david-graeber.html
Kolakowski, L. (1966) *Mennesket Uden Alternativ*. Fremad.
Krastev, I. (2014) *Democracy Disrupted – The Politics of Global Protest*. University of Pennsylvania Press.
Krishna, A. (2002) Enhancing Political Participation: What Is the Role of Social Capital? *Comparative Political Studies*, Vol. 35, Issue 4, pp. 437–460.
Kristensen, C. J. (2011) Medarbejderdrevet Innovation. In *Innovation og Entreprenørskab*. Hans Reitzel.
Kristensen, C. J. and Voxted, S. Eds. (2011). *Innovation og Entreprenørskab*. Hans Reitzel.
Kron, J. and Goodman, J. D. (2012) Online, a Distant Conflict Soars to Topic No. 1. *New York Times*. See: http://www.nytimes.com/2012/03/09/world/africa/online-joseph-kony-and-a-ugandan-conflict-soar-to-topic-no-1
Kudahl, S. and Jørgensen, J. (2013) *Borgerne vil have mere direkte indflydelse I kommunen*. Momentum.
Kymlicka, W. (2002) *Contemporary Political Philosophy – An Introduction*. Oxford: Oxford University Press.
Larsen, S. N. (2011) En Nation af Kreativitetsslaver. *Asterisk*. DPU, Aarhus Universitet.
Larsen, S. N. and Pedersen, I. K. (2011) *Sociologisk leksikon*. Hans Reitzels Forlag.
Lash, S. 1994. Reflexivity and Its Doubles: Structure, Aesthetics, Community. In U. Beck, A. Giddens and S. Lash (Eds), *Reflexive Modernization. Politics, Tradition and Aesthetics in the Modern Social Order*, pp. 110–173. Cambridge: Polity Press.
Latour, B. et al. (2012) 'The Whole Is Always Smaller than Its Parts' – A Digital Test of Gabriel Tarde's Monads. *The British Journal of Sociology*, Vol. 63, Issue 4, pp. 590–615.
Lazzarato, M. (2011) The Misfortunes of the 'Artistic Critique' and of Cultural Employment. In Raunig, Ray, and Wuggenig (Eds), *Critique of Creativity: Precarity, Subjectivity, and Resistance in the 'Creative Industries'*. Mayfly.
Lefebvre, Henri. 1991. *The Production of Space*. Oxford: Blackwell.
Lenin, V. (1960–1970) *Collected Works*. Progress Publishers.
Letki, N. (2003) Explaining Political Participation in East-Central Europe: Social Capital, Democracy and the Communist Past. Paper presented at the Annual Meeting of the American Political Science Association.

Levitas, R. (1990) *The Concept of Utopia*. London: Philip Allan.
Leys, R. (2015) The Turn to Affect: A Critique. Working paper for Conference on University of Copenhagen, May 27, 2015.
Lind, M. and Velthuis, O. Eds. (2012) *Contemporary Art and Its Commercial Markets. A Report on Current Conditions and Future Scenarios*. Berlin: Sternberg Press.
Lindekilde, L., Mouritsen, P. and Zapata-Barrero, R. (2009) The Mohhamed Cartoon Controversy in Comparative Perspective. *Ethnicities*, Vol. 9, pp. 291–313.
Luhmann, N. 1995. *Social Systems*. Stanford University Press.
Lund, A. B. and Meyer, G. (2011) *Civilsamfundets ABC*. Møller.
Lykkeberg, R. (2012) *Alle har ret – Demokrati som princip og problem*. Gyldendal.
Malantschuk, G. (1968) *Dialektik og Eksistens hos Søren Kierkegaard* [Dialectics and Existence in Søren Kierkegaard's Writing – own translation]. Copenhagen: Hans Reitzels Forlag.
Maloney and Deth (2010) *Civil Society and Activism in Europe*. Routledge.
Mannheim, K. (1968) *Ideology and Utopia*. London: Routledge and Kegan Paul Ltd.
Marin, L. (1984) *Utopics: Spatial Play*. Macmillan.
Marsh, O. and Jones (2007) *Young People and Politics in the UK*. Houndmills, Basingstoke: Palgrave Macmillan.
Mascherini, M., Saltelli, A. and Vidoni, D. (2007) *Participation in Europe: One-Size-Fits-None*. Institute for the Protection and Security of the Citizen. European Commission.
Marx, K. (1968) *Die Frühschriften*. Alfred Kröner Verlag.
Mason, P. (2012) *Why It's Kicking Off Everywhere: The New Global Revolutions*. London: Verso.
Massumi, B. (2002) *Parables for the Virtual: Movement, Affect, Sensation*. Durham, NC.
McAdam, D. (1999) *Political Proces and the Development of Black Insurgency*, 1930–1970. The University of Chacago Press.
McAdam, D. (2010) *Socil Movements: Power From Above and Below*. Talk at Fletcher Summer Institute for the Advanced Study of Non-Violent Conflict.
McAdam, D, McCarthy, J. D. and Zald, M. N. (1996) *Comparative Perspectives on Social Movements*. Cambridge University Press.
McAdam, D. and Sewell, W. H. Jr. (2001) It's About Time: Temporality in the Study of Social Movements and Revolutions. In Aminzade et al. (Eds), *Silence and Voice in the Study of Contentious Politics*, ch. 4. Cambridge University Press.
McAdam, D., Tarrow, S., and Tilly, C. (1996) To Map Contentious Politics. *Mobilization*, Vol. 1, Issue 1, pp. 17–34. San Diego State University.
McAdam, D., Tarrow, S. and Tilly, C. (2001) *Dynamics of Contention*. Cambridge University Press.
McCarthy, J. D. and Zald, M. N. (1977) Resource Mobilization and Social Movements: A Partial Theory. *The American Journal of Sociology*, Vol. 82, Issue 6, pp. 1212–1241.
McKinnon, M., Gibson, K. and Malam, L. (2008) Introduction: Critical and Hopeful Area Studies – Emerging Work in Asia and the Pacific. *Asia Pacific Viewpoint*, Vol. 49, Issue 3, pp. 273–280.
Meltzoff, A. (1990) *Foundations for Developing a Concept of Self: The Role of Imitation in Relating Self to Others and the Value of Social Mirroring, Social Modeling, and Self Practice in Infancy*. University of Chicago Press.

Melucci, A. (1989) *Nomads of the Present: Social Movements and Individual Needs in Contemporary Society* (Keane and Mier, Eds). Temple University Press.
Meyer, D. S. (2004) Protest and Political Opportunities. *Annual Review of Sociology*, Vol. 30, pp. 125–145.
Meyer, D. S. and Minkoff, D. C. (2004) Conceptualizing Political Opportunity. *Social Forces*, Vol. 82, Issue 4, pp. 1457–1492.
Miessen, M. (2011) *Nightmare of Participation*. Sternberg Press.
Milan, S. (2013) *Social Movements and their Technologies: Wiring Social Change*. Palgave Macmillan.
Miles, R., Miles, G., and Snow, C. (2005) *Collaborative Entrepreneurship*. Standford University Press.
Mintz, S. (1985) *Sweetness and Power*. Penguin.
Mohmood, S. (2005) *Politics of Piety: The Islamic Revival and the Feminist Subject*. Princeton University Press.
Moore, M. (2009) *Capitalism: A Love Story*. Dog Eat Dog Films.
More, T. (2007) *Utopia*. Sioux Falls: NuVisions Publications.
Moro (2004) *Public Institutions Interacting with Citizens' Organizations: A survey on public policies regarding civic activism in Europe* (online). Available at: http://www.activecitizenship.net/images/stories/DOCS/civic%20participation/CNEFinal_Report.pdf (accessed 20 Feb. 2010).
Morris, A. D. (1984) *The Origin of the Civil Rights Movement*. The Free Press.
Moufe, C. (2007) Artistic Activism and Agonistic Spaces. *Art & Research*, Vol. 1, Issue 2, pp. 1–5.
Moulaert, F. (2010) *Can Neighborhoods Save The City? Community Development and Social Innovation* (Chapter 1). Routledge.
Moulaert, F., MacCallum, D., Mehmood, A. and Hamdouch, A. (2013) *The International Handbook On Social Innovation – Collective Action, Social Learning, and Transdisciplinary Research*, Final Report for KARARSIS under EU FP6.
Moulier-Boutang, Y. (2011) *Cognitive Capitalism*. Polity Press.
Mueller, C. M. (1994) Conflict Networks and the Origins of Women's Liberation. In Larana, Johnston, and Gusfield (Eds), *New Social Movements*, pp. 234–263. Temple University Press.
Mulgan, G. (2007) *Social Innovation – What It Is, Why It Matters, and How It Can Be Accelerated*. The Young Foundation/The Basingstoke Press.
Neuman, W. L. (2000) *Social Research Methods – Qualitative and Quantitative Approaches* (4th ed.). Allyn & Bacon.
Newton, K. and Giebler, H. (2008). Patterns of Participation: Political and Social Participation in 22 Nations. Discussion paper for Wissenschaftscentrum Berlin für Sozialforschung. Available at: http://bibliothek.wzb.eu/pdf/2008/iv08-201.pdf.
Nielsen, H. K. (2015) Artistic Interventions in the Political Public Sphere – Democratic Potentials and Limitations. Paper Presented at the Conference The Democratic Public Sphere at Aarhus University, November 5–7, 2015.
Nielsen, H. K. and Simonsen, K.-M. (2008) *Æstetik og politik – Analyser af politiske potentialer I samtidskunsten* [Aesthetics and Politics, Analyses of the Political Potential in Contemporary Art – own translation]. Aarhus: Klim.
Nielsen, J. and Lund, E. (2015) *Journalisten der snød Gestapo*. Information.
Nowotny, S. (2011) Immanent Effects: Notes on Cre-Activity. In Raunig, Ray, and Wuggenig (Eds), *Critique of Creativity: Precarity, Subjectivity, and Resistance in the 'Creative Industries'*, pp. 9–23. Mayfly.

O'Doherty, P. D. (2007) Heidegger's unfunny and the academic text. In Westwood, R. and Rhodes, C. (Eds) *Humour, Work, and Organization*, pp. 180–204. Routledge.

Obama, Barack. 2011. "Speech from the White House on 12 February." Accessed May 14, 2013. http://www.whitehouse.gov/the-press-office/2011/02/11/remarks-president-egypt

Offe, C. (1984) *Contradiction in the Welfare States*. London: Huchington.

Olesen, T. (2007) The Porous Public and the Transnational Dialectic. The Muhammed Cartoon Conflict. *Acta Sociologica*, Vol. 50, Issue 3, pp. 295–308.

Olesen, T. (2015) *Global Injustice Symbols and Social Movements*. Palgrave.

Olesen, T. and Lindekilde, L. (2015) *Politisk protest, aktivisme og sociale bevægelser*. Hans Reitzels Forlag.

Ølgaard, D. (2015) Play, Politics, & the Practice of Resistance. *Journal of Resistance Studies*, Vol. 1, Issue 1, pp. 119–153.

Oliveira (2008) *Global Civil Society 2007/08*. LSE.

Olsen, H. (2002) *Kvalitative Kvaler – Kvalitative metoder og danske kvalitative interviewundersøgelsers kvalitet*. Akademisk Forlag.

Olson, M. (1965) *The Logic of Collective Action*. Harvard University Press.

O'Reilly, T. and Battelle, J. (2009) *Web Squared: Web 2.0 Five Years On*. O'Reilly Media Inc.

Østergaard, M. and Willig, R. (2005) *Sociale patologier*. Hans Reitzel.

Parker, M. (2002) *Utopia and Organization*. Oxford: Blackwell Publishing.

Pearce, J. (2007) Toward a Post-Representational Politics?: Participation in the 21st Century. *World Futures: The Journal of Global Education*, Vol. 63, Issue 5–6, pp. 464–478.

Pedersen, L. R. (2009) *Tidens nye tendens – social iværksætteri*. Turbulens.

Pinsky, D. (2009) *The Mirror Effect – How Celebrity Narcissism Is Seducing America*. Harper Collins Publishers.

Pirsig, R. (1974) *Zen and the Art of Motorcycle Maintenance*. William Morrow.

Plotke, D. (1990) What's So New About New Social Movements? *Socialist Review*, Vol. 20, pp. 81–102.

Popovic et al. (2007) *Canvas Core Curriculum – A Guide to Effective Nonviolent Struggle*. CANVAS.

Porter, M. and Kramer, M. (2011) *How to Fix Capitalism – And Unleash a New Wave of Growth*. Harvard Business Review.

Putnam, R. (2000) *Bowling Alone*. New York: Simon & Shuster.

Putnam, R. D. (1995) Bowling Alone: Americas Declining Social Capital. *Journal of Democracy*, Vol. 6, Issue 1, pp. 65–78.

Rabinow, P. Ed. (1997) *The Essential Works of Michel Foucault 1954–1985*. The New Press.

Radin, P. (1956) *The Trickster: A Study in American Indian Mythology*. New York: Philosophical Library.

Ragin, C. C. (1992) 'Casing' and the Process of Social Inquiry. In Ragin and Becker (Eds), *What Is a Case. Exploring the Foundations of Social Inquiry*, pp. 217–226. Cambridge University Press.

Ranciére, J. (1991) *The Nights of Labor: The Workers' Dream in Nineteen Century France*. Temple University Press.

Rancière, J. (2004) *The Politics of Aesthetics: The Distribution of the Sensible*. Continuum.

Rancière, J. (2006) *Aesthetic Separation, Aesthetic Community: Scenes from the Aesthetic Regime of Art*. Art and Research.
Rancière, J. and Panagia, D. (2000) Dissenting Words: A Conversation. *Diacritics*, Vol. 30, Issue 2, pp. 113–126.
Rasborg, L. (2014) *Spejling og jeg-støtte*. Psykologi.
Ravn, I. (2011) *Facilitering: Ledelse af møder der skaber værdi og mening*. (Hans Reitzels forlag).
Rebughini, P. (2010) Critique and Social Movements: Looking Beyond Contingency and Normativity. *European Journal of Social Theory*, Vol. 13, Issue 4, pp. 459–479. Sage.
Rehmann, J. (2013) Occupy Wall Street and the Question of Hegemony: A Gramscian Analysis. *Socialism and Democracy*, Vol. 27, Issue 1, pp. 1–18.
Reiermann, J. (2015) *Alternativet A/S*. Mandag Morgen.
Rheingold. 2005. *Technologies of the Self*. Institute for the Future.
Riley, J. E. (2000) Dunkelt men klart. See http://www.sli.uio.no-150/prosjekterv2000/vinduet/
Rochon, T. R. (1988) *Mobilizing for Peace: The Antinuclear Movements in Western Europe*. Princeton University Press.
Rochon, T. R. (1998) *Culture Moves – Ideas, Activism, and Changing Values*. Princeton University Press.
Rolnik, S. (2011) The Geopolitics of Pimping. In Raunig, Ray, and Wuggenig (Eds), *Critique of Creativity: Precarity, Subjectivity, and Resistance in the 'Creative Industries'*, pp. 23–41. Mayfly.
Rosa, H. (2005) The Speed of Global Flows and the Pace of Democratic Politics. *New Political Science*, Vol. 27, Issue 4, pp. 445–459. Routledge.
Rosa, H. (2014) *Fremmedgørelse og acceleration*. Hans Reitzels Forlag.
Rosendahl, N. Y. (2015) *Det er ikke længere nok at side I rundkreds*. Information.
Ross, K. (1988) *The Emergence of Social Space*. New York: Macmillan Press.
Rothstein, B. and Stolle, D. (2003) Introduction: Social Capital in Scandinavia. *Scandinavian Political Studies*, Vol. 25, Issue 1, pp. 1–26.
Rothstein, B. and Stolle, D. (2007). *The Quality of Government and Social Capital: A Theory of Political Institutions and Generalised trust*. QoG Working paper series no 2, Göteborg University.
Rothstein, B., Samanni, M. and Toerell, J. (2010) *Quality of Government, Political Power and the Welfare State*. QoG Working paper series no 6, Göteborg University.
Rucht, D. (1988) Themes, Logics, and Arenas of Social Movements: A Structural Approach. In Klandermans, Kriesi, and Tarrow (Eds), *International Social Movement Research*, Vol. 1, pp. 305–328.
Rucht, D. (1999) The Impact of Environmental Movements in Western Europe. In M. Giugni, D. McAdam and C. Tilly (Eds), *How Social Movements Matter*. University of Minnesota Press.
Rucht, D. (2004) The Quadruple A: Media Strategies of Protest Movements Since the 1960s. In W. van de Bonk, B. D. Loader, P. G. Nixon and D. Rucht (Eds), *Cyber Protest: New Media, Citizens, and Social Movements*, pp. 29–56. Routledge.
Sandford, M. R. (1995) *Happenings and Other Acts*. Routledge.
Sargisson, L. (1996) *Contemporary Feminist Utopianism*. Routledge.
Scharmer, O. (2009) *Theory U. Leading from the Future as It Emerges. The Social Technology of Presencing*. Berrett-Koehler Publishers, Inc.

Schlozman, K. L., Verba, S. and Brady, Henry (1995) Participation's Not a Paradox: The View from American Activists. *British Journal of Political Science*, Vol. 25, Issue 1, pp. 1–36.
Schmidt, E. and Cohen, J. (2013) *The New Digital Age: Reshaping the Future of People, Nations and Business*. New York: Knopf.
Scholten, P. (2006) *Social Return on Investment: A Guide to SROI Analysis*. Lenthe.
Scott, J. C. (1990) *Domination and the Art of Resistance 'Hidden Transcripts'*. Yale University Press.
Scott, J. C. (2012) *Two Cheers for Anarchism*. Princeton University Press.
Sennet, R. (2000) *The Corrosion of Character – The Personal Consequences of Work in the New Capitalism*. Norton and Company.
Sewell, W. (1996) Three Temporalities: Toward an Eventful Sociology. In McDonald (Ed.), *The Historic Turn in the Human Sciences*, pp. 245–280. University of Michigan Press.
Sharp, G. (1999) Nonviolent Action. In Kurtz, L. R. and Turpin, J. E. (Eds), *Encyclopedia of Violence, Peace, and Conflict*, Vol. 2, pp. 567–574. Academic Press.
Sharp, G. (2005) *Waging Nonviolent Struggle: 20th Century Practice and 21th Century Potential*. Sargent.
Shirky, C. (2010) *Here Comes Everybody – The Power of Organizing without Organizations*. Penguin Press.
Smelser, N. J. (1962) *Theory of Collective Behavior*. Free Press.
Smith, M. L. (2009) The Inequality of Participation: Re-examining the Role of Social Stratification and Post-Communism on Political Participation in Europe. *Czech Sociological Review*, Vol. 45, Issue 3, pp. 487–517.
Snow, D. and Soule, S. (2010) *A Primer on Social Movements*. Contemporary Societies.
Sohrabi-Haghighat and Mansouri (2010) 'Where's My Vote?' ICT Politics in the Aftermath of Iran's Presidential Election. *International Journal of Emerging Technologies and Society*, Vol. 8, Issue 1, pp. 24–41.
Sørensen, P. K. (2012) Project Critique – On Social Critique and Participation in Project Based Movements. *European Social Science* (forthcoming).
Sørensen, E. and Torfing, J. (Eds) (2006) *Democratic Network Governance*. Palgrave Macmillan.
Sørensen, E. and Torfing, J. (2009) Making Governance Networks Effective and Democratic Through Metagovernance. *Public Administration*, Vol. 87, Issue 2, pp. 234–258.
Sørensen, E. and Torfing, J. (2011) *Samarbejdsdrevet innovation – i den offentlige sektor*. Jurist- og økonomiforbundets forlag.
Spradley, J. (1980) *Participant Observation*. Holt, Rinehart and Winston.
Sriskandarajah, D. et al. (2014) *An Open Letter to Our Fellow Activists Around the Globae: Building From Below and Beyond Borders*. Blogs.civicus.org.
Stake, R. E. (2000) Case Studies. In N. K. Denzin and Y. S. Lincoln (Eds), *Handbook of Qualitative Research*, pp. 435–453. Thousand Oaks: Sage.
Stekelenburg, J., van, Roggeband, C. and Klandermans, B. (2013) *The Future of Social Movement Research: Dynamics, Mechanisms, and Processes*. Minneapolis: University of Minnesota Press.
Stephensen, J. L. (2008) Kunst, kreativitet og arbejde – Forskydninger I kunstens utopiske legitimering. In Nielsen and Simonsen (Eds), *Æstetik og politik – Analyser af politiske potentialer I samtidskunsten*. Klim.

Stoker, G. et al. (2011) *Prospects for Citizenship*. London, New York: Bloomsbury Academic.
St. John, G. (2008) Protestival: Global Days of Action and Carnivalized Politics in the Present. *Social Movement Studies: Journal of Social, Cultural and Political Protest*, Vol. 7, Issue 2, pp. 167–190.
Tanggaard, L. (2014) *Opfindsomhed*. Gyldendal.
Tarrow, S. (1991) *Struggle, Politics, and Reform: Collective Action, Social Movements, and Cycles of Protest*. Western Societies, Paper No. 21. Cornell.
Tarrow, S. (1998) *Power in Movement – Social Movements and Contentious Politics* (2nd ed.). Cambridge University Press.
Tarrow, S. (2012) *Strangers at the Gates – Movements and States in Contentious Politics*. Cambridge University Press.
Taylor, B. (2012) *Transformations of the American Left: Anarchism, Alterglobalization, and the New Spirit of Capitalism*, paper presented at APSA annunal meeting.
Thomassen, B. (2012) Notes Towards an Anthropology of Political Revolutions. *Comparative Studies in Science and History*, Vol. 54, Issue 3, pp. 679–706.
Thomassen, B. and Riisgaard, L. (forthcoming) *Powers of the Mask: Political Subjectivation and Rites of Transformation in Local-Global Protests*.
Thompson, S. (2006). Anger and the Struggle for Justice. In C. Hoggett and S. Thompson (Eds), *Emotion, Politics, and Society*. New York: Palgrave Macmillan, pp. 123–144.
Thornton, P. M. (2002) Framing Dissent in Contemporary China: Irony, Ambiguity and Metonymy. *The China Quarterly*, Vol. 171, pp. 661–681. Cambridge University Press.
Thrift, N. (2004) *Intensities of Feeling: Towards a Spatial Politics of Affect*. Geografiska Annaler, p. 86.
Thrift, N. (2008) *Non-Representational Theory – Space, Politics, Affect*. Routledge.
Tilly, C. (1978) *From Mobilization to Revolution*. Addition-Wesley Publishing Co.
Tilly, C. (1995) *Popular Contention in Great Britain, 1758–1834*. Harvard University Press.
Tilly, C. (2008) *Contentious Performances*. Cambridge University Press.
Tobias, S. (2005) Foucault on Freedom and Capabilities. *Theory, Culture & Society*, Vol. 22, Issue 4, pp. 65–85.
Touraine, A. (1981) *The Voice and the Eye: An Analysis of Social Movements*. Cambridge University Press.
Turner, V. (1964) Betwixt and Between. *The Proceedings of the American Ethnological Society*, pp. 4–20.
Turner, V. (1988) *The Anthropology of Performance*. New York: PAJ Publications.
Turner, R. H. and Killian, L. M. (1972) *Collective Behavior*. Prentice-Hall.
Van Deth, et. al. (2013) Using Twitter to Mobilize Protest Action. Paper for panel discussion on Transnational dimensions of protest at Johannes Gutenburg University.
Verba, S., Schlozman, K. L. and Brady, H. (1995) Participation's Not a Paradox: The View from American Activists. *British Journal of Political Science*, Vol. 25, Issue 1, pp. 1–36.
Waisanen, D. J. (2009) A Citizen's Guide to Democracy Inaction: Jon Stewart and Stephen Colbert's Comic Rhetorical Criticism. *Southern Communication Journal*, Vol. 74, Issue 2, pp. 119–140.
Warburg et al. (2014) *Discussion paper on Social Movements for ActionAid Denmarks Board Meeting 05.11.2014*. Action Aid Denmark.

Warming, H. (2007) Deltagende Observation. In Fuglsang, Hagedorn-Rasmussen, and Olsen (Eds), *Samfundsvidenskabelige Teknikker*. Samfundslitteratur.
Westwood, R. (2014) Comic Relief. *Organisation Studies*, Vol. 25, Issue 5, pp. 775–795.
Weinstein, M. M. (2009) *Measuring Success: How Robin Hood Estimates the Impact of Grants*. Robin Hood Foundation.
Whiteley, P. (2009) Is the Party Over? The Decline of Party Activism and Membership Across the Democratic World. Paper Presented at the Panel on Party Membership and Activism in Comparative Perspective, Political Studies Association Meeting, University of Manchester.
Willig, R. (2007) *Til forsvar for kritikken*. Reitzels Forlag.
Willig, R. (2009) *Umyndiggørelse*. Reitzels Forlag.
Willig, R. (2013) *Kritikkens U-vending*. Reitzels Forlag.
Wilmot, P. (2015) *Meet the Ugandan Peasant Grandmother Who Terrifies Her President*. Wagingnonviolence.org
Wolfe A. (1989) *Whose Keeper? Social Science and Moral Obligation*. San Francisco: University of California Press.
Wolff, Miles (1970) *Lunch at the 5 & 10*. Elephant Paperbacks.
Wright, E. O. (2010) *Real Envisioned Utopias*. Verso.
Young, I. M. (2003) Activist Challenges to Deliberative Democracy. In Fishkin and Laslett (Eds), *Debating Deliberative Democracy*. Blackwells.
Ziehe, Thomas (1997) Individualisering som det kulturelt forandrede selvforhold, *Social Kritik*, Vol. 52–53, pp. 129–135.
Zolberg, A. (1972) *Moments of Madness*. Politics and Society, 2: 183–207.

Index

A
Aaen, Frank, 8
Aboriginal culture, 212
acceleration society, 209–10
Action Aid Denmark, 181–4
active citizenship, 84–5
  designing, 86–9
activism
  in the 21st century, 3
  defined, 6
  in media, 6
  typology of, 81–4
  see also creative activism; participation; social movement
activist training centers, 5
Adbusters, 25–6
Adorno, Theodor, 99, 133
aesthetics and politics, 41–3
affective effect, 194
Afro-Americans, 37
Ai Weiwei, 122
al-Qaeda, 58
The Alternative, 72, 167–9
alternative principles of organization, 106–7
Alvesson, M., 155
ambivalence, 114–19, 213
American Civil Rights Movement, *see* Civil Rights Movement, United States
American Civil War, 120
anarchism as praxis, 163
Anderson, Benedict, 54
Angelica, Francisca, 86
Anonymous, 52, 62
Arab Spring, 30, 71, 126, 217
Arendt, Hannah, 198, 220
argument
  exclusion, 125–6
  interaction, 126–7
  practitioner's, 127–8
Art and Revolution, 5

artistic critique, 31
Art Workers Coalition, 27

B
Bach, Christian Friis, 197
Baisikeli, 175–6
Bakhtin, Mikhail, 104
Baldwin, James, 221
band-aid solutions, 218–19
The Battle in Seattle, 3, 56
Bauman, Zygmunt, 124, 216
Beautiful Rising, 182, 183, 185, 186
Beautiful Trouble, 181, 182, 198
Beck, Ulrich, 29
Benford, Robert D., 55
Benjamin, Walter, 198
Bennett, L. W., 56
Bergson, Henri, 101
Berlin Wall in 1989, 56
Bichlbaum, Andy, 33, 99, 100
bicycle culture, in Denmark, 217–18
bicycling activists, 197
Big Donor Show, 104–5
The Big Donorshow, 219
big politics, 127
Bildungsprozess, 123
The Billionaires for Bush, 33
Black Power salute, 49
BNN, 104
Bobel, Chris, 6
Boesen, Jakob Kirkemann, 187
Boltanski, Luc, 13, 30–1, 55, 93, 111–12, 114, 119, 131, 137, 139, 165, 172
Bonde, Lars, 86
Borch, Christian, 41
Bouazizi, Mohamed, 63–4, 217
Bourriaud, Nicolas, 222n4
Boyd, Andrew, 33, 115, 134
Brand, Karl-Werner, 28
Brecht, Bertolt, 18
Brown, Michael, 200

Brown vs. Board of Education, 38
Buddhist philosophy, change and, 209
Butler, Judith, 101–2

C
campaign, 69–71
  conditions to be met, 70
  defined, 69
  non-institutionalized, 70
  Salt March, 67
  violent and non-violent resistance, 70
campaign in Albany, Georgia, 39
campaign in Birmingham, Alabama, 39
camping critique, 216
camping site critique, 124
CANVAS, 57, 121–2, 219
capitalism
  analytically relating to, 135–8
  cognitive, 12
  effects on, 111
  lean, 112
  liberal democracy of, 28
  reflexive surface of, 131–5
  uncontinuity, 12
carbon emission countries, 88
Carlos, John, 49
Castells, Manuel, 51
caste system, United States, 37
Casually Pepper Spray Everything Cop, 26
causality, 193
Center for Artistic Activism, 27
change
  acceleration society, 209–10
  Buddhist philosophy on, 209
  defined steps, 211
  linear understanding of, 211
  measurement of, 189–221
  rethinking existing theories of, 208–21
Chenoweth, Erica, 69
Chiapello, Éve, 13, 30–1, 55, 93, 111–12, 114, 117, 119, 131, 137, 139, 165, 172
choreographers of assemblies, 56
Christiansen, Peter, 187

citizenship
  active, 84–5
  civil society and, 35
  civic activist organizations, 190–1
  civil disobedience, 70
  in India, 67
  civil right reforms, United States, 38
  Civil Rights Movement, United States, 37–40, 192, 200–1
civil society
  citizenship, 35
  decentralization process, 34
  mediating institutions, 34–6
  organized, 36
  state actors and, 34
Clinton, Hillary, 196
Coca-Cola, 86
cognitive capitalism, 12
Cohen, Leonard, 18
Cohen, Sacha Baron, 102
Colbert, Stephen, 15–16, 102, 147
Cold War, 38
comedy and satire, 102
communication technologies, 56
The Concept of Social Movement (Diani), 48
connective action, 56
Connor, Bull, 39
conscious inside stand on capitalism, 137–8
conscious outside stand on capitalism, 135–7
constructive reaction to dissatisfaction, 80
contextual epistemology, 193
cooperation, critique, cooptation and, 187–8
cooptation of social movement, 67–8
COP15 Copenhagen Climate Summit, 82, 84, 195–6, 198
COP21 in Paris in 2015, 88
corporate social responsibility (CSR), 174
cosmopolitical consciousness, 29
cotton industry, 37
country clusters, welfare provision and political institution, 77

cracks, 18–22
creative activism
  ambivalence, 114–19
  characteristics, 4–5
  cracks, 18–22
  definition, 14–18, 25
  globalization, 28–9
  measuring impact and value, 189–221
  as new phenomenon, 26–32
  as political theater, 4–6
  professionalization, see professionalization
  technological advances, 29–30
creative activists, 5
  critique, 111–14
  cynicism, 98–100
  ironic attitude, 100–5
  utopian imagination, 105–11
creative critics, 7–11
critical mirrors
  inside, 140–2
  outside, 142–4
critical strategies, 7–8
critical theory of reflection, 148–53
critique
  artistic, 31
  capitalism, 30–1
  cooperation and cooptation, 187–8
  creative critics, 111–14
  etymology, 7
  good life as a precondition for, 123–8
  social, 31
CSR, see corporate social responsibility (CSR)
cultural hegemony, 51, 61
cultural identity, 36
cultural movements, 194
cultural resistance, 28
culture
  Aboriginal, 212
  evaluating, 190–4
Cuninghame, P., 103
customer-suited service, 191
cynicism, 98–100
cynics, 98

D
The Daily Show, 102
Danida, 182, 186
Danish Bicycle Union, 217
Danish cartoon crisis in 2005–6, 55
Danish Islamic community, 55
Danish Roskilde Festival, *see* Roskilde Festival inDenmark
Dawson, Arthur Potts, 36
deadline, 120–2
Debord, Guy, 5
decision-making process, 162
Delanty, Gerard, 84
deliberative democracy, 29
  normative principles of, 33
  principles of, 79, 85, 86
  theories of, 33
demobilization of social movement, 67–8
democracy
  direct forms of, 35
  self-expression and, 73
dependent variable, 222–3
Derrida, Jacques, 105
détournement, 5, 25
  memes, 25–6
Dialectics of Enlightenment (Horkheimer and Adorno), 133
Diani, Mario, 31–2, 48, 68–9, 98
diffusion mechanisms, 57
digital communication platforms, 56
dissatisfaction
  constructive reaction to, 80
  cross-country comparison of, 76
  personal, and structural condition, 73–81
  welfare states, 75–80
Dixiecrats, 37
'Dome of Vision,' 164–5
Domination and the Art of Resistance (Scott), 61
drum circle, 164
Dugnad, 178
Duncombe, Stephen, 18, 21, 27, 108–9
Dutton, Michael, 113–14
Dynamics of Contention (McAdam, Tilly, Tarrow), 55
dystopianism, 105

Index

E
effective affect, 194
Egyptian Revolution, 56
18th Brumaire of Louis Bonaparte (Marx), 41
Eisinger, P., 52
Ejrnæs, Anders, 226
Elbæk, Uffe, 167–8
English Defense League, 58
Engström, Richard Georg, 178
Epstein, Barbara, 202
Esping-Andersen, G., 77
ethical spectacle, 116
ethnographic participatory observations, 206–7
European Union, 72
eutopia, 109, 110, 117
eventful protests, 18
events, defined, 17–18
evocative transcripts, 62
exclusion argument, 125–6
extra-parliamentary participation, 77–8

F
Facebook, 56
facilitator, 32
  in corporate context, 32
  training, 32
Fair Trade movement, 175
financial crisis, United States, 37, 56
Flacks, R., 55
Flames of War (video), 22
Folke, Steen, 187
Forbes, Steve, 217
Foucault, M., 8–9, 54, 64, 98, 120, 121, 136–9, 143, 152
Fournier, Valérie, 107
Frankfurt School, 121
Fraser, Nancy, 10, 89, 120, 128–31, 137, 140, 150–5, 157, 158, 224
Freedom Riders, 38
Freire, Paulo, 201
French Revolution, 50
Fukuyama, F., 118

G
Gadsden, Walter, 39
gag laws, 88

Gandhi, Mohandas, 26, 67
Ganz, Marshall, 34
Gennep, Arnold van, 212
Gerbauso, Paolo, 56
Giddens, Anthony, 39–40, 85
Gladwell, Malcolm, 30, 205, 209, 218, 2019
globalization, 28–9, 56
Gore, Al, 136
Graeber, David, 40, 202
Grameen Bank, 172–3
Gramsci, Antonio, 51
Great Depression, 37
Greenpeace, 52, 144, 166, 195–8
guerilla marketing, 116
Guernica (Picasso), 20

H
Habermas, Jürgen, 10, 85, 102, 125, 135
Hakim Bey, *see* Wilson, Peter Lamborn
happening, defined, 17
Hare Krishna, 52
Hariman, Robert, 101
Hayes, Rutherford B., 37
headlines, 120–2
Hegel, 123, 124
Heifetz, Ronald A., 211
Hess, David, 18
heterotopology of mirroring counter strategies, 138–40
hidden transcripts, 61
Highlander Institute, 180
hippie movement, 200
hippies, 200
Hirschman, Albert, 63
home-grown insurgency, 71
Honneth, Axel, 123–4, 125, 135
Horkheimer, Max, 133
Horton, Myles, 180
human development theory, 73
humor, and irony, 100–5
Humphrey, Carol, 62

I
identity correction, 99
identity politics, 43
ideological integrity, 191

ideology and utopia, 110
'I have a dream' (King), 38
immanent critique, 10
The Inconvenient Truth, 136
independent variable, 223
India, civil disobedience in, 67
Indignados, 52
Information, 102
infrapolitics, 63, 64, 101
Inglehart, Ronald, 73
innovation, 172–3
  social, 173–4
insurgency
  armed, 70
  home-grown, 71
interaction argument, 126–7
interdisciplinary approach, 22–4
Internet, 56
Internet data, 207
interventions, 207
interview/interviewing, 206
ironic attitude of creative activists, 100–5

J
Jameson, Fredric, 109
Jesus, 26
Jim Crow system, 37, 38
Jordan, John, 3, 36, 152–3
journalists, politicians and, 6
Justesen, Dines, 187
justice, social, 128–31

K
Kant, Immanuel, 8–9, 14, 124, 151
Keer, Joanna, 183
Kennedy, John F., 39
Kierkegaard, Søren, 101
King, Martin Luther, 26, 38–9, 180
King, Rodney, 57
Kliman, Andrew, 40–1
Kolakowski, Leszek, 127, 128
Kony, Joseph, 16–17
KONY 2012, 16–17, 146, 205, 219
Kotter, John, 211
Krastev, Ivan, 204
Ku Klux Klan, 39
Kurdi, Aylan, 39

L
Lagos, Richard, 63
Lambert, Steve, 27
leadership, 34
leafleting, 80
lean capitalism, 112
Lehman Brothers, 56
Lenin, V., 51
liberal democracy of capitalism, 28
life
  pace of, acceleration, 210
  rituals accompanying transitional stages in, 212
lifestyle movements, 218
liminality, 212–13
Lings, L.H.M., 41
Livia award, 201
Lord's Resistance Army in Uganda, 16
Luk Lejren event, 43
Lunacharsky, Anatoly, 113

M
Mannheim, Karl, 110
Manning, Bradley, 57
Marin, Louis, 19, 106
Martin, Brian, 18
Marx, Karl, 8, 51
mass culture, 51
mass media, 56–7
McAdam, Doug, 27, 55, 219
McAlpine, Robin, 192
Mead, Margaret, 40
Melucci, Alberto, 51
memes, 25–6
meta-activism, 87–8
meta-political misframing, 151
meta-political misrepresentation, 129
Middle East, 64
Miessen, Marcus, 170
Milošević regime in Serbia, 121, 219
mirror effect, 194
mirroring
  adults, 225
  defined, 225
  heterotopology of, 138–40
  infants, 225
  neurons, 224–5
  psychological technique, 225
mirroring neuron, 135, 224–5

mirrors
 critical, 140–4
 proposing, 145–8
mobilization
 dynamics of, 67
 phases, 66–7
Modernization, Cultural Change, and Democracy (Inglehart and Welzel), 73
Montgomery bus boycott, 38
More, Thomas, 109
More Than Music, 19, 107
Moufe, Chantall, 172
movement of 1977 in Italy, 27
Msonza, Natasha, 182
multi-modular digital networks, 57

N
NAACP, *see* National Association for the Advancement of Colored People (NAACP)
National Association for the Advancement of Colored People (NAACP), 38
NCC, *see* Nordic Construction Company (NCC)
Neighborhood Moms, 201–2
neophytes, 213
New Life festival, 86
new partnership, 180–7
new social movements (NSM), 54
The New Spirit of Capitalism (Boltanski and Chiapello), 13, 93
The New York Times by Yes Men, 108, 109
Nielsen, Henrik Kaare, 220, 222
Nielsen, Kai, 87
Nightmare of Participation (Miessen), 170
non-violent resistance, 70
Nordic Construction Company (NCC), 164–5
NSM, *see* new social movements (NSM)

O
Obama, Barack, 108
Occupy World Street (OWS), 39, 192, 202–4

Ølgaard, Daniel, 135
Olympics in Mexico City (1968), 49
Open Utopia (Duncombe), 108
Operation First Casualty, 110
ordinary misrepresentation, 129
organ donors in Holland, 104–5
organization, alternative principles of, 106–7
ou-topia, 109
Outze, Børge, 102–3
Oxford English Dictionary, 6

P
pace of life acceleration, 210
parity of participation, 129
Parker, Martin, 106
Parks, Rosa, 38, 180
participation, 162–70
 democratic, 163
 democratic value, 167
 extra-parliamentary, 77–8
 facilitated, 165–6, 170
 paradoxes of, 72–89
 political, 32–4
 prioritizing, 164
participatory democracy, 29
partnership, 180–7
Pearce, Jenny, 95
performative surprise, 104
personal dissatisfaction and structural condition, 73–81
personal revelation through art, 28
philosophical sociology, 42
physical distance, 214
Picasso, Pablo, 20
Pinochet, Augusto, 63
Pirsig, Robert, 214
political opportunities, 52–3
political participation, facilitating, 32–4
See also participation
politicians, media and, 6
politics
 aesthetics and, 41–3
 contentious, 52
 depolitization of, 153
 identity, 43

Popovic, Srdja, 100
Porta, Donatella Della, 18, 31–2, 68–9, 98
post-industrial democracies, 66–7
practitioner's argument, 127–8
prisons, logic of, 121
Pritchett, Laurie, 39
private consultants, 163
process-oriented activism, 95
professional integrity, 191
professionalization
  cooptation and, 187–8
  new partnership, 180–7
  overview, 161–2
  social business, 171–9
  top-down bottom-up inclusion, 162–70
project-based activism, 95–6
project-organized networks, 56
Promises, 215
proposing mirror
  inside, 145–6
  outside, 146–8
The Protester, 183
public opinion, 224
punk rock, Russia, 124
Pussy Riot, 105, 122, 124
Putin, Vladimir, 124

R
racism, United States, 38
Radin, Paul, 212–13
Rally to Restore Sanity and/or Fear, 15–16
Rancière, Jacques, 21, 42, 43, 105
Rasmussen, Lars Løkke, 196
Ravnborg, Helle Munk, 185
Rebughini, Paola, 10, 121, 155
Reclaim the Streets, 42
recognition, 128
recuperation of social movement, 68
redistribution, 128
reflection
  critical theory, 148–53
  framing, 128–31
refugee crisis, 39
Rehmann, Jan, 203

representation, 129
  meta-political misrepresentation, 129
  misframing, 129
  ordinary misrepresentation, 129
representative democracy, 28
resistance
  hidden transcripts, 61
  practices of, 61
resource mobilization theories, 51–2
revitalization, 28
Riley, John Erik, 115
Rizzolati, Giacomo, 224
Rochon, Thomas, 49, 68, 215
Roosevelt, Franklin D., 37–8
Rosa, Hartmut, 121, 133, 215–16
Rosendahl, N. Y., 225
Rosengaard, Martin, 34
Roskilde Festival inDenmark, 19, 107–8
Russian State Broadcasting, 58
Rwodzi, Francis, 183

S
sacred poverty, 213
Salt March campaign, 67
Samson, Kristine, 41–2
Scales of Justice (Fraser), 129
Scandinavian countries, patterns of participation in, 79
Scharmer, Otto, 125–6, 127, 128
Schmidt, Eric, 204
School for Creative Activism, 16, 21
Scott, James C., 61–4, 116, 163
Seeger, Pete, 180
Segerberg, A., 56
self-expression, 73
self-initiative, 191
Sennett, Richard, 165
Sewell, William H., 17
shared value creation, 174
Sharp, G. P., 69, 70
Situationist International, 5, 27
Sköldberg, K., 155
small politics, 127
Smapp, 226
Smelser, N. J., 51
Smith, Tommie, 49
Snow, David A., 55

social acceleration, *see* acceleration society
social activism, 26
social architects, 87
social business, 171–9
  innovative, 172
social change, acceleration of, 210
social critique, 31
social entrepreneur, 173
social innovation, 173–4
social justice, 128–31, 155–6
  recognition, 128–9
  redistribution, 128
  reflection, 130–1
  representation, 129
social media, 226
social mobilization, 37
social movement, 47–8
  activists, 48
  collective action, 53–4
  contentious collective action, 48
  cycles of contention, 59–71
  demobilization of, 67–8
  Diani on, 48
  empirical properties of, 47
  international attention, 56
  leaders in, 48
  literature on, 48, 53
  Marx, 51
  measuring efficacy of, 189–221
  nineteenth-century scholars on, 50–1
  repertoire, 49–50
  resource mobilization theories, 51–2
  theories on, 48–9
  traditional repertoire, 49–50
social sculpture, 98–9
sociological encyclopedia, 51
Socrates, 101
Solnit, David, 5, 33, 88
Søndergaard, Kasper, 43
Sophists, 101
Soviet Union, 38
Spark, 171–2
spectacles, defined, 18
Stacey, Ralph, 211
state-employed actors, 163
Stephan, Maria J., 69

Stewart, Jon, 15–16, 102, 147
structuration, theory of, 39–40
sustainability, 172

T
Tarrow, Sidney, 47, 52, 53, 55, 60, 65, 66, 68
technical acceleration, 209–10
technological advances, 29–30
Theatrum Mundi, 165
theory of structuration, 39–40
Thornton, Patricia M., 116
Thrift, Nigel, 42
Tiananmen Square, 55
Tilly, Charles, 49, 52, 55
Time Magazine, 3, 183
Todd, Andrew, 165
top-down bottom-up inclusion, 162–70
totalitarianism, 110
Touraine, Alain, 54
"Tour de Future," 197
traditional media, 56
training facilitator, 32
Transitional Council, 168–9
Truman, Harry S., 38
trust, 191
Turner, Victor W., 213
Tweets and Streets (Gerbauso), 56
Twitter, 56

U
Uganda, 99
Unboss, 175–6
ungleichseitigkeit, 224
United Nations, 29
United States
  caste system, 37
  civil rights movement, 37–40, 192, 200–1
  Dixiecrats, 37
  financial crisis, 37, 56
United Victorian Workers, 110
uprisings, 213
Ushahidi, 145–6, 156
Utopia (More), 109
utopian critique, 10
utopian imagination, 105–11
utopianism, 105

V

variables, 194–204
Village Project, 98–9
violent resistance, 70
voluntary labor, 5
von Hornsleth, Christian, 98–9

W

"We are all Khaled Said," 56
welfare states, 75–80
Welzel, Christian, 73
Why Civil Resistance Works: The Strategic Logic of Nonviolent Struggle (Chenoweth and Stephan), 69
Wikileaks, 57
Willig, Rasmus, 7, 122, 134
Wilson, Peter Lamborn, 107
Woodly, Deva, 57, 113
Wooloo, 86–8, 167, 224
World Trade Organization (WTO), 3

Y

Yes Lab, 33
Yes Men, 33, 86, 99–100, 108
Yunus, Muhammed, 172–3

Z

Zapatista movement in Mexico, 110
Zapatistas subcommandante Marcos, 62
Zen and the Art of Motorcycle Maintenance (Pirsig), 214
Zimbabwe, 183
Žižek, Slavoj, 105

The manufacturer's authorised representative in the EU is Springer Nature Customer Service Centre GmbH, Europaplatz 3, 69115 Heidelberg, Germany. If you have any concerns regarding our products, please contact ProductSafety@springernature.com

Printed and bound by CPI Group (UK) Ltd, Croydon, CR0 4YY

23/03/2026

02076398-0006